CONSUMER FINANCIAL DISPUTE RESOLUTION IN A COMPARATIVE CONTEXT

Nearly all major global financial centres have developed systems of consumer financial dispute resolution. Such systems aim to assist parties to resolve a growing number of monetary disputes with financial institutions. How governments and self-regulatory organisations design and administer financial dispute resolution mechanisms in the context of increasingly turbulent financial markets is a new area for research and practice.

Consumer Financial Dispute Resolution in a Comparative Context presents comparative research about the development and design of these mechanisms in East Asia, North America and Europe. Using a comparative methodology and drawing on empirical findings from a multi-jurisdictional survey, Shahla F. Ali examines the emergence of global principles that influence the design of financial dispute resolution models, considers the structural variations between the ombuds and arbitration systems and offers practical proposals for reform.

SHAHLA F. ALI is an assistant professor of law at the University of Hong Kong Faculty of Law, where her teaching and research focus on arbitration and dispute resolution, law and development and commercial transactions in a comparative context.

CONSUMER FINANCIAL DISPUTE RESOLUTION IN A COMPARATIVE CONTEXT

Principles, Systems and Practice

SHAHLA F. ALI

CAMBRIDGE UNIVERSITY PRESS

CAMBRIDGE UNIVERSITY PRESS
Cambridge, New York, Melbourne, Madrid, Cape Town,
Singapore, São Paulo, Delhi, Mexico City

Cambridge University Press
The Edinburgh Building, Cambridge CB2 8RU, UK

Published in the United States of America by Cambridge University Press, New York

www.cambridge.org
Information on this title: www.cambridge.org/9781107028715

First published 2013

Printed and bound in the United Kingdom by the MPG Books Group

A catalogue record for this publication is available from the British Library

Library of Congress Cataloguing in Publication data
Ali, Shahla F., author.
Consumer financial dispute resolution in a comparative context :
principles, systems and practice / Shahla F. Ali.
p.   cm.
Includes bibliographical references and index.
ISBN 978-1-107-02871-5 (hardback)
1. Arbitration and award.   2. Financial services industry–Law and legislation.
3. Dispute resolution (Law)   4. Consumer protection–Law and legislation.
5. Arbitration and award.   6. Ombudspersons.   I. Title.
K2405.B35A45 2013
346.07–dc23
2012040694

ISBN 978-1-107-02871-5 Hardback

The capacity of any institution to effect and manage change, and to respond creatively to challenges that lie before it, entails the development of a number of critical skills. These include the ability to ... properly assess the resources of the community ... [and] to uphold standards of fairness and equity.

(BIC, May, 2001 Integrity in Public Institutions)

CONTENTS

FIGURES

TABLES

ACKNOWLEDGEMENTS

The research for this book has been made possible by funds from the Government of Hong Kong's Research Grants Council, Public Policy Research Grant (7001-PPR-10). Without the valuable input and views from practitioners, ombudsmen, mediators and arbitrators from the Asia Pacific, Europe and America, the practical insights in this book would not be possible.

Many people have helped with this book. Finola O'Sullivan, editor at Cambridge University Press, made valuable suggestions at the initial stages of the manuscript and saw it through to its final completion. Anonymous reviewers provided helpful input at the early stages of the project. Special thanks to an outstanding team of research assistants, including Antonio Da Roza, Alison Choy, Silvia Hui, Perry J. H. Sea and Cynthianna Yau. Juliet Binns and Abigail Fiddes provided expert publishing assistance and Kim Hughes and Richard Woodham produced the final manuscript with thoughtful and attentive care.

Many colleagues have contributed valuable insights that have improved the book. At the University of Hong Kong Department of Law, I am grateful for the kind support of colleagues in the dispute resolution field, including Fu Hualing, Katherine Lynch, Alex Mak, Tony Carty, Gu Weixia, Richard Holt, Anna Koo, James Fry and Zhao Yun. I am also thankful to our Dean Johannes Chan and Department Head Douglas Arner for providing a supportive research environment and our Asian Institute for International and Financial Law (AIIFL) and our Center for Comparative and Public Law (CCPL) for providing valuable institutional support. I am also grateful to participants who shared valuable feedback at the following conferences: the 2nd East Asian Law and Society Conference 2011 (Seoul, Korea), the CCL/HKU Conference From Economic Development to Human Flourishing: The Case of China (Hong Kong SAR), the 3rd NUS-AsianSIL Young Scholars Workshop (Singapore), the Law and Society Association Annual Conference (San Francisco, CA), the Asia Pacific Mediation Forum (Bangkok, Thailand) and the Soochow

International Law Conference (Taipei). I am also grateful for a fruitful exchange with Professor Robin Hui Huang and Professor Yang Dong and his graduate students from Renmin University, Michael Hwang and with Professors Russell Korobkin and Daniel Bussel at UCLA's School of Law. The Hong Kong chapter also benefited from insights from the Hong Kong Government's RGC grant, 'Enhancing Hong Kong's Future as a Leading International Financial Centre' (T31–717/12-R).

A special note of thanks to my family. I am grateful to my husband Victor Ali for suggesting I explore this topic in 2008, and for his always helpful insights and constant support. Thanks also to my daughter Martha for her always bright spirit and efficient help tearing up old drafts. Though an ocean separates me from my immediate family, I feel the support of my mom, Charleen and her husband Steve; my mother and father-in-law, Claudine and Nabil; my brothers and sisters-in-law; and especially my dad and grandmother for their love and support from the realm beyond.

All that is positive in this book reflects the generosity and support of colleagues, research assistants, survey participants, friends and associates. All errors and omissions are, of course, my own.

~

Introduction

The present financial crisis has had significant repercussions throughout the global economy. It has provided an impetus for examining effective avenues for the resolution of financial disputes. As yet, however, there is little consensus worldwide as to how the effects of such crises can best be addressed through effective systems of financial dispute resolution.

This book presents an examination of how governments and self-regulatory organisations in major global financial centres have increasingly employed alternative dispute resolution mechanisms including ombuds models, arbitration, direct settlement negotiation and mediation to address consumer complaints against retail banks and financial institutions as a form of 'responsive banking'. The results of a comparative cross-jurisdictional analysis of consumer financial dispute resolution centres in seven jurisdictions shed light on the underlying structural design, policy orientation, complaint procedures, financing and oversight of financial dispute resolution centres as established in diverse regions. The findings indicate that such centres in general offer a flexible and relatively fast way to resolve financial disputes, but are not without their challenges. Such challenges include the potential for mismatch between regulatory consistency and individualised case handling.[1] Determining how best to overcome such challenges while addressing a growing number of finance-related disputes are pressing questions facing governments, legislatures and aggrieved citizens.

A financial crisis with global proportions

Beginning in early 2007, the indicators of what would soon become the most severe financial crisis since the Great Depression in the 1930s became increasingly evident. In the summer of 2007, investment banks such as Bear Stearns and BNP Paribus warned investors that they would

---

[1] See Arner, Hsu and Da Roza (2010) 'Financial regulation in Hong Kong: Time for a Change', *As. J.C.L.*, 5, pp. 71–114.

be unable to retrieve money invested in sub-prime mortgages hedge funds. Later in September, there was a bank run on Northern Rock – the biggest run on a British bank for more than a century. By 2008, Northern Rock was nationalised. Banks such as the Union Bank of Switzerland ('UBS'), Merrill Lynch and Citigroup also started announcing losses due to heavy investments in sub-prime mortgages. In response to the growing crisis, central banks in Europe, Canada, the United Kingdom, the United States and Japan intervened to boost liquidity in the financial markets by reducing interest rates and increasing monetary supply.[2]

To prevent a collapse of the US housing market, financial authorities in the United States stepped in with one of the largest bailouts in history of Fannie Mae and Freddie Mac. On 15 September 2008, Lehman Brothers filed for bankruptcy. Ripple effects were immediately felt throughout the world. Countries successively announced details of rescue packages for individual banks as well as the banking system as a whole and emergency interest rates were further cut. The United States initiated a $700 billion Troubled Asset Relief Program to rescue the financial sector and the Federal Reserve also injected a further $800 billion into the economy to stabilise the system and encourage lending. It also extended insurance to money market accounts via a temporary guarantee.[3] By early 2009, the United Kingdom, the European Union and the United States had officially slipped into recession.

Governments across the world implemented economic stimulus packages and promised to guarantee loans. The International Monetary Fund ('IMF') estimated that banks in total lost $2.8 trillion from toxic assets and bad loans between 2007 and 2010.[4] There was also a severe decline in assets as stock indices worldwide fell along with housing prices in the United States and the United Kingdom.[5]

The global reach of the financial crisis calls for renewed investigation of how governments and self-regulatory organisations in major financial centres can effectively employ dispute resolution mechanisms to address citizen complaints arising from financial dislocation. Such an examination is

---

[2] BBC News (7 August 2009) 'Credit crunch to downturn', available at: http://news.bbc.co.uk/2/hi/business/7521250.stm [accessed 29 December 2010].

[3] D. Gullapalli, and S. Anand (20 September 2008) 'Bailout of money funds seems to stanch outflow', *The Wall Street Journal*, available at: http://online.wsj.com/article/SB122186683086958875.html?mod=article-outset-box [accessed 29 December 2010].

[4] D. Cutler, S. Slater and E. Comlay (5 November 2009) 'US, European Bank writedowns, credit losses', *Reuters*, available at: www.reuters.com/article/idCNL554155620091105?rpc=44 [accessed 29 December 2010].

[5] BBC News, 'Credit crunch to downturn'.

important not only to help us understand the dynamics of resolving complex consumer disputes in times of financial crisis, but also to prepare us to apply lessons learned to the design of more robust, fair and efficient centres for the prevention and resolution of future financial disputes.

Viewing consumer financial dispute resolution in a theoretical context

The question of how systems of consumer financial dispute resolution can be designed in diverse contexts to effectively and fairly administer the resolution of financial disputes, how such centres can draw on emerging global principles of accessibility, efficiency, impartiality and fairness and how such centres might consequently contribute to the health of the broader economic environment touch on three primary bodies of scholarship: work in the law and development field; studies in dispute system design; and work examining the impact of globalisation on international legal practice.

Law and development literature has long puzzled over the relationship between systems of dispute resolution and economic growth. Much of this literature has focused on formal systems of dispute resolution including litigation and arbitration and economic development.[6] Informal structures have traditionally been framed as outside the shadows of formal law,[7] and somewhat antithetical to growth.[8] Work focusing on East Asia has traditionally framed the debate in terms of whether economic growth has occurred in spite of, or because of, the later development of formal legal structures in the region.[9] However, thus far, none of these studies

---

[6] See for example: M. Weber (1968) *On Charisma And Institution Building*, S. N. Eisenstadt (ed.), (University of Chicago Press); D. M. Trubek (1972) 'Toward a social theory of law: an essay on the study of law & development', *Yale L. J.*, 82, p. 1; D. M. Trubek (1973) 'Max Weber on law and the rise of capitalism', *Wisconsin Law Review*, 3, p. 720; D. North (1990) *Institutions, Institutional Change And Economic Growth* (New York: Cambridge University Press).

[7] See for example: L. Bernstein (2001) 'Private commercial law in the cotton industry: creating cooperation through rules, norms and institutions', *Michigan L. Rev.*, 99, p. 1724; R. Ellickson (1991) *Order Without Law: How Neighbors Settle Disputes* (Harvard University Press).

[8] See for example: M. Weber, *On Charisma and Institution Building*; D. North, *Institutions, Institutional Change and Economic Growth*.

[9] See for example: A. Rosette and L. Cheng (1991) 'Contract with a Chinese face: socially embedded factors in the transformation from hierarchy to market, 1978–1989', *J. Chin. L.*, 5, pp. 219–233; D. C. Clarke (2003) 'Economic development and the rights hypothesis: the China problem', *Am. J. Comp. L.*, 51, p. 89; F. Upham (2002) 'Mythmaking in the rule of law orthodoxy, Carnegie Endowment for international peace', Rule of Law Series, Democracy and Rule of Law Project, Number 30; T. Ginsburg (2000) 'Does law matter for economic development? Evidence from East Asia', *Law and Society Review*, 34(3).

have directly traced the impact of institutional forms of alternative dispute resolution on the health of the broader economy and consumer confidence. This book will contribute to this discussion by examining the contribution of institutional alternative dispute resolution, including mediation and ombuds fact-finding processes to financial stability and development.

This book also speaks to recent work regarding the design of effective and efficient systems of dispute resolution in resolving polycentric disputes. Recent work has offered insights into the design of institutional dispute resolution mechanisms for a variety of public and private settings,[10] as well as complex multi-party disputes.[11] Thus far there has been limited

---

[10] See for example: William L. Ury, Jeanne M. Brett and Stephen B. Goldberg (1988) *Getting Disputes Resolved: Designing Systems to Cut the Cost of Conflict* (Jossey-Bass) pp. 41–64; Janet Martinez and Stephanie Smith (2009) 'An analytic framework for dispute system design', *Harvard Negotiation Law Review*, 14, p. 123; Cathy A. Costantino and Christina Sickles Merchant (1996), *Designing Conflict Management Systems: A Guide to Creating Productive and Healthy Organizations* (Jossey-Bass); Lisa Blomgren Bingham, Cynthia J. Hallberlin, Denise A. Walker and Won-Tae Chung (2009) 'Dispute system design and justice in employment dispute resolution: mediation at the workplace', *Harvard Negotiation Law Review*, 14, pp. 1–50; Lawrence Susskind, Sarah McKearnan and Jennifer Thomas-Larmer (1999) *The Consensus Building Handbook: A Comprehensive Guide To Reaching Agreement* (SAGE), pp. 61–168; Richard C. Reuben (2005) 'Democracy and dispute resolution: systems design and the new workplace', *Harvard Negotiation Law Review*, 10, p. 11; Jill Gross (2006) 'Securities mediation: dispute resolution for the individual investor', *Ohio State Journal on Dispute Resolution*, 21(2), pp. 329–381; John Lande (2002) 'Using dispute system design methods to promote good-faith participation in court-connected mediation programs', *UCLA Law Review*, 50, pp. 69–141; Sharon Press (1992–1993) 'Building and maintaining a statewide mediation program: a view from the field', *Kentucky Law Journal*, 81, pp. 1029–1065; Ellen E. Deason (2004) 'Procedural rules for complementary systems of litigation and mediation – worldwide', *Notre Dame Law Review*, 80, available at: http://papers.ssrn.com/sol3/papers.cfm?abstract_id=583141 [accessed 25 May 2012]; Andrea Kupfer Schneider (2008) 'The Intersection of Dispute Systems Design and Transitional Justice', *Harvard Negotiation Law Review*, available at: http://papers.ssrn.com/sol3/papers.cfm?abstract_id=1296183 [accessed 25 May 2012]; Carrie J. Menkel-Meadow (2009) 'Are there systemic ethics issues in dispute system design? And what we should [not] do about it: Lessons from international and domestic fronts', *Harvard Negotiation Law Review*, 14, pp. 195–231; Kagan, Robert A. (2003) *Adversarial Legalism and American Government: The American Way of Life* (Harvard University Press); Malcom M. Feeley (1989) *Court Reform on Trial: Why Simple Solutions Fail* (Basic Books); D. Caron and L. Caplan (2010) *The 2010 UNCITRAL Arbitration Rules: A Commentary* (Oxford University Press); Katherine Lynch (2003) *The Forces of Economic Globalization: Challenges to the Regime of International Commercial Arbitration* The Hague, Netherlands: Kluwer Law International).

[11] See for example: S. Sturn and H. Gadlin (2007) 'Conflict resolution and systemic change', *J. Disp. Resol.*, 1, p. 1; S. A. Wiegand (1996) 'A just and lasting peace: supplanting mediation with the ombuds model', *Ohio St. J. on Disp. Resol.*, 12, p. 95.

work focused on the design of institutional alternative dispute resolution mechanisms in addressing consumer financial disputes. Systems design literature has also examined, from a socio-legal perspective, the larger socio-legal dispute processing debate investigating how mechanisms may be developed to limit the effect of the power/knowledge gap of 'repeat players' in institutional dispute resolution settings through appropriate regulations and policies. Previous studies in respect of litigation tend to suggest that 'haves' (i.e. large businesses, high socio-economic status groups) tend to fare better in courts than 'have nots'.[12] Therefore attention to procedural safeguards aimed at addressing structural inequities in the design and development of such systems is necessary if such disputes are to be effectively addressed.

At the global level, literature examining the impact of globalisation on domestic legal practices has relevance to the question of how domestic legislation effectively integrates relevant global standards and principles. This literature provides a helpful grounding in emerging questions of how global norms interact with national law-making processes,[13] the interaction between processes of 'convergence' and 'informed divergence' in the development of public law,[14] and the interplay between principles and systems in commercial dispute resolution design.[15] Such insights are useful in understanding the extent to which emergent global principles may inform the design and structure of newly emerging consumer financial dispute resolution systems.

This book, drawing on comparative cross-jurisdictional analysis, will make practical proposals for reform which will aim to contribute to the development of systems of transparent and equitable dispute resolution capable of responding to financial dislocation.

Overview of methodology

This book will identify and analyse factors and processes that give rise to the development of accessible, efficient and equitable financial dispute

---

[12] See M. Galanter (1974) 'Why the "haves" come out ahead: speculations on the limits of legal change', *Law & Society Review*, 9(1), pp. 95–160.

[13] T. Halliday and B. Carruthers (2007) 'The recursivity of law: global norm-making and national law-making in the globalization of corporate insolvency regimes', *American Journal of Sociology*, 112 p. 1135.

[14] See A. M. Slaughter (2004) *A New World Order* (Princeton University Press).

[15] See for example: J. Braithwaite and P. Drahos (2000) *Global Business Regulation* (Cambridge University Press).

resolution mechanisms. It will examine comparative institutional dispute resolution structures and results in selected financial centres in East Asia, North America and Europe in order to glean best practices. Given the near global impact of the current financial crisis, a unique opportunity exists to examine and test the efficacy of diverse dispute resolution approaches to addressing a common global challenge.

Two methodological principles characterise the research process used to examine the primary questions under analysis: a comparative framework and a triangulating approach.

A principal orientation of the research process focuses on comparative methodology. Through comparison among corresponding financial dispute resolution centres in seven jurisdictions, the aim of the research is to understand how these jurisdictions address investor complaints through unique structures of financial dispute resolution including ombuds, arbitration and multi-tier processes.

The second methodological principle parallels the process of 'triangulation' used by geological surveyors in cases where direct measurement of physical heights or spaces is impossible. Based on the assumption that any one research method alone can be subject to bias, contemporary researchers have found that multiple research techniques can, to a large extent, compensate for each other's deficiencies and provide a broader foundation for critical analysis (Cook and Fonow, 1990; Eckstein, 1992). Therefore the methodological approach employed here similarly draws on three complementary qualitative and quantitative data collection methods. These include the following:

> *Secondary academic research*: Empirical research by other scholars concerning institutional alternative dispute resolution of financial disputes, including mediation and negotiation is accumulated, reviewed and examined in the conventional fashion.
>
> *On-site data collection*: A variety of data from financial alternative dispute resolution centres in East Asia, North America and Europe is collected in order to conduct comparative content analysis of alternative dispute resolution processes, methods, ground rules and preparation in order to glean best practices.
>
> *Survey*: In order to assess how arbitrators and ombuds view the benefits of their particular method of consumer financial dispute resolution, its benefits, challenges and suggestions for improvement, a survey was conducted between the autumn of 2011 and the summer of 2012. Nearly 100 survey questionnaires were distributed to practitioners throughout the world. A total of 48 arbitrators and ombuds people from East Asia, North America, Europe, the Middle East and Africa responded. The

participants represented highly experienced practitioners, members of government regulatory ombuds services and private arbitration commissions. The majority of those surveyed (44 per cent) had worked for institutions involved in consumer financial dispute resolution for more than four years.

The survey results are described in Part II (Ombuds systems), on arbitration and ombuds practices respectively, which in summary are as follows: practitioners of consumer financial dispute resolution view ombuds processes as particularly useful in providing an independent and free review service for financial customers. At the same time the service also helps to identify areas for further improvement by banks and regulatory agencies.[16] Perhaps as a result of such benefits, the use of ombuds processes has been increasing in recent years. The majority of respondents (89 per cent) indicated that they had in fact seen an increase in the use of ombuds processes in consumer financial dispute resolution in recent years. At the same time, practitioners acknowledged areas for continued improvement including the need for greater public education[17] and oversight and quality assurance of ombuds processes.[18]

Arbitration practitioners likewise viewed the benefits of arbitration services in consumer financial disputes as providing disputants with technical expertise 'where the parties are not arguing over the law, but application of financial/accounting principles'.[19] Among the challenges include 'proof issues, imbalance of power and information, lack of full discovery options/rights'.[20] Concerns about such disparities were echoed by other participants who noted the prevalence of perceptions that 'large institutions have "repeat-user" advantage'.[21] Practitioners noted suggestions for improvement including the need for '[g]ood program design [including] exit evaluations [and a] grievance process to allow parties to file complaints against neutrals who do not perform well'. In addition, 'a code of ethics for neutrals' was suggested along with 'anything that supports procedural due process'.[22] These findings are elaborated on in greater depth in Part II.

[16] Survey No. 1 (July 2011–March 2012).
[17] Survey No. 1 (July 2011–March 2012).
[18] Survey No. 4 (July 2011–March 2012).
[19] Survey No. 8 (July 2011–March 2012).
[20] Survey No. 10 (July 2011–March 2012).
[21] Survey No. 14 (July 2011–March 2012).
[22] Survey No. 10 (July 2011–March 2012).

Structure of the book

The book is divided into three parts: following an introduction, Part I (Principles) explores the emergence of global principles that influence to varying degrees the design of consumer financial dispute resolution systems in diverse societies. A number of emerging standards, gleaned from the Equator Principles, the Basel Accords, the UN Millennium Development Goals, global deliberative processes and general rule of law principles, including the need for accessible grievance mechanisms, financial dispute prevention through transparent risk disclosure and risk mitigation, impartiality, equity, accountability and fairness, provide helpful guidance in the development of consumer financial dispute resolution systems.

Parts II and III (Ombuds systems and Arbitration systems) then examine the two major systems of consumer financial dispute resolution: the ombuds process and the arbitration system. Part II examines the structure and function of ombuds-based consumer financial dispute resolution centres in the United Kingdom, Australia and Japan. Part III then goes on to examine arbitration-based models in the United States, Singapore and Hong Kong as well as emerging systems in China. These jurisdictions are selected because they represent two very different forms of consumer financial dispute resolution in relatively well established markets and therefore provide a basis for comparison. These sections systematically examine the structural design, policy orientation, complaint procedures, financing and oversight of financial dispute resolution centres as established within each region.

Part IV (Practice), drawing on comparative cross-jurisdictional analysis of regional models and empirical findings of consumer financial dispute resolution practitioners, presents policy recommendations, including investigating the efficacy of developing interventions that aim to minimise the power/knowledge gap of 'repeat players' in institutional dispute resolution settings through appropriate regulations and policies. As will be seen in the chapters that follow, the ombuds and arbitration models of consumer financial dispute resolution implement principles of impartiality, equity, accountability and fairness to varying degrees, based on the unique mandate, regulatory function and objectives of each mechanism.

In examining financial dispute resolution models in the jurisdictions studied, this research finds that at the global level, due to the fact that such non-binding global principles allow diverse consumer financial dispute resolution mechanisms the option of opting into such standards, at the substantive level, divergence in costs, regulatory role and the binding nature of awards can, to a large extent, co-exist with a relatively high degree of convergence in relation to the multi-tier structure of most consumer financial dispute resolution processes.

In addition, the findings indicate that the appropriateness of a dispute resolution method is arguably informed by the extent to which it takes on a regulatory role. Regulatory dispute resolution modes such as the ombudsman model that take on inquisitorial elements may be preferred when displacing the judicial function as they incorporate safeguards for disputants against third party discretion. But even for non-regulatory schemes, inquisitorial elements aimed at addressing the power/knowledge gap, including suggesting the provision of information regarding relevant standards and rules, at least as touchstones, may still be incorporated into consensual models of dispute resolution, in order to ensure a de minimis level of fairness and confidence in the process.

PART I

Principles

1

Principles of consumer financial dispute resolution in a global context

Introduction

The question of how global standards and principles interact with domestic legal institutions has been the subject of ongoing scholarship. Recent financial dislocation indicates that in many respects the world's financial markets are increasingly operating as a single integrated whole. Both the economic fallout of the financial crisis as well as the global response reflects the significant degree of interchange characterising cross-border exchange. Many global financial centres were directly impacted by the financial crisis, and responded with their own unique regulatory mix that drew on global experience.

A number of relevant standards, gleaned from the Equator Principles, the Basel Accords, the UN Millennium Development Goals, global deliberative processes and general rule of law standards, including the need for accessible grievance mechanisms, financial dispute prevention through transparent risk disclosure and risk mitigation, impartiality, equity, accountability and fairness, provide helpful guidance in the development of consumer financial dispute resolution systems.

This chapter will first examine the theoretical perspectives regarding the impact of globalisation on international legal practice. Then it will turn to an examination of existing international standards developed by global entities such as the United Nations, the Basel Committee, the IFC/World Bank, as well as members of civil society that have informed the development of consumer financial dispute resolution services.

As will be seen in the chapters that follow, the ombuds and arbitration models of consumer financial dispute resolution implement such global principles to varying degrees, based on the unique mandate, regulatory function and objectives of each mechanism. For example, as will be seen in the examination of the ombuds models of consumer financial dispute resolution, the principles of accessibility, accountability and fairness may be given greater importance, while in the arbitration model, principles of finality may take precedence.

In examining financial dispute resolution models in the jurisdictions studied, this research finds that at the global level, due to the fact that such non-binding global principles allow diverse consumer financial dispute resolution mechanisms the option of opting in to particular standards, at the substantive level, divergence in costs, regulatory role and the binding nature of awards can co-exist, to a large extent, with a relatively high degree of convergence in relation to the multi-tier structure of most consumer financial dispute resolution processes.

Theoretical perspectives on the impact of globalisation on international legal practice

In examining the dynamic nature of financial governance in the context of diverse societies, it is helpful to review the impact of globalisation on international legal practice.

Addressing the conceptual challenges brought about by globalisation,[1] scholars within an emerging field examining the internationalisation of the practice of law have begun to explore questions such as the impact of globalisation on the legal profession, the changing landscape of the international practice of law in various countries and the impact of globalisation on international dispute resolution mechanisms.[2] This literature provides a helpful grounding in emerging questions of global dispute resolution procedure, the dynamics of global enforcement of international agreements and the mechanisms that are best suited to resolving particular types of commercial disputes. For example, John Braithwaite and Peter Drahos, in their book *Global Business Regulation*, investigate global business regulation through examining underlying principles that constitute the global context.[3] Such principles are not exclusively legal principles, but rather emerge from the values and practices of a given community of actors. Through this lens, Drahos and Braithwaite examine how the regulation of business has shifted from national to global institutions in the areas of contract, intellectual property and corporations law, and the role played by global institutions as well as various NGOs and significant

[1] See generally, S. Ali (2010) *Resolving Disputes in the Asia Pacific Region: International Arbitration and Mediation in East Asia and the West* (Routledge).
[2] J. Drolshammer and M. Pfeifer (2001) *The Internationalization Of The Practice Of Law* (The Hauge: Kluwer Law International).
[3] J. Braithwaite and P. Drahos, *Global Business Regulation*.

individuals.[4] Braithwaite and Drahos' contribution to the study of private global business regulation offers a helpful framework for examining the development of private international regulation and corresponding implementation at the local level.

Recent socio-legal work by Terrence Halliday and Bruce Carruthers (2007, 2009) regarding the recursivity of law in global norm making and national law-making has made an important contribution to examining the dynamic mechanisms by which global norms interact with national law-making processes in the corporate insolvency regime.[5]

In addition, responding to the question of how emerging global legal norms respond to national diversity while crossing international borders, A. M. Slaughter describes how legal networks such as those associated with international arbitration have proliferated in recent years.[6] Such networks offer 'a flexible and relatively fast way to conduct the business of global governance, coordinating and even harmonising national government action while initiating and monitoring different solutions to global problems'.[7] On the one hand, these networks promote 'convergence', while on the other hand they also allow for 'informed divergence'.[8] Such interactions are founded on the basis of what Slaughter calls the foundational norm of 'global deliberative equality' derived from the basic moral precept that 'our species is one, and each of the individuals who compose it is entitled to equal moral consideration'.[9]

The bodies of literature described above provide some useful insights into the nature of regulatory practices in a transnational context. In particular, Braithwaite and Drahos' insights into the interplay between underlying global principles and business regulation,[10] Halliday and Carruthers' scholarship regarding the recursivity of law in global norm making,[11] and Slaughter's findings regarding the dynamic interaction of processes of 'convergence' and 'informed divergence' in the global legal sphere[12] are particularly helpful in framing the question of how emerging

---

[4] Ibid.

[5] T. Halliday and B. Carruthers (2007) 'The recursivity of law: global norm-making and national law-making in the globalization of corporate insolvency regimes'; see also: T. Halliday and B. Carruthers (2009) *Bankrupt: Global Lawmaking and Systemic Financial Crisis* (Stanford University Press).

[6] See A. M. Slaughter, *A New World Order*, p. 11.

[7] Ibid.   [8] Ibid.   [9] Ibid., p. 245.

[10] J. Braithwaite and P. Drahos, *Global Business Regulation*.

[11] T. Halliday and B. Carruthers, 'The recursivity of law: global norm-making and national law-making in the globalization of corporate insolvency regimes'.

[12] A. M. Slaughter, *A New World Order*.

global principles in the realm of financial regulation operate in a diverse global context.

Principles of consumer financial dispute resolution

Since the mid-twentieth century, international standards developed by global entities such as the United Nations, the Basel Committee, the IFC/World Bank, as well as principles of fairness and transparency advanced by members of civil society and rule of law scholars have indirectly informed the development of consumer financial dispute resolution services.

Such principles and standards, while globally influential, lack the enforceability of binding laws or regulations. Be it by institutions, member states of diverse organisations, or societal initiatives, these concepts share the aim of achieving the just resolution of financial disputes at both the local and international level. Such goals are advanced through provision of better access to legal justice (*UN Consumer Protection Principles, Millennium Development Goals* and *Rules of Law Principles*); the creation of review mechanisms (*Equator Principles*); improving the discipline and monitoring of financial institutions (*Equator Principles, Basel Accords*); or social deliberation on the part of the public for states and institutions to approach and resolve financial disputes in a fair and accountable manner (*Global Deliberation*).

Many of these concepts have been developed in response to the financial crisis of the late-2000s as financial institutions and states saw the need to restore the confidence of investors (e.g. *Basel Accords*). While it is true that such concepts are valuable to the prevention and resolution of financial disputes, it must also be noted that there are various institutional and jurisdictional limitations that these concepts potentially fail to encounter. They may depend on the voluntary participation of financial institutions (*Equator Principles*), or require local legal implementation and enforcement (*UN Consumer Protection Principles* and *Basel Accords*), or perhaps only suggest broad-brush legal and social justice principles that are only as effective as the local economic, political and legal systems provide (*Global Deliberation, Millennium Development Goals* and *Rules of Law Principles*).

For each of the principles, this chapter will review its content and applicability to the resolution of financial disputes, progress in achieving its goals, if any, and limitations of such standards in informing the development of consumer financial dispute resolution institutions.

Equator principles – the need for 'adequate grievance mechanisms'

The need for adequate grievance mechanisms to voice complaints regarding unsustainable practices of financial institutions is articulated in the Equator Principles ('EPs').[13] The EPs are the result of an initiative by various financial institutions to evaluate and manage risks of project finance transactions. The EPs include Principle 6, which requires a grievance mechanism for borrowers to review a decision against their financing application. The EPs were updated twice, in 2006 and 2010, and continue to depend solely on the voluntary participation of financial institutions, with no apparent sanctions for non-compliance.

The EPs are 'a credit risk management framework for determining, assessing and managing ... risk in project finance transactions. The EPs are adopted voluntarily by financial institutions and are primarily intended to provide a minimum standard for due diligence to support responsible risk decision-making.'[14]

The Equator Principles Association adopted the guidelines used by the International Finance Corporation ('IFC'), the private sector arm of the World Bank Group.[15] These 10 principles are essentially a pledge by the 73 adopting financial institutions[16] including Bank of America, Barclays, BNP Paribas, Citigroup, HSBC, RBS and Standard Chartered to 'not provide loans to projects where the borrower will not or is unable to comply with [the] respective ... policies and procedures that implement the Equator Principles'.[17]

---

[13] See The Equator Principles Association (EPA), 'History of the Equator Principles', (updated January 2012), available at: www.equator-principles.com/index.php/history [accessed 25 April 2012]. For a number of years, banks working in the Project Finance sector had been seeking ways to assess and manage the environmental and social risks associated with such investment activities. In October 2002, nine international banks convened in London, together with the IFC, to discuss these issues. The banks volunteered jointly to develop a banking industry framework for addressing environmental and social risks in project financing that could be applied globally and across all industry sectors. The EPs were launched in Washington DC on 4 June 2003.

[14] The Equator Principles Association (EPA), 'About the Equator Principles' (updated 2011), available at: www.equator-principles.com/index.php/about-the-equator-principles [accessed 25 April 2012].

[15] Available at: www.ifc.org/ifcext/sustainability.nsf/Content/EHSGuidelines [accessed 25 April 2012].

[16] Full list of EPFIs can be seen from The Equator Principles Association (EPA), 'Members & Reporting' (updated September 2011), available at: www.equator-principles.com/index. php/members-reporting [accessed 25 April 2012].

[17] The Equator Principles Association (EPA), 'The Equator Principles' (June 2006), available at: www.equator-principles.com/resources/equator_principles.pdf [accessed 2 May 2012].

Specific to the resolution of financial disputes is Principle 6, and to some extent Principle 7. Principle 6 provides that:

> the borrower will, scaled to the risks and adverse impacts of the project, establish a grievance mechanism as part of the management system. This will allow the borrower to receive and facilitate the resolution of concerns and grievances raised by individuals or groups from among project-affected communities. The borrower will inform the affected communities about the mechanism in the course of its community engagement process and ensure that the mechanism addresses concerns promptly and transparently, in a culturally appropriate manner, and is readily accessible to all segments of the affected communities.[18]

Other than requiring that the initial review and consultation process be independent (Principle 7), the principles do not elaborate on the particular characteristics of the grievance mechanism, and appear to offer a great deal of liberty to financial institutions to decide how they will establish the mechanism according to this provision.

The main limitation of the EPs is that they do not 'create any rights in, or liability to, any person, public or private'.[19] Rather, institutions implement these principles voluntarily and independently, without reliance on or recourse to the IFC or the World Bank.[20]

UN guidelines for consumer protection

The United Nations Guidelines for Consumer Protection address issues relevant to the resolution of consumer financial disputes through provisions addressing information, representation, redress and consumer education. Each of these elements is seen as key to protecting consumers and building on a growing trend of international cooperation in facilitating cross-border remediation in consumer protection. The Guidelines have to be enacted and enforced locally. Observers comment that the success of consumer protection largely depends on educated consumers, well-resourced institutions, and well-trained and neutral law enforcers.[21]

---

[18] Full list of EPFIs can be seen from EPA, 'Members & Reporting' (updated September 2011), available at: www.equator-principles.com/index.php/members-reporting [accessed 25 April 2012].

[19] As stated in the disclaimer immediately after the Principles are provided. EPA, *supra* note 17, p. 6.

[20] As stated in the disclaimer immediately after the Principles are provided. EPA, *supra* note 17, p. 6.

[21] UN Department of Economic and Social Affairs (1999) 'Part II', *UN Guidelines for Consumer Protection*, available at: www.un.org/esa/sustdev/publications/consumption_en.pdf [accessed 25 April 2012].

The United Nations Guidelines for Consumer Protection constitute a non-binding declaration, which provides a framework for implementation of consumer protection laws at a national level. It calls upon governments (particularly developing countries) to develop, strengthen and maintain a strong consumer policy, and provide for enhanced protection of consumers by enunciating various steps and measures around the issues[22] of standards, redress, education and information.

In the twenty-five years since the Guidelines were first enacted, commentators and policy makers have come to describe the principles in the language of consumer 'rights'.[23] In this regard, a common restatement of the Guidelines can be found in the Charter of Consumers International which renders the Guidelines as consumer rights. They include the: 1) Right to redress; 2) Right to information; 3) Right to consumer education; 4) Right to representation.[24]

Of particular interest is the right to obtain redress. The guidelines provide that,

> [g]overnments should establish or maintain legal and/or administrative measures to enable consumers or, as appropriate, relevant organisations to obtain redress through formal or informal procedures that are expeditious, fair, inexpensive and accessible. Such procedures should take particular account of the needs of low-income consumers.[25]
>
> In addition, the guidelines further state that '[g]overnments should encourage all enterprises to resolve consumer disputes in a fair, expeditious and informal manner, and to establish voluntary mechanisms, including advisory services and informal complaints procedures, which can provide assistance to consumers.'[26] Importantly, '[i]nformation on available redress and other dispute-resolving procedures should be made available to consumers.'[27]

John Wood provides some useful insights into how consumer protection laws can be crafted in order to realise these 'rights'.[28] He explains that consumer laws should: 1) provide consumers with a right to compensation as a result of faulty services; 2) provide a mechanism through which consumers can channel their complaints and grievances to government;

---

[22] Ibid.
[23] R. Brown (2011) 'The UN Guidelines for Consumer Protection: making them work in developing countries', *Paper for Consumers' International Congress*, p.4, available at: http://a2knetwork.org/sites/default/files/un_guidelines_r_brown_paper.doc [accessed 25 April 2012].
[24] Ibid.   [25] Ibid.   [26] Ibid.   [27] Ibid.
[28] J. Wood, 'What consumer laws should do (based upon consumers' international's eight consumer rights)', quoted in R. Brown, ibid., Appendix 1.

3) ensure that consumers are properly compensated for any loss suffered if their consumer rights are contravened; 4) protect consumers from intimidation or harassment if they seek to enforce their rights; and 5) establish effective post-sale consumer protection. When national laws fully reflect such guidelines they provide the legal basis for upholding the consumer rights contained in the UN Guidelines.

In 1985, the United Nations General Assembly adopted the United Nations Guidelines for Consumer Protection (Resolution 39/85). The Guidelines constitute a comprehensive policy framework outlining what governments need to do to promote consumer protection[29] in a number of areas including: information, choice, representation, redress and consumer education. While not legally binding, the Guidelines provide an internationally recognised set of basic objectives. The Guidelines are particularly designed for governments to use in structuring and strengthening consumer protection policies and legislation. The Guidelines were adopted in recognition that consumers often face imbalances in economic terms, education levels and bargaining power. Consumer protection guidelines aim at addressing not only the issues of product safety and economic efficiency, but also social justice and economic development.[30]

Looking forward, not only do the Guidelines call for local implementation, international cooperation is also extensively provided in Part IV.

> For example, the International Consumer Protection and Enforcement Network ('ICPEN'), which includes the United States' and more than thirty other countries' trade practices enforcement agencies, seeks to promote gathering and sharing of information concerning consumer protection issues (including legislation and enforcement policies and practices), addressing cross-border violation of consumer protection laws, facilitating cross-border remedies, promoting enforcement of consumer protection laws, and encouraging wider cooperation among consumer protection enforcement organs. ICPEN has established mechanisms for

[29] Consumers International, 'Consumer Rights', available at: www.consumersinternational.org/who-we-are/consumer-rights [accessed 25 April 2012]; US President John F. Kennedy delivered a historic address to the US Congress in 1962, which outlined his vision of consumer rights. This was said to be the first time any politician had formerly set out such principles. He said, 'Consumers by definition, include us all, they are the largest economic group, affecting and affected by almost every public and private economic decision. Yet they are the only important group … whose views are often not heard.'

[30] UN Division for Sustainable Development Department of Economic and Social Affairs (1998) 'Consumer protection and sustainable consumption: new guidelines for the global consumer', *Background paper for the United Nations inter-regional expert group meeting*, available at: www.un.org/esa/sustdev/sdissues/consumption/cppgoph4.htm [accessed 25 April 2012].

consumer complaints about online international transactions and a collaborative database to aid member states' enforcement agencies.[31]

Many see the Consumer Protection guidelines as a 'guide for governments committed to protecting the ... economic rights of their citizens as consumers. They recognise the right to be protected ... from fraudulent, deceptive, or restrictive business practices, the right to information necessary – to make informed choices and the freedom to organise consumer groups and to have their views represented.'[32]

Brown suggests that the resolution of consumer disputes with clear rules 'will not be sufficient for effective protection of consumers, advancement of their interests and the achievement of sustainable consumption and efficient allocation of resources'.[33] He believes three additional criteria are critical: the market should be disciplined by a proportion of educated and informed consumers; the institutions administering the rules need to be well designed and well resourced; and the people responsible for complaint resolution and regulatory enforcement must be not only well trained, but be able to act uninfluenced and be prepared to take some risks.[34]

Hence, local implementation of the Guidelines is necessary in order for them to be useful. They must also be enforced, with well trained and independent individuals and institutions in order to truly protect the basic rights of the consumers.

Basel Accords: transparent risk disclosure and risk minimisation

The Basel Accords provide guidelines that aim at preventing consumer financial disputes from occurring through 1) transparent risk disclosure on the part of banking institutions; and 2) risk minimisation through adequate capital reserves. The Basel Committee on Banking Supervision provides a forum for regular cooperation among banks, and develops guidelines and standards for banking matters and cross-border banking

---

[31] J. Delisle and E. Trujillo (Suppl. 2010) 'Consumer protection in transnational contexts', *Am. J. Comp. L.*, 58, 135, p. 24, available at: http://papers.ssrn.com/sol3/papers.cfm?abstract_id=1673945 [accessed 25 April 2012].

[32] The Reagan Administration and Multinationals (August 1984) *Multinational Monitor* 5(8), available at: www.multinationalmonitor.org/hyper/issues/1984/08/reagan.html [accessed 25 April 2012].

[33] R. Brown, 'The UN Guidelines for Consumer Protection: making them work in developing countries', p. 5.

[34] Ibid.

supervision. It does not possess any legal authority but formulates supervisory best practice standards and guidelines for local authorities to implement nationally. The latest instalment of the Basel Accords, 'Basel III', is a response to the late-2010s financial crisis and aims at improving the banking sector's ability to absorb shocks arising from financial and economic stress, improve risk management and governance, and strengthen banks' transparency and disclosures. It is suggested that if jurisdictions and their institutions comply with the capital requirements and disclosure and risk management standards as suggested by the Accords, investors will be better protected and the need for a massive bailout by the public sector may be less likely.[35]

As noted, the Committee does not possess any formal supervisory authority, and its conclusions do not have legal force. Rather, it formulates broad supervisory standards and guidelines and recommends statements of best practice in the expectation that individual authorities will take steps to implement them through detailed arrangements – statutory or otherwise – which are best suited to their own national systems. The Committee encourages convergence towards common approaches and standards without attempting detailed harmonisation of member countries' supervisory techniques.[36]

The Committee attributed a major cause of the economic and financial crisis in the late-2010s to the excessive on- and off-balance sheet leverage in the banking and shadow banking sectors of many countries. Due to a gradual erosion of the level and quality of the capital base and the fact that many banks were holding insufficient liquidity buffers, the banking system was hence incapable of absorbing the resulting systemic trading and credit losses.[37] As a result, the market lost confidence in the solvency and liquidity of many banking institutions. The weaknesses in the banking

---

[35] Bank for International Settlements, 'About the Basel Committee', available at: www.bis.org/bcbs/about.htm [accessed 25 April 2012]. The Basel Committee's objective is to enhance understanding of key supervisory issues and improve the quality of banking supervision worldwide. It attempts to do so by exchanging information on national supervisory issues, approaches and techniques, with a view to promoting common understanding. The Committee also uses this common understanding to develop guidelines and supervisory standards. The Committee is best known for its international standards on capital adequacy; the Core Principles for Effective Banking Supervision; and the Concordat on cross-border banking supervision.

[36] Bank for International Settlements, 'History of the Basel Committee and its Membership', available at: www.bis.org/bcbs/history.htm [accessed 25 April 2012].

[37] Basel Committee of Banking Supervision (Revised June 2011) 'Basel III: A global regulatory framework for more resilient banks and banking systems', p. 5, available at: www.

sector were rapidly transmitted to the rest of the financial system and the real economy, which led to a massive contraction of liquidity and credit availability. Eventually, the public sector had to step in with unprecedented injections of liquidity, capital support and guarantees, which led to taxpayers suffering large losses.[38]

To address the market failures by the largely under regulated banking sector, the Committee introduced a number of fundamental reforms[39] to the international regulatory framework, now known as 'Basel III'.[40] Among the measures recommended in Basel III include enhanced risk disclosure and greater transparency on the part of the banks.[41] In many

---

bis.org/publ/bcbs189.pdf [accessed 25 April 2012]. Nor could it withstand the reintermediation of large off-balance sheet exposures that had built up in the shadow banking system. Moreover, the crisis was further amplified by a procyclical deleveraging process and by the interconnectedness of systemic institutions through an array of complex transactions.

[38] Basel Committee of Banking Supervision, 'Basel III: A global regulatory framework for more resilient banks and banking systems', p. 5.

[39] Ibid. The reforms aim to strengthen bank-level, or microprudential, regulation, which will help raise the resilience of individual banking institutions to periods of stress. The reforms also have a macroprudential focus, addressing system-wide risks that can build up across the banking sector as well as the procyclical amplification of these risks over time. These micro and macroprudential approaches to supervision are interrelated, as greater resilience at the individual bank level can additionally reduce the risk of system-wide shocks.

[40] Moody's Analytics (2011) 'Implementing Basel III: Challenges, Options & Opportunities', *White Paper September 2011*, p. 3, available at: www.moodysanalytics.com/Contact-Us/ERM/Contact-Form-Basel-III-Implementation/~/media/Insight/Regulatory/Basel-III/Thought-Leadership/2011/11-01-09-Implementing-Basel-III-Whitepaper.ashx [accessed 25 April 2012]. Basel III is part of the Committee's continuous effort to enhance the banking regulatory framework, building on the International Convergence of Capital Measurement and Capital Standards document ('Basel II').

[41] Bank for International Settlements, 'International regulatory framework for banks (Basel III)', available at: www.bis.org/bcbs/basel3.htm [accessed 25 April 2012]. It is a 'comprehensive set of reform measures, developed by the Basel Committee on Banking Supervision, to strengthen the regulation, supervision and risk management of the banking sector. These measures aim to:

• improve the banking sector's ability to absorb shocks arising from financial and economic stress, whatever the source
• improve risk management and governance
• strengthen banks' transparency and disclosures.

The reforms target:

• bank-level, or microprudential, regulation, which will help raise the resilience of individual banking institutions to periods of stress.
• macroprudential, system wide risks that can build up across the banking sector as well as the procyclical amplification of these risks over time.

jurisdictions, including Hong Kong and Singapore, among the most significant complaints voiced by aggrieved purchasers of Lehman Minibond notes were that the banks did note sufficiently disclose the risks associated with the purchase of such Minibonds.

Naturally, once member states legislate or implement the Basel rules, banks will come under the governance of such local laws and regulations with the aim of preventing financial disputes with increased capital (security) requirements, and preventing excessive leverage, so that investor risk is minimised.

The implementation of Basel III has occurred to a varying extent throughout the world.[42] The EU has been consistent in its adoption of past

---

These two approaches to supervision are complementary as greater resilience at the individual bank level reduces the risk of system wide shocks.'

[42] Ibid. The central bank Governors of the Group of Ten countries established the Basel Committee at the end of 1974. They meet regularly four times a year, and have four main working groups which also meet regularly.

The Committee's members come from Argentina, Australia, Belgium, Brazil, Canada, China, France, Germany, Hong Kong SAR, India, Indonesia, Italy, Japan, Luxembourg, Mexico, the Netherlands, Russia, Saudi Arabia, Singapore, South Africa, South Korea, Spain, Sweden, Switzerland, Turkey, the United Kingdom and the United States. Countries are represented by their central banks or the equivalent authority with the formal responsibility for the prudential supervision of banking business. On the other hand, the Committee reports to the central bank Governors and Heads of Supervision of its member countries and seeks their endorsement for its major initiatives.

A central goal of the Committee is to close gaps in international supervisory coverage in pursuit of two basic principles: no foreign banking establishment should escape supervision; and that supervision should be adequate. To achieve this, the Committee has issued a long series of documents since 1975.

In 1988, the Committee introduced a capital measurement system commonly referred to as the 'Basel Capital Accord'. This system provided for the implementation of a credit risk measurement framework with a minimum capital standard of 8 per cent by 1992. This framework has been progressively introduced not only in member countries but also in virtually all other countries with internationally active banks. The Committee proposed a revised Capital Adequacy Framework in 1999, which consists of three 'pillars': minimum capital requirements, which refine the standardised rules set forth in the 1988 Accord; supervisory review of an institution's internal assessment process and capital adequacy; and effective use of disclosure to strengthen market discipline as a complement to supervisory efforts. Following extensive interaction with banks, industry groups and supervisory authorities that are not members of the Committee, the revised framework ('Basel II') was issued on 26 June 2004.

Over the past few years, the Committee are said to be more aggressive in their bid to promote sound supervisory standards worldwide. In response to the late-2010s financial crisis, the Committee and its oversight body, the Group of Governors and Heads of Supervision, have developed a reform programme to address the lessons of the crisis, which delivers on the mandates for banking sector reforms established by the G20 at

Basel Accords and therefore aims to seamlessly migrate from Basel II to Basel III.[43] Japan, Hong Kong, Singapore and Australia are well advanced and on a par with the European Union. The United States aims to build on the foundations of Basel I with the widely publicised Dodd-Frank Act.[44]

In 2010, some banks cautioned that the Basel Accords and other reforms could cause a 3 per cent reduction in economic growth over the next five years in the United States, Euro Zone and Japan, resulting in the loss of almost ten million jobs. However, the OECD published its study soon after, which estimated that Basel III rules will only affect economic growth by 0.05 to 0.15 percentage points a year.[45] The additional costs for disclosure and review, as well as maintenance of capital to satisfy the new requirements, are said to be an essential and necessary trade-off in order to prevent financial disputes and, more importantly, another credit crisis.

Global deliberation

In recent times, public deliberation efforts among members of civil society have highlighted the principles of access to justice, equity and fairness in the context of the resolution of financial disputes worldwide. Facilitated by a growing use of social networks, recent movements, such as the Occupy movement, have focused attention on the lack of financial oversight and regulation of high-risk investments.[46]

Global deliberation can take many forms. It may be defined as 'an approach to politics in which citizens, not just experts or politicians, are deeply involved in community problem solving and public decision making'.[47]

---

their 2009 Pittsburgh summit. Collectively, the new global standards to address risks on both on the levels of individual firms and the broader banking systems have been referred to as 'Basel III'.

[43] Moody's Analytics, 'Implementing Basel III: Challenges, Options & Opportunities', p. 4.

[44] The extra-territorial impact of the Dodd Frank Act and in particular the Volker Rule was recently addressed in an AIIFL talk by Jeffrey H. Chen (Spring 2012).

[45] H. Jones and D. Hulmes (15 February 2011) 'Basel rules to have little impact on economy – OECD', *Reuters*, available at: www.reuters.com/article/2011/02/16/oecd-basel-idUSLDE71E23Q20110216 [accessed 25 April 2012].

[46] M. Muskal (15 November 2011) 'Occupy Wall Street camps are today's Hoovervilles', *The Los Angeles Times*.

[47] Center for Public Deliberation, 'What is deliberation?', available at: www.cpd.colostate.edu/what.html [accessed 25 April 2012].

In the backdrop of the Global Financial Crisis in the late-2000s and with the aid of social networks and a 'non-binding consensus based collective decision-making tool',[48] the Occupy movement quickly caught on and spread to nearly 100 cities in the United States and over 1,500 cities globally and has become a 'factor in the national political debate'.[49] Among the major issues voiced by the movement include access to justice, fairness and equity.[50]

The importance of fairness as advocated in the Occupy movement is well summarised by former British Prime Minister Gordon Brown: 'Anti-Wall Street protests … are driven by concerns over "what's fair and what's responsible … It's not about the extremes in this debate".'[51] 'There are voices in the middle who say, "Look, we can build a better financial system that is more sustainable, that is based on a better and proportionate sense of what's just and fair and where people don't take reckless risks or, if they do, they're penalised for doing so,"' Brown said.[52]

The principles of accountability and fairness addressed by the movement have opened up a dialogue on how such principles might be integrated into government policy. While there has been no apparent legal development *as a result* of the Occupy movement, during this same time, many policy makers have put forward suggestions on ways to reform the financial market to make it an environment characterised by greater transparency and fairness. For example, Joseph Petrick offers a number of suggestions on how the financial markets can be better regulated in response to general calls for greater fairness.[53] In addition, the proposed EU Financial Transaction Tax,[54] which aims to tax all financial transactions in the EU in order to increase the contribution of financial services to support failing social structures and limit market volatility, earmarking the funds for poverty reduction and other public programmes, emerged

---

[48] Occupy Wall Street, 'About', available at: www.occupywallst.org/about/ [accessed 25 April 2012].

[49] M. Muskal, 'Occupy Wall Street camps are today's Hoovervilles'.

[50] Occupy Wall Street (29 September 2011) 'Declaration of the Occupation of New York City', available at: www.nycga.net/resources/declaration/ [accessed 25 April 2012].

[51] Bloomberg (21 October 2011) 'Ex-British Chief Brown Says Wall Street Protestors Seek Fairness', available at: www.bloomberg.com/news/2011-10-21/ex-british-chief-brown-says-wall-street-protests-seek-fairness.html [accessed 25 April 2012].

[52] Ibid.

[53] J. A. Petrick (2011) 'Sustainable stakeholder capitalism: a moral vision of responsible global financial risk management', *J. Bus. Ethics*, 99(1), pp. 93–109.

[54] A more targeted reform is suggested in the recent article: John Vella, Clemens Fuest and Tim Schmidt-Eisenlohr (2011) 'The EU Commission's Proposal for a Financial Transaction Tax', *British Tax Review*, 6.

following general calls for greater equity and transparency in the financial industry.[55]

UN millennium development goals – objective 8a: to develop an open, rule-based trading system

The UN Millennium Declaration, adopted in September 2000[56] with input from NGOs and civil society, puts forward a number of goals[57] and targets[58] aimed at advancing global development. Among the goals

---

[55] L. Beeston (11 October 2011) 'The ballerina and the bull', *The Link*, available at: http://thelinknewspaper.ca/article/1951 [accessed 25 April 2012]. See also J. Vella (26 March 2012), *The EU's Commission for a Proposed Financial Transaction Tax*, HKU, for discussion of alternative methods such as a banking tax.

[56] Millennium Project, 'What they are', available at: www.unmillenniumproject.org/goals/index.htm [accessed 25 April 2012].

[57] The United Nations, 'Background', available at: www.un.org/millenniumgoals/bkgd.shtml [accessed 25 April 2012]. The eight Millennium Development Goals ('MDGs') range from halving extreme poverty to stopping the spread of HIV/AIDS and providing universal primary education by the target date of 2015 form a blueprint agreed to by all the world's countries and all the world's leading development institutions in 2000.

These eight goals are further divided into eighteen targets, which are complemented by forty-eight technical indicators to measure their progress. These indicators have since been adopted by a consensus of experts from the United Nations, International Monetary Fund ('IMF'), the Organisation for Economic Co-operation and Development ('OECD') and the World Bank. The Goals are rather self-explanatory, and perhaps only Goal 8 is relevant to our purposes. The first seven Goals are provided below, together with Goal 8 and its first target (Target 12, otherwise known as Objective 8A).

- Goal 1: Eradicate extreme poverty and hunger
- Goal 2: Achieve universal primary education
- Goal 3: Promote gender equality and empower women
- Goal 4: Reduce child mortality
- Goal 5: Improve maternal health
- Goal 6: Combat HIV/AIDS, malaria and other diseases
- Goal 7: Ensure environmental sustainability
- Goal 8: Develop a global partnership for development
    • Target 12: Develop further an open, rule-based, predictable, non-discriminatory trading and financial system (includes a commitment to good governance, development, and poverty reduction bother nationally and internationally)

There are indicators that are used to measure the success of achieving these goals. For instance, for Targets 12–15, indicators include the statistics gathered on official development assistance ('ODA'), market access, and debt sustainability. It must be noted that none of these address Target 12 specifically.

[58] Millennium Project (2006) 'Goals, Targets and Indicators', available at: www.unmillenniumproject.org/goals/gti.htm [accessed 25 April 2012].

include the aim of 'develop[ing] further an open, rule-based, predictable, non-discriminatory ... financial system' (Goal 8a). On this basis, no individual or nation is to be denied the chance to benefit from development and global challenges are to be managed in a way that distributes the costs and benefits fairly.[59]

The goals reflect an underlying view that rising inequity leads to more financial instability and vulnerability to external economic shocks. As a result, low- and middle-income earners with falling wages have to maintain or increase their consumption by relying on borrowed funds.[60]

Progress towards the goal of achieving an 'open, rule-based, predictable, non-discriminatory ... financial system' (Goal 8a) has been advanced through increasing global coordination through the International Monetary Fund which engages in ongoing research regarding financial stability, country-level and regional macro-economic analysis, review, consultation and policy formation.

Rule of law principles: impartiality, fairness, transparency and consistency

Rule of law principles, including principles of impartiality, fairness, transparency and consistency, are directly relevant to the design and development of consumer financial dispute resolution mechanisms.[61]

It is clear that the general principles of the rule of law provide the standards by which most disputes, including financial disputes, are prevented

---

[59] Overseas Development Institute ('ODI') (April 2010) 'The MDGs fundamentals: improving equity for development', *Briefing Paper*, available at: www.odi.org.uk/resources/docs/5833.pdf [accessed 25 April 2012].

[60] Ibid., with reference to G. Turner (2008) *The Credit Crunch: Housing Bubbles, Globalization and the Worldwide Economic Crisis* (London: Pluto Press). When lending practices are poorly regulated, as in the late-2000s global financial crisis, rising demand for borrowing fuels unsustainable debt levels. In the short run, the credit-fuelled boom offset the social and political tensions of increased inequity. But once borrowers defaulted, boom turned to bust. Individuals with growing debt would then have increased vulnerability to external shocks such as illness, unemployment and natural disaster.

[61] A. V. Dicey (1915) *Introduction to the Study of the Law of the Constitution*, 8th edn (Macmillan,), p. vi. The rule of law is an old concept, originating with Aristotle's idea that 'law should govern'. Popularising the term 'rule of law' was English jurist and theorist Albert Dicey in the late-nineteenth century. Dicey identified a few essential characteristics of law:

    i. The supremacy of law. All persons (individuals and government) are subject to law
   ii. A concept of justice which emphasises interpersonal adjudication, law based on standards and the importance of procedures

and resolved.[62] At the global level, the United Nations defines rule of law as 'principles of ... equality before the law, accountability to the law, fairness in the application of the law ... participation in decision-making, legal certainty, avoidance of arbitrariness and procedural and legal transparency'.[63] Scholars have suggested that the applicability of the rule of law to the international level will depend on that ideal 'serving a function rather than defining a status [as] [s]uch a vision of the rule of law more accurately reflects the development of the rule of law in national jurisdictions'.[64]

Theorists such as Lon Fuller, Joseph Raz and H.L.A. Hart have also contributed to the development of the concept of rule of law in the later decades of the twentieth century. Such principles of legality[65] include the idea that laws must be general, prospective, clear and non-contradictory,[66] justice must be accessible[67] and all must be bound by and act consistently with the law.[68]

Theorists have provided important accounts of the importance of the rule of law to a market-economy, and hence presumably, to the resolution of financial disputes.[69] Based on this view, with the rule of law, individuals can feel assured that their disputes will be resolved fairly and consistently. Under the rule of law, individuals are able to invest and plan for the future, believing that they can be assured of the security of their returns.[70]

   iii. Restrictions on discretionary power
   iv. The doctrine of judicial precedent
   v. Legislation should be prospective and not retrospective.
   vi. An independent judiciary
   vii. An underlying moral basis for all law

     Dicey's considerations are understandably focused on the English setting. It did, however, present a general framework for understanding the concept of rule of law, which was followed by theorists such as Fuller and Raz.

[62] B. Tamanaha, 'A concise guide to the rule of law', *Legal Studies Research Paper Series Paper # 07–0082*, p. 2, available at http://ssrn.com/abstract=1012051 [accessed 25 April 2012]. For fuller discussion, see B. Tamanaha (2004) *On Rule of Law: History, Politics, Theory* (Cambridge University Press).

[63] United Nations Rule of Law (2004), 'What is the rule of law?', quoted from *Report Of The Secretary-General: The Rule Of Law And Transitional Justice In Conflict And Post-Conflict Societies*, available at: www.unrol.org/article.aspx?article_id=3 [accessed 25 April 2012].

[64] Simon Chesterman (2008) 'An International Rule of Law?' *American Journal of Comparative Law*, 56, pp. 331–361.

[65] C. Murphy (2005) 'Lon Fuller and the moral value of the rule of law', *Law and Philosophy*, 24, p. 240.

[66] L. Fuller (1969) *Morality of Law*, rev. edn (New Haven: Yale University Press), p. 39.

[67] J. Raz, *Authority of Law* (Oxford: Clarendon Press), p. 213.

[68] B. Tamanaha, 'A concise guide to the rule of law', p. 3.

[69] F. A. Hayek (1944) *The Road to Serfdom* (University of Chicago Press), pp. 80–96.

[70] Ibid.

Tamanaha also provides insights into how the rule of law enhances certainty, predictability and security in the realm of property and contracts.[71] At the core of such principles is a common concern regarding safeguarding individuals against arbitrary decision making.[72] Providing new insight into the functioning of legal rules from a ground-up, technical and participatory level, Riles demonstrates that such technicalities are the core element of regulation and must be understood more broadly to engage the wider public in efforts to improve global financial governance.[73]

Given the nature of private dispute resolution, on the surface, many of the principles of the rule of law would seem to conflict with the theory and methodology of private disputing. Cases are treated on an individualised basis; precedent and formal rules play a limited role in decision making. Yet, there is a growing scholarship that alternative dispute resolution and rule of law principles may not be fundamentally at odds.[74] For example,

[71] B. Tamanaha, 'A concise guide to the rule of law', p. 2. For fuller discussion, see B. Tamanaha, *On Rule of Law: History, Politics, Theory*. First, if economic actors can better predict the anticipated costs and benefits of prospective transactions, they are hence more able to make more efficient decisions. Parties can enter into contracts with the confidence that the other party will live up to the terms of the contract (or they will get a remedy from the legal system). Hence, it is reasoned that because of this confidence bestowed by the rule of law, contracts with strangers or parties at a distance are possible, which expands the range and frequency of commercial and financial interactions, hence increasing the overall economic movement. Second, as Locke suggests, the protection of property (and persons) conferred by legal rules offers an assurance that the fruits of one's labour will be protected. This security allows individuals to put in their efforts to additional productive activity, and to enjoying its benefits, rather than expending time and effort on protecting existing gains.

[72] World Justice Project (2011) 'Rule of Law Index', the full index is available at: http://worldjusticeproject.org/rule-of-law-index-data [accessed 25 April 2012]. The World Justice Project ('WJP') attempts to give an objective quantitative assessment calculating the 'Rule of Law Index' in sixty-six major jurisdictions. The WJP identified nine key areas of rule of law and the relative performances of the jurisdictions in them. The areas are:

1. Limited Government Powers
2. Absence of Corruption
3. Order and Security
4. Fundamental Rights
5. Open Government
6. Effective Regulatory Enforcement
7. Access to Civil Justice
8. Effective Criminal Justice
9. Informal Justice

[73] A. Riles (2011) *Collateral Knowledge*. Chicago, Ill.: University of Chicago Press.

[74] See for example: R. C. Reuben (15 October 2010) 'How ADR can foster the rule of law: beyond the fundamental tension', Symposium on ADR and the Rule of Law: Making the Connection, Missouri School of Law,.

given the integration of alternative dispute resolution practices in judicial and regulatory decision making, and the dependence of core alternative dispute resolution processes such as arbitration, mediation and ombuds-based determination on law to secure enforcement, confidentiality and legitimacy, the relationship between the rule of law and alternative dispute resolution is often more closely integrated than it might appear on the surface.[75]

Summary

A number of helpful principles, useful to the development of consumer financial dispute resolution, can be gleaned from the Equator Principles, the Basel Accords, the UN Millennium Development Goals, global deliberative processes and general rule of law principles. They include the need for an accessible grievance mechanisms, financial dispute prevention through transparent risk disclosure and risk mitigation, justice, equity, accountability and fairness.

As will be seen in the chapters that follow, the ombuds and arbitration models of consumer financial dispute resolution implement such principles to varying degrees, based on the unique mandate, regulatory function and objectives of the mechanism. For example, as will be seen in the examination of the ombuds models of consumer financial dispute resolution, the principles of accessibility, accountability and fairness may be given greater importance, while in the arbitration model, principles of finality may take precedence.

In the context of observing the dynamic interaction of convergence and informed divergence at the global level, due to the fact that such non-binding global principles allow diverse consumer financial dispute resolution systems the option of opting in to particular standards, at the substantive level, divergence in costs, regulatory interplay and the binding nature of awards can co-exist with the three tier structure of most consumer financial dispute resolution processes.

In the chapters that follow, two major systems of consumer financial dispute resolution – the ombuds process and the arbitration system – will be examined, alongside the structural design, policy orientation, complaint procedures, financing and oversight of financial dispute resolution centres as established within each region.

---

[75] Ibid.

PART II

Ombuds systems

Part II examines the structure and function of ombuds-based consumer financial dispute resolution centres in the United Kingdom, Australia and Japan. The chapters systematically examine the structural design, policy orientation, complaint procedures, financing and oversight of financial dispute resolution centres as established within each region. Survey findings regarding the benefits, challenges and suggestions for improving the delivery of ombuds services in consumer financial disputes are presented at the end of this Part.

2

Financial dispute resolution in the United Kingdom

Introduction

As will be seen in this chapter, the United Kingdom ombudsman service operates on the basis of a number of important principles. These include: accessibility, efficiency and equity. In particular, the system aims to mitigate the often unequal bargaining position of claimants and large financial institutions by providing that decisions are made without prejudice to the claimant who retains the ability to pursue his/her claims in court. In addition, the service is free for eligible complainants, and enjoys high levels of compliance by financial services firms.[1] At the same time, the ombudsman service faces a number of challenges, including what some argue as limited oversight by the courts. These will be discussed in greater detail below.

Ombudsmen in the United Kingdom

The history of ombudsmen in the United Kingdom is a long one, traditionally associated with the handling of concerns about the national government and allegations of maladministration. The first such organisation was the Parliamentary and Health Service Ombudsman, which is comprised of the Parliamentary Commissioner for Administration and the Health Service Commissioner for England, created in 1967 by the Parliamentary Commissioner Act of that year. The Local Government Ombudsman for England and Wales was created in 1973, and a similar Ombudsman for Scotland was established in 1974.

In addition to the oversight of the government, there are also many industry-specific ombudsmen in the United Kingdom, including the Office of the Telecommunications Ombudsman, the Pensions Ombudsman and the Financial Ombudsman Service.

---

[1] E. Morris (2008) 'The Financial Ombudsman Service and the Hunt Review: continuing evolution in dispute resolution', *J.B.L.*, 8, pp. 785–808.

Alternative dispute resolution in the United Kingdom

Alternative dispute resolution is well established in the United Kingdom, with London being a leading centre of arbitration. Alternative dispute resolution ('ADR') more generally has long been incorporated into the civil procedure of the UK courts. The concept of active case management, for example, includes the court encouraging parties to use ADR and, where appropriate, to facilitate the use of ADR.[2] Parties can, in the course of civil proceedings, make a written request for a stay of proceedings while settlement via ADR is attempted; alternatively, the court may of its own initiative, make such an order if it considers that appropriate.[3] In respect of mediation specifically, where a party unreasonably refuses to mediate, they may be penalised in the court's order on costs.[4] Further efforts to increase the use of ADR include the government's pledge to consider and use ADR in all suitable cases where the other party accepts it,[5] court-backed mediation schemes,[6] and the Ministry of Justice's National Mediation Helpline.

---

[2] According to Civil Procedure Rules rule 1.4(2)(e) and 1.4(2)(f),

    (2) Active case management includes –
        (e) encouraging the parties to use an alternative dispute resolution procedure if the court considers that appropriate and facilitating the use of such procedure;
        (f) helping the parties to settle the whole or part of the case.

[3] See Civil Procedure Rules rule 26.4(1) and 26.4(2)(b), which states that:

    (1) A party may, when filing the completed allocation questionnaire, make a written request for the proceedings to be stayed while the parties try to settle the case by alternative dispute resolution or other means.
    (2)(b) [Where] the court, of its own initiative, considers that such a stay would be appropriate, the court will direct that the proceedings, either in whole or in part, be stayed for one month, or for such specified period as it considers appropriate.

[4] See Civil Procedure Rules rule 44.5(3)(a)(ii):

    (3) The court must also have regard to –
        (a) the conduct of all the parties, including in particular –
    (ii) the efforts made, if any, before and during the proceedings in order to try to resolve the dispute.

    For further, see *Halsey* v. *Milton Keynes General NHS Trust* [2004] 1 WLR 3002.

[5] 'Settlement of government disputes through ADR' pledge 2001 – see Ministry of Justice (March 2010) *Annual Pledge Report 2008–9: Monitoring the effectiveness of the government's commitment to using alternative dispute resolution 2/3/10*, available at: www. justice.gov.uk/publications/docs/alternative-dispute-resolution-08-09.pdf [accessed 15 February 2012].

[6] E.g. Automatic Referral to Mediation Scheme – Central London county court; Court of Appeal mediation scheme, etc.

In the wider regulatory context, as a member of the European Union, the United Kingdom is subject to the Mediation Directive.[7] The Directive only applies to cross-border disputes where two parties are domiciled in two different member states, but one commentator has remarked that 'the spread of compulsory mediation is foreshadowed by the European Mediation Directive … nothing in the Directive prevents Member States from extending the scope of any implementation legislation they pass to cover domestic disputes'.[8]

However, while there has been a marked increase in the use of mediation in the United Kingdom, it does not appear to have spread as rapidly as 'it might have done'. Reasons include misconceptions about mediation, the lack of education, and conservatism in the legal profession restraining its greater use.[9] In the final report for the Civil Litigation Costs Review, Lord Justice Jackson concludes: 'What is now needed is a serious campaign (a) to ensure that all litigation lawyers and judges (not just some litigation lawyers and judges) are properly informed about the benefits which ADR can bring and (b) to alert the public and small businesses to the benefits of ADR.'[10]

The Financial Ombudsman Service and the Financial Services and Markets Act

The Financial Services and Markets Act 2000 consolidated the regulation of financial services and markets under the Financial Services Authority ('FSA'), a single regulator for the entire financial industry. A consolidated statutory dispute resolution scheme was also created – the Financial Ombudsman Service ('FOS').

Into the FOS was incorporated eight independent ombudsmen and complaint-handling schemes, including the Insurance Ombudsman Bureau (as the insurance division of the FOS), the Personal Investment Authority and the Securities and Futures Authority Complaints Bureau (as the investment division of the FOS), and the Banking Ombudsman and the Building Societies Ombudsman (as the banking and loans division of the FOS).[11]

---

[7] Directive 2008/52/EC of the European Parliament and the Council of 21 May 2008 on certain aspects of mediation in civil and commercial matters OJ L136/3 24.5.2008.

[8] R. Clift (2009) 'The phenomenon of mediation: judicial perspectives and an eye on the future', *The Journal of International Maritime Law*, 15 pp. 508–517.

[9] Ibid.   [10] Ibid.

[11] Financial Ombudsman Service. (1999–2000) *Annual Report 1999/2000: Laying the foundations*, available at: www.financial-ombudsman.org.uk/publications/first-annual-report/ar-1999–2000.pdf [accessed 8 February 2012].

The Financial Services Compensation Scheme

In addition to the Financial Ombudsman Service, the Financial Services and Markets Act 2000 also established the Financial Services Compensation Scheme.[12] The Scheme was created to compensate customers of authorised financial services firms in the event of insolvency, and is a consolidation of previous compensation schemes. The Scheme covers deposits, insurance policies, insurance brokering, investments, mortgages and mortgage arrangement, and pays compensation up to certain limits when a firm is unable to pay claims against it because it has stopped trading or is in default.

A period of transition

Financial regulation and dispute resolution in the United Kingdom is presently undergoing a massive transition in the aftermath of the financial crisis. First, in June 2007, a review of pensions institutions for the Department for Work and Pensions recommended operational integration of the Pensions Ombudsman with the FOS, while maintaining a separate jurisdiction.

---

[12] The Scheme was established under s. 213 of the Financial Services and Markets Acts 2000:

  (1) The Authority must by rules establish a scheme for compensating persons in cases where relevant persons are unable, or are likely to be unable, to satisfy claims against them.

  (2) The rules are to be known as the Financial Services Compensation Scheme (but are referred to in this Act as 'the compensation scheme').

  (3) The compensation scheme must, in particular, provide for the scheme manager–
    (a) to assess and pay compensation, in accordance with the scheme, to claimants in respect of claims made in connection with regulated activities carried on (whether or not with permission) by relevant persons; and
    (b) to have power to impose levies on authorised persons, or any class of authorised person, for the purpose of meeting its expenses (including in particular expenses incurred, or expected to be incurred, in paying compensation, borrowing or insuring risks).

  (4) The compensation scheme may provide for the scheme manager to have power to impose levies on authorised persons, or any class of authorised person, for the purpose of recovering the cost (whenever incurred) of establishing the scheme.

  (5) In making any provision of the scheme by virtue of subsection (3)(b), the Authority must take account of the desirability of ensuring that the amount of the levies imposed on a particular class of authorised person reflects, so far as practicable, the amount of the claims made, or likely to be made, in respect of that class of person.

Second, in 2008, Lord Hunt's review of the FOS was published, focusing on the openness and accessibility of the FOS and recommending certain changes, some of which have since been implemented.

Third, new powers were conferred upon the FSA by the Financial Services Act 2010, as a result of the financial crisis – in particular, the Turner Review: A Regulatory Response to the Global Banking Crisis published in March 2009 and the HM Treasury White Paper entitled Reforming Financial Markets published in July 2009. These powers include the ability to order firms to carry out past business reviews (which assess if customers have been mistreated in breach of regulatory obligations, have suffered loss and deserve redress) – complaints which may also be directed to the FOS under the new s. 404B.[13]

---

[13] Section 404B of the Financial Services Act 2010 provides that:

    (1) If—

        (a) a consumer makes a complaint under the ombudsman scheme in respect of an act or omission of a relevant firm, and

        (b) at the time the complaint is made, the subject-matter of the complaint fails to be dealt with (or has been dealt with) under a consumer redress scheme, the way in which the complaint is to be determined by the ombudsman is to be as mentioned in subsection (4).

    (2) If a consumer—

        (a) is not satisfied with a determination made by a relevant firm under a consumer redress scheme, or

        (b) considers that a relevant firm has failed to make a determination in accordance with a consumer redress scheme, the consumer may, in respect of that determination or failure, make a complaint under the ombudsman scheme.

    (3) A complaint mentioned in subsection (1) or (2) is referred to in the following provisions of this section as a 'relevant complaint'.

    (4) A relevant complaint is to be determined by reference to what, in the opinion of the ombudsman, the determination under the consumer redress scheme should be or should have been (subject to subsection (5)).

    (5) If, in determining a relevant complaint, the ombudsman determines that the firm should make (or should have made) a payment of an amount to the consumer, the amount awarded by the ombudsman (a 'money award') must not exceed the monetary limit (within the meaning of section 229).

    (6) But the ombudsman may recommend that the firm pay a larger amount.

       ...

    (8) If, in determining a relevant complaint, the ombudsman determines that the firm should take (or should have taken) particular action in relation to the consumer, the ombudsman may direct the firm to take that action.

    (9) Compliance with a direction under subsection (8) is enforceable, on the application of the consumer, by an injunction or, in Scotland, by an order for specific performance under section 45 of the Court of Session Act 1988.

       ...

   (11) The compulsory jurisdiction of the ombudsman scheme is to include the jurisdiction resulting from this section.

It is worth noting that collective action by consumers in the financial services sector was debated as part of these reforms, but ultimately abandoned due to controversy – though the possibility of the introduction of such actions remains, with deep implications for financial dispute resolution.

Fourth, in June 2010, the abolition of the FSA was announced. Under the new system of financial regulation, the Bank of England will be in charge of macro-prudential regulation. A new Prudential Regulation Authority will be created as a subsidiary of the Bank, and will conduct prudential regulation. A new Consumer Protection and Regulatory Authority will be created to take on the regulation of the conduct of all financial services businesses, and take over responsibility for the Financial Ombudsman Service and the Financial Services Compensation Scheme. There will also be an Economic Crime Agency, responsible for the investigation of and bringing criminal prosecution for economic crimes such as insider dealing, market manipulation, etc.

In light of these possible developments, the role, jurisdiction and processes of the FOS will undoubtedly continue to develop and change.

Financial alternative dispute resolution programmes

Financial Ombudsman Service Limited

The Financial Ombudsman Service scheme is administered by a body corporate under s. 225 of the Financial Services and Markets Act 2000 as the scheme operator, the Financial Ombudsman Service Limited.[14] It is a public body, set up by Parliament, to carry out statutory functions on a non-commercial, not-for-profit basis.

Range of disputes

Complaints that are brought before the FOS are broadly separated into the following headings: banking and credit (including current accounts, credit

---

[14] Section 225 provides that:

  (1) This Part provides for a scheme under which certain disputes may be resolved quickly and with minimum formality by an independent person.
  (2) The scheme is to be administered by a body corporate ('the scheme operator').
  (3) The scheme is to be operated under a name chosen by the scheme operator but is referred to in this Act as 'the ombudsman scheme'.
  (4) Schedule 17 makes provision in connection with the ombudsman scheme and the scheme operator.

cards, mortgages, unsecured loans, consumer-credit products and services, savings accounts and other banking services); insurance (including payment protection, motor insurance, buildings insurance, travel insurance, contents insurance, extended warranties, commercial and business protection, income protection, critical illness, legal expenses, private medical and other insurance matters); and investments and pensions (including whole-of-life policies and savings endowments, unit-linked bonds, personal pension plans, stockbroking, investment ISAs, 'with-profits' bonds, portfolio management, guaranteed-income bonds, annuities, small self-administered schemes and self-invested pensions, derivatives, unit trusts, structured and other products – mortgage endowment complaints were included under investments and pensions in 2009).[15]

Structure

The casework of the FOS is dealt with in three stages: front-line enquiries and initial complaints (customer contact division); adjudicators who settle complaints informally (casework operations); and ombudsmen making formal decisions (a large panel of ombudsmen led by three lead ombudsman for insurance and investments, banking, loans, consumer credit and mortgages, and legal policy, under two principal ombudsman and the chief executive and chief ombudsman of the FOS).[16]

Underlying legal mandate

Under Part XVI and Sch. 17 of the Financial Services and Markets Act 2000, and s. 59 of the Consumer Credit Act 2006,[17] the FOS is set up as the statutory dispute resolution scheme.

Part XVI provides for the creation of the scheme and the scheme operator, the scheme's compulsory and voluntary jurisdiction, determination

---

[15] Financial Ombudsman Service. (2009–2010) *Annual Review 2009/2010*, available at: www.financial-ombudsman.org.uk/publications/ar10/ar10.pdf [accessed 8 February 2012].

[16] Financial Ombudsman Service. Our Organisation Chart, available at: www.financial-ombudsman.org.uk/about/organisation-chart.htm [accessed 8 February 2012].

[17] Section 59 of the Consumer Credit Act 2006 provides that:

(1) After section 226 of the 2000 Act insert—

'226A Consumer credit jurisdiction

(1) A complaint which relates to an act or omission of a person ('the respondent') is to be dealt with under the ombudsman scheme if the conditions mentioned in subsection (2) are satisfied.

of complaints under the compulsory jurisdiction, awards, costs, powers in respect of information and protection of data, and funding of the scheme by the financial industry. Both the compulsory and voluntary jurisdiction of the scheme are determined by way of rules, but the statutory power to determine complaints under the compulsory jurisdiction should be noted: 'A complaint is to be determined by reference to what is, in the opinion of the ombudsman, fair and reasonable in all the circumstances of the case.'[18]

Under Sch. 17, the body corporate that exercises the scheme operator must be established by the FSA.[19] The scheme operator must make a report to the FSA at least once a year as to the discharge of its functions, and the Chief Ombudsman is also required to do the same.[20] In respect of the compulsory jurisdiction, the FSA is empowered to make

    (2) The conditions are that—
        (a) the complainant is eligible and wishes to have the complaint dealt with under the scheme;
        (b) the complaint falls within a description specified in consumer credit rules;
        (c) at the time of the act or omission the respondent was the licensee under a standard licence or was authorised to carry on an activity by virtue of section 34A of the Consumer Credit Act 1974;
        (d) the act or omission occurred in the course of a business being carried on by the respondent which was of a type mentioned in subsection (3);
        (e) at the time of the act or omission that type of business was specified in an order made by the Secretary of State; and
        (f) the complaint cannot be dealt with under the compulsory jurisdiction.
    (3) The types of business referred to in subsection (2)(d) are—
        (a) a consumer credit business;
        (b) a consumer hire business;
        ...
    (4) A complainant is eligible if—
        (a) he is—
            (i) an individual; or
            (ii) a surety in relation to a security provided to the respondent in connection with the business mentioned in subsection (2)(d); and
        (b) he falls within a class of person specified in consumer credit rules.
    (5) The approval of the Treasury is required for an order under subsection (2)(e).
    (6) The jurisdiction of the scheme which results from this section is referred to in this Act as the 'consumer credit jurisdiction'.

[18] See s. 228(2) of the Financial Services and Markets Act 2000.
[19] See s. 2 of Sch. 17 of the Financial Services and Markets Act 2000: '(1) The Authority must establish a body corporate to exercise the functions conferred on the scheme operator by or under this Act.'
[20] See s. 7 of Sch 17 of the Financial Services and Markets Act 2000:

    (1) At least once a year–
        (a) the scheme operator must make a report to the Authority on the discharge of its functions; and

rules in respect of the time limit for bringing complaints.[21] While the scheme operator makes rules which set out the procedure for dealing with complaints, the consent of the FSA is required before such rules may be made.[22] Similarly, the terms of reference in respect of the voluntary jurisdiction are determined by the scheme operator with the approval of the FSA.[23]

Financial services firms authorised by the FSA are required to adhere to rules published by the FSA in its Handbook – rules pertaining to the FOS are found in the section of the Handbook, Dispute resolution: complaints. The first chapter contains rules and guidance on how authorised firms should deal with complaints promptly and fairly. The second, third and fourth chapters detail how the FOS deals with unresolved complaints.

Determining jurisdiction

The scope of the FOS' jurisdiction is determined with reference to the type of activity a complaint relates to, the place where the activity complained of is carried on, the eligibility of the complainant, and whether or not the complaint was referred to the FOS in time.[24]

An eligible complainant is a person who is a consumer, a micro-enterprise, a charity with an annual income of less than £1 million or a trustee of a

---

(b) the Chief Ombudsman must make a report to the Authority on the discharge of his functions.

[21] See s. 13 of Sch. 17 of the Financial Services and Markets Act 2000: '(1) The Authority must make rules providing that a complaint is not to be entertained unless the complainant has referred it under the ombudsman scheme before the applicable time limit (determined in accordance with the rules) has expired.'

[22] See s. 14 of Sch. 17 of the Financial Services and Markets Act 2000: '(1) The scheme operator must make rules, to be known as "scheme rules", which are to set out the procedure for reference of complaints and for their investigation, consideration and determination by an ombudsman.'

[23] See s. 18 of Sch. 17 of the Financial Services and Markets Act 2000:

(1) Complaints are to be dealt with and determined under the voluntary jurisdiction on standard terms fixed by the scheme operator with the approval of the Authority.
(2) Different standard terms may be fixed with respect to different matters or in relation to different cases.
...
(4) The scheme operator may not vary any of the standard terms or add or remove terms without the approval of the Authority.

[24] See DISP 2.2 of the FSA Handbook.

trust with a net asset value of less than £1 million.[25] The complainant must be a customer, a payment service user, a holder or a beneficial owner of a collective investment scheme, a beneficiary of a personal pension scheme or stakeholder pension scheme, a guarantor of a mortgage or loan or a beneficiary of a trust or estate of the establishment complained against.[26]

Certain types of complainant are excluded under the Rules, for example, a firm, a payment service provider, an electronic money holder, a professional client the complaint of which falls within the compulsory jurisdiction or a body corporate or certain types of partnership the complaint of which falls within the compulsory jurisdiction.[27]

The FOS will only consider complaints where the establishment complained against has already sent the complainant its final response in respect of the complaint, or eight weeks have elapsed since the establishment received the complaint.[28] The FOS cannot consider complaints

---

[25] See DISP 2.7.3 of the FSA Handbook:
An eligible complainant must be a person that is:

   (1) a consumer;
   (2) a micro-enterprise;
     (a) in relation to a complaint relating wholly or partly to payment services, either at the time of the conclusion of the payment service contract or at the time the complainant refers the complaint to the respondent; or
     (b) otherwise, at the time the complainant refers the complaint to the respondent;
   (3) a charity which has an annual income of less than £1 million at the time the complainant refers the complaint to the respondent; or
   (4) a trustee of a trust which has a net asset value of less than £1 million at the time the complainant refers the complaint to the respondent.

[26] Only an overview of the most common types of eligible complainant is listed here. For the full list of types of eligible complainant and further details, please refer to DISP 2.7.6 of the FSA Handbook.

[27] For further, see DISP 2.7.9 of the FSA Handbook:
The following are not eligible complainants:

   (1) (in all jurisdictions) a firm, payment service provider, electronic money issuer, licensee or VJ participant whose complaint relates in any way to an activity which:
     (a) the firm itself has permission to carry on; or
     (ab) the firm, payment service provider or electronic money issuer itself is entitled to carry on under the Payment Services Regulations or the Electronic Money Regulations; or
     (b) the licensee or VJ participant itself conducts;

and which is subject to the Compulsory Jurisdiction, the Consumer Credit Jurisdiction or the Voluntary Jurisdiction; ...

[28] See DISP 2.8.1 of the FSA Handbook:
The Ombudsman can only consider a complaint if:

   (1) the respondent has already sent the complainant its final response; or
   (2) eight weeks have elapsed since the respondent received the complaint; ...

more than six months after the date on which the final response was sent or more than six years from the date the complainant reasonably ought to have become aware of the cause for complaint. The FOS is empowered certain discretion in respect of the time limits.[29] There are also exceptions to the time limits in respect of reviews of past business[30] and mortgage endowment complaints.[31]

Compulsory jurisdiction

The activities to which the compulsory jurisdiction applies are regulated activities (see s. 22 of the Financial Services and Markets Act 2000[32]), payment services, consumer credit activities, lending money secured by a charge on land, lending money, paying money by plastic card, providing ancillary banking services or any ancillary activities including advice.[33] The territorial scope of the compulsory jurisdiction is restricted to activities carried on from an establishment in the United Kingdom.[34]

---

[29] See DISP 2.8.2–2.8.4 of the FSA Handbook:
2.8.2 The Ombudsman cannot consider a complaint if the complainant refers it to the Financial Ombudsman Service:

   (1) more than six months after the date on which the respondent sent the complainant its final response or redress determination; or
   (2) more than:
      (a) six years after the event complained of; or (if later)
      (b) three years from the date on which the complainant became aware (or ought reasonably to have become aware) that he had cause for complaint;
...
2.8.3 The six-month time limit is only triggered by a response which is a final response. A final response must tell the complainant about the six-month time limit that the complainant has to refer a complaint to the Financial Ombudsman Service.
2.8.4 An example of exceptional circumstances might be where the complainant has been or is incapacitated.

[30] See DISP 2.8.5 of the FSA Handbook.
[31] See DISP 2.8.6–2.8.7 of the FSA Handbook.
[32] See s. 22 of the Financial Services and Markets Act 2000:

   (1) An activity is a regulated activity for the purposes of this Act if it is an activity of a specified kind which is carried on by way of business and—
      (a) relates to an investment of a specified kind; or
      (b) in the case of an activity of a kind which is also specified for the purposes of this paragraph, is carried on in relation to property of any kind.

[33] See DISP 2.3.1 of the FSA Handbook.
[34] See DISP 2.6.1 of the FSA Handbook:

   (1) The Compulsory Jurisdiction covers complaints about the activities of a firm (including its appointed representatives), of a payment service provider (including agents of

Consumer credit jurisdiction

The consumer credit jurisdiction applies where the activity is not covered by the compulsory jurisdiction and relates to acts or omissions by a licensee under the Consumer Credit Act 1974 carrying on consumer credit activities or ancillary activities including advice.[35] The consumer credit jurisdiction covers activities carried on by an establishment in the United Kingdom.[36]

Voluntary jurisdiction

The voluntary jurisdiction applies to a list of activities similar to those listed under the compulsory jurisdiction, but not covered by either the compulsory jurisdiction or the consumer credit jurisdiction. The person carrying on the activities must be subject to the voluntary jurisdiction by contract.[37] The voluntary jurisdiction covers the activities of

a payment institution) or of an electronic money issuer (including agents of an electronic money institution) carried on from an establishment in the United Kingdom.

[35] See DISP 2.4.1 of the FSA Handbook:
The Ombudsman can consider a complaint under the Consumer Credit Jurisdiction if:

(1) it is not covered by the Compulsory Jurisdiction; and
(2) it relates to an act or omission by a licensee in carrying on
(a) one or more consumer credit activities; or
(b) any ancillary activities, including advice, carried on by the licensee in connection with them.

[36] See DISP 2.6.3 of the FSA Handbook: 'The Consumer Credit Jurisdiction covers only complaints about the activities of a licensee carried on from an establishment in the United Kingdom.'

[37] See DISP 2.5.1 of the FSA Handbook:
The Ombudsman can consider a complaint under the Voluntary Jurisdiction if:

(1) it is not covered by the Compulsory Jurisdiction or the Consumer Credit Jurisdiction; and
(2) it relates to an act or omission by a VJ participant in carrying on one or more of the following activities:
(a) an activity carried on after 28 April 1988 which:
(i) was not a regulated activity at the time of the act or omission, but
(ii) was a regulated activity when the VJ participant joined the Voluntary Jurisdiction (or became an authorised person, if later);
(b) a financial services activity carried on after commencement by a VJ participant which was covered in respect of that activity by a former scheme immediately before the commencement day;
(c) activities which (at 30 April 2011) were regulated activities or would be regulated activities if they were carried on from an establishment in the United Kingdom (these activities are listed in DISP 2 Annex 1 G); ...

an establishment in the United Kingdom or elsewhere in the European Economic Area if the activity is directed at the United Kingdom, the contracts governing the activity are made under UK law, and the relevant establishment has notified appropriate regulators in its home state of its intention to participate in the voluntary jurisdiction.[38]

Procedures of the Financial Ombudsman Service

The approach of the FOS will depend on the facts of the complaint, but generally, the FOS will attempt to settle the complaint informally through mediation or conciliation. If such conciliation or mediation is not possible, based on the relevant documents, an adjudicator's view on how the case should be resolved is given in writing to both sides. Where one side is unhappy with the adjudicator's view, they can ask for a review and final decision by an ombudsman. At this stage, a request for a hearing would be considered, and the ombudsman will perform an independent review of the complaint. Where the ombudsman's decision is accepted by the complainant, it is binding on both parties, but if not, neither party is bound by the decision and the complainant is free to take out court proceedings.[39]

As has been noted above, the Ombudsman will determine complaints by reference to what is fair and reasonable in the circumstances.[40] In

---

[38] See DISP 2.6.4 of the FSA Handbook:
The Voluntary Jurisdiction covers only complaints about the activities of a VJ participant carried on from an establishment:

(1) in the United Kingdom; or
(2) elsewhere in the EEA if the following conditions are met:
   (a) the activity is directed wholly or partly at the United Kingdom (or part of it);
   (b) contracts governing the activity are (or, in the case of a potential customer, would have been) made under the law of England and Wales, Scotland or Northern Ireland; and
   (c) the VJ participant has notified appropriate regulators in its Home State of its intention to participate in the Voluntary Jurisdiction.

[39] Financial Ombudsman Service. A quick guide to how we handle disputes between businesses and consumers, available at: www.financial-ombudsman.org.uk/publications/technical_notes/QG7.pdf [accessed 8 February 2012].
[40] See FSA Handbook DISP 3.6.1: 'The Ombudsman will determine a complaint by reference to what is, in his opinion, fair and reasonable in all the circumstances of the case.' See also s. 228 of the Financial Services and Markets Act 2000:

(1) This section applies only in relation to the compulsory jurisdiction and to the consumer credit jurisdiction.
(2) A complaint is to be determined by reference to what is, in the opinion of the ombudsman, fair and reasonable in all the circumstances of the case.

determining what is fair and reasonable, the Ombudsman will have regard for the relevant laws and regulations, regulators' rules, guidance and standards, codes of practice, and what the Ombudsman considers to be good industry practice at the relevant time.[41]

A complaint may be dismissed without having its merits considered where it is considered that the complainant is unlikely to suffer financial loss, material distress or inconvenience, the complaint is frivolous or vexatious, or has no reasonable prospect of success, the establishment complained against has already made an offer of compensation or goodwill payment that is fair and reasonable in the circumstances and still open for acceptance, the subject matter of the complaint has been or is being dealt with by court proceedings, or is more suitably dealt with by the court or other arbitration or complaints scheme, if the complaint is about a legitimate exercise of commercial judgment, employment matters, investment performance, an exercise of discretion under a will or trust, a pure landlord and tenant issue arising out of a regulated sale and rent back agreement.[42]

Complaints may also be dismissed without consideration of the merits in order to allow a court to consider the complaint a test case if the FOS receives from the establishment complained against a written statement about how and why the complaint raises an important or novel point of law with significant consequences, and undertakes to pay the complainant's costs and disbursements within six months of the complaint being dismissed by the court. A test case may also be brought where the FOS considers the complaint raises important or novel points of law with important consequences that would be more suitably dealt with by the courts.[43]

---

[41] See DISP 3.6.4 of the FSA Handbook:
> In considering what is fair and reasonable in all the circumstances of the case, the *Ombudsman* will take into account:
>
> (1) relevant:
>   (a) law and regulations;
>   (b) regulators' rules, guidance and standards;
>   (c) codes of practice; and
> (2) (where appropriate) what he considers to have been good industry practice at the relevant time.

[42] See DISP 3.3.4 of the FSA Handbook.
[43] See DISP 3.3.5 of the FSA Handbook:
> The Ombudsman may dismiss a complaint without considering its merits, so that a court may consider it as a test case, if:
>
> (1) before he has made a determination, he has received in writing from the respondent:
>   (a) a detailed statement of how and why, in the respondent's opinion, the complaint raises an important or novel point of law with significant consequences; and

Awards

The maximum money award the Ombudsman may make is £100,000,[44] from which costs, interest on the principal award and interest on costs are excluded.[45] However, the Rules expressly set out that complainants should not need to have professional advisers to bring complaints, and thus awards of costs should be uncommon.[46] If the Ombudsman considers fair compensation requires payment of a larger amount, it may recommend that the complainant be paid the balance.[47] In addition to money awards, interest awards and costs awards, the Ombudsman is also empowered to give directions in respect of steps to be taken by the establishment complained against as the Ombudsman considers just and appropriate, regardless of whether or not a court could have made such an order.[48]

Awards are enforceable by complainants through the courts.[49]

...

(2) the Ombudsman considers that the complaint:
    (a) raises an important or novel point of law, which has important consequences; and
    (b) would more suitably be dealt with by a court as a test case.

[44] See DISP 3.7.4 of the FSA Handbook: 'The maximum money award which the Ombudsman may make is £150,000 (including costs and interest).'

[45] See DISP 3.7.5 of the FSA Handbook:
For the purpose of calculating the maximum money award, the following are excluded:

(1) any interest awarded on the amount payable under a money award;
(2) any costs awarded; and
(3) any interest awarded on costs.

[46] See DISP 3.7.10 of the FSA Handbook: 'In most cases complainants should not need to have professional advisers to bring complaints to the Financial Ombudsman Service, so awards of costs are unlikely to be common.'

[47] See DISP 3.7.6 of the FSA Handbook:

3.7.6 If the Ombudsman considers that fair compensation requires payment of a larger amount, he may recommend that the respondent pays the complainant the balance. The effect of section 404B(6) of the Act is that this is also the case in relation to a complaint the subject matter of which falls to be dealt with (or has properly been dealt with) under a consumer redress scheme.

[48] See DISP 3.7.11 of the FSA Handbook:

Except in relation to a complaint the subject matter of which falls to be dealt with (or has properly been dealt with) under a consumer redress scheme, a3 direction may require the respondent to take such steps in relation to the complainant as the Ombudsman considers just and appropriate (whether or not a court could order those steps to be taken).

[49] See DISP 3.7.13 of the FSA Handbook: 'Under the Act, a complainant can enforce through the courts a money award registered by the Ombudsman or a direction made by the Ombudsman.'

Terms of reference for voluntary jurisdiction participants

The Rules provide for the standard terms on which voluntary jurisdiction participants agree to be subject to the FOS scheme. Rules contained in DISP 1–3 apply to participants, except DISP 1.9–1.11 and 2.3–2.4.[50] The same award powers of the Ombudsman also apply to participants.[51] Agreeing to participate under the voluntary jurisdiction is retroactive in effect, applying to acts and omissions of the participant that occurred even before the agreement to the voluntary jurisdiction.[52]

A participant may not withdraw from the voluntary jurisdiction unless it has submitted to the FOS a written plan for notifying its customers of the intention to withdraw and handling complaints against it before the withdrawal, paid the general levy for the year, and both the plan and date of withdrawal are approved by the FOS.[53]

Statistics

For the year 2009–2010, the FOS handled 925,095 initial enquiries, a 17 per cent increase from the year before. Of these, there were 163,012 new substantive cases.

The FOS resolved 166,321 cases, resulting in compensation for consumers in 50 per cent of the cases. 38 per cent of the disputes were resolved within three months, while 67 per cent were resolved within six months. 155,591 cases were resolved by the FOS adjudicators through mediation,

---

[50] See DISP 4.2.3 of the FSA Handbook.

[51] See DISP 4.2.4 of the FSA Handbook: 'The Ombudsman has the same powers to make determinations and awards under the Voluntary Jurisdiction as he has under the Compulsory Jurisdiction (see DISP 3.7 (Awards by the Ombudsman)).'

[52] See DISP 4.2.2 of the FSA Handbook: 'By agreeing to participate, a VJ participant also agrees that the Voluntary Jurisdiction covers an act or omission that occurred before the VJ participant was participating in the Voluntary Jurisdiction, whether the act or omission occurred before or after commencement.'

[53] See DISP 4.2.7 of the FSA Handbook:

A VJ participant may not withdraw from the Voluntary Jurisdiction unless:

(1) the VJ participant has submitted to FOS Ltd a written plan for:
   (a) notifying its existing customers of its intention to withdraw; and
   (b) handling complaints against it before its withdrawal;
(2) the VJ participant has paid the general levy for the year in which it withdraws and any other fees payable; and
(3) FOS Ltd has approved in writing both the VJ Participant's plan and the date of withdrawal (which must be at least six months from the date of the approval of the plan).

recommended settlements and adjudications, while 10,730 cases were resolved by Ombudsman formal decisions.[54]

Service providers

Consumers do not pay to bring complaints to the FOS. The FOS is funded by levies and case fees required to be paid by law from the businesses it covers. Levies are adjusted in accordance with the size of the business, and are payable even if no formal complaints have been referred. Businesses do not pay case fees in respect of the first three complaints settled during a year, but there is a fee of £500 for the fourth and each subsequent complaint.[55]

Oversight

As noted above, under s. 7 of Sch. 17 of the Financial Services and Markets Act 2000, both the scheme operator and the Chief Ombudsman are required to report to the FSA annually in respect of the discharge of their functions.[56] A memorandum of understanding between the FSA and the FOS further sets out that:

- both organisations will seek to dispel confusions and misunderstandings about their different roles;[57]
- consult each other at an early stage on issues which may have significant implications for the other organisation;[58]
- the FOS will inform the FSA of issues that appear likely to have significant regulatory implications;[59]
- the FOS will give the FSA information the FSA reasonably requires to enable it to discharge its statutory obligations in respect of the scheme;[60]
- the FOS will routinely give the FSA regular information about the number and types of complaints handled;[61]

---

[54] Financial Ombudsman Service. *Annual Review 2009/2010.*
[55] Financial Ombudsman Service. Frequently-asked Questions, available at: www.financial-ombudsman.org.uk/faq/answers/research_a5.html [accessed 8 February 2012].
[56] For s. 7 of Sch. 17, see footnote 20 above.
[57] Para. 11(a), Memorandum of Understanding between the Financial Services Authority and the Financial Ombudsman Service Limited, 6/4/07.
[58] Paragraph 11(d), ibid.   [59] Paragraph 12, ibid.
[60] Paragraph 15(a), ibid.   [61] Paragraph 15(b), ibid.

- where concerns arise, the FOS will give the FSA information in respect of shortcomings in a firm's complaint-handling, fitness and propriety of a firm or other issues that may require action by the FSA;[62] and
- the FSA may request information about the number and types of complaints and specific initial and final decisions in respect of a firm where there is contemplated regulatory action against the firm.[63]

A similar memorandum exists between the FOS and the Office of Fair Trading in respect of the overlapping jurisdiction between the two entities under the Consumer Credit Act 2006 as well as the enforcement of the Competition Act 1998, the Enterprise Act 2002, the Unfair Terms in Consumer Contracts Regulations 1999 and certain provisions of the Financial Services and Markets Act 2000 as relates to competition and financial services firms. Parallel provisions to the ones set out above may be found at paras. 13(a), 13(d), 14, 19(a), 19(b), 19(c) and 19(d) of the memorandum respectively.

Strengths

In comparison with the resolution of disputes by way of litigation, the strengths of the FOS include the fact that it is free for eligible complainants, more efficient given the documents-based process, enjoys high levels of compliance by financial services firms, and in particular, has the power to 'draw on a range of extra-legal standards in a manner which operates to the benefit of consumers by mitigating the inequality of bargaining power and unfair substantive legal provisions encountered in parts of the financial services business, notably the banking and insurance sectors'.[64]

Multi-tiered dispute resolution

While the majority of disputes resolved by the FOS are resolved at the conciliation and adjudication stage, the multi-tiered structure involving adjudicators and ombudsmen provides what has been described as 'effectively an internal right of appeal in FOS procedures'.[65]

The internal review of initial views on merits is of particular importance in the context of the statutory power to resolve disputes with

---

[62] Paragraph 15(c), ibid.   [63] Paragraph 15(d), ibid.

[64] E. Morris, 'The Financial Ombudsman Service and the Hunt Review: continuing evolution in dispute resolution'.

[65] Ibid.

reference to what is fair and reasonable. While the determinations of the Ombudsmen are subject to judicial review, 'thus far has a narrow focus in terms of intervention being confined to instances of irrationality rather than the courts substituting their opinion on the merits for that of an ombudsman'.[66] The policy of non-intervention from the courts serves to strengthen the authority of the determinations of the Ombudsmen and enhances the finality of their decisions, particularly as against financial services firms. At the same time, consumers can have the benefit of having the merits of their complaints reviewed by both an adjudicator and an ombudsman.

Dealing with cases of wider implication

In contrast with the limitations imposed on Australian schemes of financial dispute resolution, the FOS retains the power to resolve cases that raise wider implications, as well as information-sharing arrangements with the FSA and Office of Fair Trading where they may take action. There is also a test case procedure to refer cases involving new legal issues to the courts.

Benefits of merging schemes

In merging pre-existing dispute resolution schemes of the financial industry together under the FOS, the FOS has from the outset maintained that it would continue the virtues of accessibility and specialised dispute resolution expertise that its predecessors had provided, while adding the value of a single point of entry, uniform treatment of complaints, as well as a strong relationship with the industry regulator and a business-facing management culture.[67]

Advantages over litigation

Studies in respect of litigation tend to suggest that 'haves', i.e. government units, large businesses, high socio-economic status groups, tend to fare better in courts than 'have nots'. It is suggested that an explanation for this is the fact that 'repeat players' tend to fare better than individuals

[66] Ibid.
[67] Financial Ombudsman Service. *Annual Report 1999/2000.*

or 'one shotters' in court as a result of structural advantages and institutional limitations of the adversarial court system. Repeat players tend to have enhanced access to specialised resources and expertise devoted to handling similar, recurrent disputes, are likely to develop informal relationships with courts and other dispute resolution forums, and can be strategic in the management of individual disputes since each individual case is of lower relative importance to them.[68]

A study which applied these hypotheses to the FOS, however, found that larger or more experienced firms are not necessarily more successful in defending complaints against them, an explanation for which is that because of the informal and ad hoc nature of FOS adjudications, large firms were less capable of playing for rules. Furthermore, professionally represented complainants were less likely to win, perhaps because of the perception on the part of an adjudicator that legally represented complainants might have weaker complaints, and rather than strengthening the complainant's position, a legal representative might equally attempt to play for the rules. The study also found that there was no higher success rate at the FOS for complaints filed by more economically resourced socio-economic groups.

One conclusion that can thus be drawn is that the informal dispute resolution as carried out by the FOS is explicitly designed to offset some of the advantages enjoyed by repeat players in court litigation, thus providing consumers with a level playing field.[69]

Expectation management

Another empirical study has shown that the approach of adjudicators at the FOS and their own perception of their role is not only to handle complaints, but also to manage expectations of consumers – to bridge the gap between a professional analysis of retail-finance complaints and the complainant's perception of mistreatment and expectation for redress.

By using very personal methods of communication with complainants, the FOS' complaint handlers are often able to reshape the complainant's expectations for redress, avoiding prematurely raising expectations and thus mitigating dissatisfaction with adverse decisions.

---

[68] M. Galanter, 'Why the "haves" come out ahead: speculations on the limits of legal change', pp. 95–160.

[69] S. Gilad (2010) 'Why the "haves" do not necessarily come out ahead in informal dispute resolution' *Law & Policy*, 32(3), pp. 283–312.

In this way, the FOS process does not merely involve holding service providers to account but also shifting consumer expectation and attitudes.[70] While this may appear to be contradictory to the role of accountability the FOS plays, it is arguable that such intervention is necessary in the management of excessive expectation on the part of consumers as well as the engendering of confidence in the complaint-handling process.

Challenges

Integration of the Pensions Ombudsman

The FOS maintains a jurisdiction over complaints about pensions[71] as part of its jurisdiction to deal with complaints about businesses providing activities regulated by the FSA. Its predecessor, the Personal Investment Authority Ombudsman Bureau, previously dealt with complaints in respect of personal pensions. The Pensions Ombudsman ('PO') also exists to investigate pension complaints, in particular those concerning occupational pensions. A memorandum of understanding between the FOS and PO confirming this division of pensions jurisdiction, as well as the introduction of stakeholder pensions and employers involvement in personal pension schemes, was reached in 2002.

In his review of pensions institutions for the Department for Work and Pensions, Thornton recommended operational integration between the FOS and the Pensions Ombudsman.[72] This recommendation was welcomed by the FOS to end potential confusion.[73]

In addition to the usual challenges one might expect to encounter in the merging of two ombudsmen, there is an issue of increased oversight by the courts over the FOS. While, 'judicial policy thus far has been fairly deferential to FOS autonomy, by positing a narrow irrational test for intervention ... the policy consideration driving judicial restraint is one of a concern by the courts to avoid substituting their opinion on the merits for

[70] S. Gilad (2008) 'Accountability or expectations management? The role of the ombudsman in financial regulation' *Law & Policy*, 30(2), pp. 227–253.
[71] The types of complaint the FOS will receive in respect of pensions can be seen here: www.financial-ombudsman.org.uk/publications/technical_notes/pensions.html [accessed 25 April 2012].
[72] P. Thornton (June 2007) 'A Review of Pensions Institutions: An Independent Report to the Department for Work and Pensions', Recommendation 29.
[73] Ombudsman News Issue 62, June/July 2007, available at: www.financial-ombudsman.org.uk/publications/ombudsman-news/62/62.htm [accessed 8 February 2012].

that of the FOS',[74] the Pensions Ombudsman's decisions can be appealed to the High Court on points of law. The negative views on statutory rights of appeal being incorporated into the jurisdiction of the FOS in the Hunt Review[75] may well be tested. As Morris comments: 'There is no guarantee that in statutory rights of appeal the courts will defer to FOS autonomy and its distinctive ADR role: the experience of such rights in the context of the pensions ombudsman suggests that an antagonistic relationship emerges, with the courts regularly overruling the ombudsman on points of law and in general displaying little sympathy for the unique nature of an ombudsman's jurisdiction.'[76]

The Hunt Review

Lord Hunt was commissioned by the FOS in 2008 to perform a review, which focused broadly on issues of accessibility and transparency. Some have noted that due to the fact that the review was conducted by a single individual who held no public hearings and commissioned no hard, empirical evidence to support its recommendations, some limitations may exist in the findings.[77]

A quasi-regulatory role?

The FOS has always maintained that it does not play a regulatory role, and in his review, Lord Hunt called upon the FOS to guard against assuming a quasi-regulatory role. This has been criticised as being disingenuous and misleading:

> Viewed in the round it is clear that the FOS in practice performs an indirect, circumscribed regulatory role: it performs an early warning function, identifying patterns in its case work which may necessitate FSA regulatory or disciplinary action; it regularly applies in its case work regulatory

---

[74] E. Morris, 'The Financial Ombudsman Service and the Hunt Review: continuing evolution in dispute resolution'.

[75] Hunt Review (2008) at para. 4.15.

[76] See E. Morris, 'The Financial Ombudsman Service and the Hunt Review: continuing evolution in dispute resolution'.

[77] Ibid. 'This type of management consultancy oriented review (albeit one that has major practical implications and inherent capacity for speedy implementation compared with traditional law reform inquiries) according to internal pre-ordained precepts is ill suited to a thorough evaluation of fundamental issues which bear on all dimensions of the FOS' activities, including its future role in a rapidly changing regulatory and business landscape.'

guidance and sectoral codes, often with a gloss added, transforming them into binding obligations; and it has started to build a corpus of persuasive precedent designed to improve standards of business practice.[78]

The recommendation against assuming a quasi-regulatory role appears to be contradicted by the recommendation in the Hunt Review for the development of a guidebook of principles and precedents as well as publishing detailed decisions. Morris identifies these recommendations with the criticisms from financial services firms of the lack of consistency in FOS decision-making and its power to make determinations on extra-legal bases, particularly the notion of what is considered to be fair and reasonable. In this regard, it is commented: 'the pleas of business should be treated with caution: the fair and reasonable standard is statutorily prescribed as the ultimate norm in FOS dispute resolution; it is inherently subjective; and a valuable doctrinal and practical resource in tackling unfair business practices.'[79]

This underlying tension between the need for predictability in FOS determinations and the statutory discretion of the Ombudsmen raises the issue of whether or not recommendations such as the development of precedents and publishing of decisions would have the effect of eroding the otherwise unfettered discretion of the FOS, even if only by self-imposed rules of policy.

Morris concludes rather strongly that 'it is arguable that FOS practice on receipt of complaints is too passive; that its role would be bolstered by independent investigatory powers concerning problems in particular firms or with specific products without necessarily having to wait for individual complaints to be made. This early identification and rectification of such problems may prevent them subsequently escalating into large-scale consumer grievance or regulatory problems.'[80] Whether or not it is desirable for the FOS to take on a more regulatory role, particularly in light of ongoing changes to the powers of the FSA and FOS and indeed the entire regulatory structure of the financial industry in the United Kingdom remains to be seen.

Hunt's recommendations in respect of marketing strategy, advertising campaigns and outreach strategies, as well as a change in name, are all directed at increasing the public profile and awareness of the work and jurisdiction of the FOS.[81]

---

[78] Ibid.   [79] Ibid.   [80] Ibid.   [81] Ibid.

The Hunt Review also makes recommendations in respect of: case work advisers trained to assist the most vulnerable consumers through FOS procedures; developing measures to handle abuse of consumer complainants by claims management companies; and an empirical review of the £100,000 limit on compensation. The lack of revision of this sum since 1981 has also been commented upon elsewhere.[82]

Financial Services Act 2010

In the aftermath of the financial crisis, the regulatory powers of the FSA were strengthened by the Financial Services Act 2010. While the abolition of the FSA (see below) is inevitable, these changes to financial regulation are likely to remain relevant for some time to come. First, the likely period of transition from the current regulatory system to the proposed new structure is likely to take some time, despite commitment by the present coalition government to getting the primary legislation through Parliament within two years. Second, it is likely that the transition will involve the transplant of powers, including those created by the Financial Services Act 2010, to the newly created regulators.

Of relevance to the FOS is the strengthening of both the FSA's and its own powers to deal with past business reviews:

> The 2010 Act strengthens the FSA's power to make authorised firms carry out past business reviews, with a view to providing redress for consumers who have not been treated fairly. Before the 2010 Act came into force, the FSA had no express power of its own to order firms to carry out past business reviews (the point of such reviews being to assess which of a given firm's customers had been mistreated in contravention of the firm's regulatory obligations, suffered loss and deserved redress) ... However, the 2010 Act has laid the ground for the FSA to acquire its own power to order firms to carry out such reviews ... Equally, however, consumers who are unsatisfied by a firm's determination following its past business review may make a complaint to the Financial Ombudsman Service, under

---

[82] A. Samuel (2010) 'With arbitration facing restrictions, it's time to look at a UK solution for consumer disputes', *Alternatives to the High Cost of Litigation: the Newsletter of the International Institute for Conflict Prevention & Resolution*, 28, pp. 111–113. Morris has commented in respect of these recommendations that they highlight a fundamental weakness – the extensive control the FSA exercises over the content of the rules of the FOS. 'In essence the FSA enjoys exclusive control over internal complaints procedures relating to the core compulsory jurisdiction and its approval is required for FOS rules on this concerning the voluntary and consumer credit jurisdictions' – raising issues of how truly independent the FOS is.

s.404B.[83] Consumers may also complain to FOS if they feel an underlying matter has simply not been dealt with by a past business review.[84]

How this power will be exercised by the FSA remains to be seen – it appears extraneous and encroaching upon the jurisdiction of the FOS to deal with complaints by empowering the regulator to simply order such reviews.

Class actions or mass claims

The fact that the ombudsman scheme is not well designed to handle mass complaints has been commented on, though 'it may be the best of a number of bad alternatives'.[85]

It has been noted that proposals to create class actions against financial services firms were originally included under the Financial Services Act 2010, only to be removed in order to ensure its passing before the change in government.[86] 'This would have facilitated a route for mass claims in court where FSA-ordered redress may not have been viable. In short, firms would have faced a redoubled threat on two fronts – from the regulator and the consumer.'[87]

This would not be the first time that such a form of action has been proposed – and rejected – in the United Kingdom. The government, in July 2009, rejected a proposal by the Civil Justice Council to introduce class-action rules. In rejecting the proposal, the government stated that such changes should be made on a sectoral basis and involve reviews of the ADR and regulatory options in each sector.[88]

Although able to bring forward the interests of large groups of complainants at the same time, criticisms of this form of lawsuit include their cost (which make it unlikely to be the first option if others, particularly ADR, are available); the risk of abuse, and difficulties in coping with certain types of cases, 'such as where individual issues (reliance, causation

---

[83] For s. 404B, see footnote 13 above.

[84] Willmott (2010) 'Equipping the modern regulator: assessing the new regulatory powers under the Financial Services Act 2010', *Compliance Officer Bulletin*, 78, pp. 1–28.

[85] A. Samuel, 'With arbitration facing restrictions, it's time to look at a UK solution for consumer disputes'.

[86] N. Willmott, 'Equipping the modern regulator: assessing the new regulatory powers under the Financial Services Act 2010'.

[87] Ibid.

[88] C. Hodges (2010) 'Collective redress in Europe: the new model', *Civil Justice Quarterly*, 29(3), pp. 370–395.

or damage) vary widely between members of the group, and predominate over general issues, such as in product liability or some misrepresentation claims, or over quantification, validation or distribution of small individual sums'[89] – a description that may be applied to complaints against financial services firms.

The possible introduction of class actions, particularly in the financial sector, should not be dismissed out of hand, and one can speculate as to the effect the introduction of such litigation may have on ADR, including discouraging complainants from engaging in ADR in favour of collectively taking the merits of their case to court. Hodges writes about the growing interest in this form of litigation in Europe,[90] and the weakness of an individualised approach to complaints in the FOS is its inability to cope with mass complaints. Pertinent examples of such mass complaints are seen in respect of the Lehman Minibonds in Hong Kong and Singapore that required government and regulator intervention in order to achieve compensation for complainants. In this regard, another criticism of ADR techniques in the financial sector (which may not specifically apply to the FOS due to the system of adjudication and determination) is highlighted by Hodges: 'Disadvantages of ADR are said to be that settlements can bear little relationship to underlying merits of disputes, and that mediators can potentially exert improper pressure in reaching settlements.'[91]

At present, it appears that the system of test cases may be sufficient, as the bank charges litigation in the United Kingdom illustrates:

> Many individual complaints over allegedly unfair bank charges were initially dealt with by the FOS, and either dismissed or settled. The fact that that Service had found in favour of a claimant in some cases was then used to found claims in the county courts as having binding legal effect, when it did not. The courts became clogged, and the impasse was unscrambled when the banks and a regulator agreed to bring a test case, which had the effect of freezing all individual cases.[92]

Hodges comments that there is a crucial difference between the American and European systems that will need to be overcome if class-action litigation is to be deployed in the same way as it is in the United States: 'The whole point of the US private enforcement system is to facilitate actions in the courts as the primary means of regulatory control: if

---

[89] Ibid.   [90] Ibid.   [91] Ibid.   [92] Ibid.

some settlements involve over-compensation or are unfair, this still has an intended deterrent effect on markets and actors generally.'[93]

Abolition of FSA

The most significant change that has been announced in respect of the financial regulatory system of the United Kingdom is that of the abolition of the FSA and the division of its powers and roles between a number of new institutions.

Under the proposals, the Bank of England will deal with 'macro-prudential' regulation. This will be carried out by a new Financial Policy Committee, which will be responsible for identifying and taking action to mitigate potential systemic risks to the market.

The FSA will be disbanded and its powers split up between three new statutory bodies:

1. The Prudential Regulation Authority, which will be a subsidiary of the Bank of England, will be responsible for ensuring individual financial services firms are soundly managed and maintain adequate financial resources – 'micro-prudential regulation';
2. The Consumer Protection and Markets Authority will be responsible for ensuring retail and wholesale firms comply with business conduct rules on a day-to-day basis, as well as ensuring that listed companies comply with their regulatory duties; and
3. The Economic Crime Agency will be responsible for investigating and bringing criminal prosecutions for economic crimes in the UK, including insider dealing, market manipulation, etc.[94]

The CPMA will retain the FSA's responsibility for the FOS and the Financial Services Compensation Scheme.[95] There will undoubtedly be a major impact on the financial sector of the United Kingdom as a whole – certainly, the strong relationship of the FOS with the industry regulator will now have to be reconsidered in light of the fragmentation of that regulatory jurisdiction. Areas such as cases of wider implication will almost certainly be affected given that their impact on macro- and micro-prudential issues will be overseen by the Bank of England.

---

[93] Ibid.
[94] Willmott, 'Equipping the modern regulator: assessing the new regulatory powers under the Financial Services Act 2010'.
[95] *Tolley's Company Law and Insolvency Newsletter* (July 2010) Vol. 10, Bulletin 1.

Lessons learned

The OXERA review

As part of the Financial Services and Markets Act 2000 two-year review, the Office of Fair Trading employed OXERA to undertake an in-depth assessment of the impact of the Act on competition in financial services. The Review rejected the idea of an appeals mechanism but explored the possibility of provisions for test cases being taken to court.[96] It appears that the test-case mechanism arose from this Review.

The need for hearing

Under the FOS procedure, hearings are rare, and this position has been commended in the Hunt Review. Morris, however, has pointed out that the right to fair trial under Article 6 of the European Convention on Human Rights may require formal hearings that are accessible to the public, and that arguments that such proceedings would detract from speedy resolution and confidentiality in the ADR process have been rejected by Strasbourg.[97]

The matter appears to have been settled in the recent case of *Heather Moor & Edgecomb* [2008] EWCA Civ 642, in which a firm challenged the FOS' refusal for a hearing under Article 6 of the European Convention on Human Rights. The Court of Appeal acknowledged that Article 6 does apply to the FOS, but because the processes of the FOS were safeguarded by a right to judicial review, the FOS was in compliance with the Article. It remains to be seen whether or not the discretion the FOS can exercise in resolving matters with reference to what is fair and reasonable will lead to a challenge under the need for a public hearing under the right to fair trial.

Conclusion: the UK Ombuds Model and its contribution to consumer confidence

Drawing on the results of a number of independent reviews of the UK Ombuds scheme, several of its features, including its accessibility, the

[96] Ibid.
[97] E. Morris, 'The Financial Ombudsman Service and the Hunt Review: continuing evolution in dispute resolution'.

competency of its adjudicators and the process of decision making without prejudice to the complainant, have been found to contribute to overall financial stability. The OXERA review concluded that the Act had a positive impact on competition and in particular, the FOS and Financial Services Compensation Scheme were beneficial as they built consumer confidence.[98] This contribution to consumer confidence has also been remarked upon in 'Collective Redress in Europe: The New Model'.[99] Another commentator has noted the perception of fairness for consumers due to the inquisitorial approach adopted by the FOS.[100]

One empirical study has shown that the FOS dispute resolution process has been able to offset some of the advantages enjoyed by repeat users in civil litigation, providing consumers with a level playing field.[101] Another empirical study has shown that the FOS process actively involves the management of consumer expectations, which in turn can enhance confidence in the complaint process even if the outcome is adverse for the consumer.[102]

Hodges has commented upon the evidence of the effectiveness of ombudsmen and other independent authorities in preventing high percentages of meritless claims going forward and avoiding litigation costs where there is basis for voluntary settlement.[103] Each of these contributions, including levelling the playing field and expectation management through consumer education, have resulted in contributing to lowering litigation costs and increasing consumer confidence in the resolution of financial disputes in the United Kingdom.

---

[98] *Tolley's Company Law and Insolvency Newsletter* (February 2005) Vol. 4, Bulletin 8.

[99] C. Hodges, 'Collective redress in Europe: the new model'.

[100] A. Samuel, 'With arbitration facing restrictions, it's time to look at a UK solution for consumer disputes'.

[101] S. Gilad, 'Why the "haves" do not necessarily come out ahead in informal dispute resolution'.

[102] S. Gilad, 'Accountability or expectations management? The role of the ombudsman in financial regulation'.

[103] C. Hodges, 'Collective redress in Europe: the new model'.

3

Financial dispute resolution in Australia

Introduction

The Australian ombudsman schemes of the Financial Ombudsman Service ('FOS') and the Credit Ombudsman Services Limited ('COSL') operate on the basis of a number of important principles including: accessibility, transparency and efficiency. In general the two programmes have achieved success in providing accessible, cost-effective dispute resolution for consumers. At the same time, the programmes continue to seek ways to refine services in areas including: improving the reporting of annual complaints data;[1] providing parties with an early summary of contentions and articulation of key issues;[2] increasing its jurisdictional limit;[3] and increasing the Ombudsman's compensation power.[4] These issues will be discussed in greater detail below.

Ombudsmen in Australia

The use of ombudsmen in Australia as a free means of resolving disputes outside the court systems is well established and has a long history. The Commonwealth Ombudsman, for example, was established in 1976 and investigates complaints about the actions and decisions of Australian government departments and agencies as well as overseeing complaint investigations conducted by the Australian Federal Police. Many states in Australia also have state Ombudsmen carrying out similar functions in respect of local governments.

In addition to the government-run ombudsman services, industry-based ombudsmen are also well established in Australia. Examples of

---

[1] See Australian Securities and Investment Commission (ASIC), 'Feedback from Submissions to the Financial Ombudsman Service Limited's New Terms of Reference (Report 182)', December 2009.
[2] Recommendation 16, ibid.   [3] Recommendation 35, ibid
[4] Recommendation 36, ibid.

industries with established ombudsmen include the energy sector, the telecommunications industry and the financial industry.

Alternative dispute resolution in Australia

Alternative dispute resolution ('ADR') mechanisms in Australia initially operated independently of the court system, but court-annexed and court-referred ADR initiatives are now widespread.[5] The power of Australian courts to refer matters to compulsory mediation can be found in the Federal Court of Australia Act 1976 s. 53A, which grants the Court the power to make an order to refer proceedings in the Court for an ADR process;[6] the Federal Magistrates Act 1999 ss. 34 and 35, which enable the Federal Magistrate Court to refer matters arising out of proceedings for mediation and arbitration respectively;[7] the Civil Procedure Act 2005 s. 26, which states that the Court may refer any proceedings before it for mediation with or without the parties' consent;[8] the Magistrates

---

[5] See The Hon McClellan J, 'Civil Justice in Australia – Changes in the Trial Process', 'Civil Justice Reform – What Has It Achieved?', jointly hosted by the University of Hong Kong and the University College of London on 15–16 April 2010 in Hong Kong, p. 26.

[6] Section 53A of the Federal Court of Australia Act 1976 provides that:

    (1) The Court may, by order, refer proceedings in the Court, or any part of them or any matter arising out of them:
       (a) to an arbitrator for arbitration; or
       (b) to a mediator for mediation; or
       (c) to a suitable person for resolution by an alternative dispute resolution process;
    in accordance with the Rules of Court.
    ...
    (3) This section does not apply to criminal proceedings.

[7] Section 34 of the Federal Magistrates Act 1999 provides that:

    (1) The Federal Magistrates Court may, by order, refer proceedings in the Federal Magistrates Court, or any part of them or any matter arising out of them, to a mediator for mediation in accordance with the Rules of Court.
    (2) Subsection (1) has effect subject to the Rules of Court.
    (3) Referrals under subsection (1) to a mediator may be made with or without the consent of the parties to the proceedings.

    Section 35 of the Federal Magistrates Act 1999 provides that:

    (1) The Federal Magistrates Court may, by order, refer proceedings in the Federal Magistrates Court, or any part of them or any matter arising out of them, to an arbitrator for arbitration in accordance with the Rules of Court.

[8] Section 26 of the Civil Procedure Act 2005 provides that: (1) If it considers the circumstances appropriate, the Court may, by order, refer any proceedings before it, or part of

Court Act 1991 s. 27(1), which empowers the Court to refer an action for mediation and appoint a mediator with or without the parties' consent depending on the constitution of the Court;[9] the District Court Act 1991 s. 32(1), which similar to the Magistrates Court Act 1991 s. 27(1), empowers the Court to refer an action for mediation and appoint a mediator; the Supreme Court Act 1935 s. 65, which stipulates the Court's powers to refer a civil proceeding for mediation and to appoint a mediator for that purpose;[10] the Supreme Court Rules 2000 r. 518,[11] which empowers the Court to order at any stage of a proceeding a referral of the proceeding with or without the parties' consent; and the Court Procedures Rules 2006 r. 1179, which allows the court to order, on application by a party or on its own initiative, a referral of a proceeding for mediation or neutral evaluation.[12]

any such proceedings, for mediation by a mediator, and may do so either with or without the consent of the parties to the proceedings concerned.

[9] Section 27(1) of the Magistrates Court Act 1991 provides that: 'Subject to and in accordance with the rules, the Court constituted of a Magistrate (whether sitting with assessors or not) may, with or without the consent of the parties, and any other judicial officer or a Registrar may, with the consent of the parties, appoint a mediator and refer an action or any issues arising in an action for mediation by the mediator.'

[10] Section 65 of the Supreme Court Act 1935 provides that:

(1) Subject to and in accordance with the rules of court, the court constituted of a judge may, with or without the consent of the parties, and a master or the registrar may, with the consent of the parties, appoint a mediator and refer a civil proceeding or any issues arising in a civil proceeding for mediation by the mediator.

(2) A mediator appointed under this section has the privileges and immunities of a judge and such of the powers of the court as the court may delegate.

...

(4) The court may itself endeavour to achieve a negotiated settlement of a civil proceeding or resolution of any issues arising in a civil proceeding.

[11] Rule 518 of the Supreme Court Rules 2000 provides that:

(1) At any stage in a proceeding a judge, with or without the consent of any party, may order that the proceeding or any part of it be referred for mediation.

(2) If a matter is referred to mediation, the mediator is to be –
  (a) the Principal Registrar; or
  (b) a suitable person appointed by the Principal Registrar.

(3) Unless otherwise ordered, an order under subrule (1) does not operate as a stay of proceedings.

[12] Rule 1179 of the Court Procedures Rules 2006 provides that:

(1) The court may, by order, refer a proceeding, or any part of a proceeding, for mediation or neutral evaluation.

(2) The court may make an order on application by a party to the proceeding or on its own initiative.

Statistics on the settlement rates of court-annexed ADR schemes are generally high.[13] Despite the concerns in respect of ADR, e.g. the lack of an independent and impartial third party during negotiations, that such processes may mask inbuilt power inequalities between the parties, the lack of strong empirical data to suggest ADR is quicker and cheaper than traditional court-based processes, and the cost consequences in the event that ADR processes break down and necessitate court intervention,[14] its benefits, including improved access to justice, faster resolution of cases, time and cost savings, and its confidential nature, have led to high degrees of satisfaction in its use in Australia.[15]

Ombudsmen for financial service providers

Financial service providers in Australia are required to have internal complaints procedures to handle disputes with consumers. Where these procedures fail to resolve the dispute, an external dispute resolution ('EDR') scheme is subscribed to. There are only two external dispute resolution schemes approved by the Australian Securities and Investment Commission: the FOS and the COSL.[16]

The Financial Ombudsman Service

On 1 July 2008, three of the largest existing complaints schemes in the financial services industry of Australia were consolidated into a centralised financial dispute resolution scheme. The Banking and Financial Services Ombudsman, the Insurance Ombudsman Service and the Financial Industry Complaints Service were merged into a single external dispute resolution service under a newly created company. Subsequently, on 1 January 2009, the Credit Union Dispute Resolution Centre and Insurance Brokers Disputes Limited were also merged to become the Mutuals division and the Insurance Broking division respectively.[17]

---

[13] National Alternative Dispute Resolution Advisory Council (2003) 'ADR Statistics – Published Statistics on Alternative Dispute Resolution in Australia', available at: www.nadrac.gov.au [accessed 8 February 2012]; see also Federal Court of Australia (2008–2009) *Annual Report 2008–2009*, p. 32 and Supreme Court of New South Wales (2008) *Annual Review 2008*, p. 28.

[14] See The Hon McClellan J, 'Civil Justice in Australia – Changes in the Trial Process', p. 65.

[15] See Victorian Law Reform Commission (2008) *Civil Justice Review: Final Report*, p. 214.

[16] Australian Securities and Investments Commission ('ASIC'), 'ASIC-approved external dispute resolution schemes', available at: www.asic.gov.au [accessed 25 April 2012].

[17] Financial Ombudsman Service, 'The Financial Ombudsman Service establishes Mutuals and Insurance Broking divisions', available at: www.fos.org.au [accessed 8 February 2012].

The Predecessor Schemes

The Banking and Financial Services Ombudsman resolved complaints from individuals and small businesses in respect of financial services provided by banks and financial service providers. Its decisions were binding on the service providers, and its dispute resolution process was free to complainants. Claims were limited to amounts less than AU$280,000, and its jurisdiction excluded disputes in respect of general policies (e.g. interest rates, fees, branch closures).[18]

The Insurance Ombudsman Service resolved disputes between consumers and participating companies (insurers and other financial service providers). It was an independent national external dispute resolution body approved by the Australian Securities and Investments Commission, and provided dispute resolution free of charge to consumers. The Service also handled enquiries about general insurance matters, which included: home building, home contents, motor vehicle, travel, sickness and accident, consumer credit, pleasurecraft, valuables and personal property, medical indemnity insurance, residential strata title policies, certain small business policies and third party motor vehicle disputes if the consumer in question was uninsured and the property damage was less than AU$3,000.[19]

The Financial Industry Complaints Service resolved complaints against members of the financial services industry (e.g. life insurance, superannuation, funds management, financial advice, investment and sales and stock broking of financial or investment products).[20]

The Credit Union Dispute Resolution Centre was established in 1996 to resolve disputes between credit unions and their members.[21]

Insurance Brokers Disputes Limited previously provided dispute resolution services between life and general insurance brokers and their clients. Its jurisdiction was claims below AU$100,000.[22]

---

[18] Banking and Financial Services Ombudsman (February 2008) *Review of Australia's Consumer Policy Framework, Production Commission Discussion Paper*, available at: www.pc.gov.au/__data/assets/pdf_file/0010/89092/subdr170.pdf [accessed 2 May 2012].

[19] Carter Newell Insurance Ombudsman Service Fact Sheet 2, available at: www.carternewell.com/media/799149/fact%20sheet%202%20-%20new.pdf [accessed 2 May 2012].

[20] New South Wales ('NSW') Government Lawlink, Other complaint handling agencies, available at: www.lawlink.nsw.gov.au/lawlink/olsc/ll_olsc.nsf/vwPrint1/OLSC_othercomplaint [accessed 2 May 2012].

[21] Credit Union Dispute Resolution Centre (2005–2006) *2005–2006 Annual Report*, available at: www.fos.org.au/public/download.jsp?id=36] [accessed 2 May 2012].

[22] M. Attard, 'Resolution of Insurance Disputes', *The Law Handbook*, available at: www.lawhandbook.org.au/handbook/ch23s01s10.php# [accessed 8 February 2012].

Transitional arrangements

The Terms of Reference, processes, procedures and guidelines of the three ombudsmen and two other schemes continued to apply for a transitional period, but were reviewed and replaced by a standard set of terms of reference, procedures and policies that applied across the board at the beginning of 2010.[23]

From 1 January 2010, the Financial Ombudsman Service Terms of Reference were in effect, and apply to disputes lodged on or after the date on which the Terms of Reference came into force.[24]

The new terms are directed at increasing consistency in treatment of consumers as well as financial service providers, and replace five separate sets of rules and guidance procedures. For general insurance claims, the jurisdiction of the FOS has been increased from AU$280,000 to amounts under AU$500,000 – but compensation payments remain capped at AU$280,000. Clients of insurance brokers will also be able to bring claims of up to AU$500,000, a large increase from the previous limit of AU$100,000. Compensation also remains capped at AU$100,000, but increased to AU$150,000 on 1 January 2012.[25] Consequential losses and interest may also be added to compensation awards. For further information in respect of the Terms of Reference, please see *Types of dispute* below.

Expanded jurisdiction?

The merger of the Banking, Insurance and Financial Industry Complaints Services has expanded its jurisdiction beyond that of its predecessors. The ability of the Financial Ombudsman Service to make determinations against Australian Financial Service ('AFS') licensees in respect of complaints about matters not included in the definition of 'financial services' under the Corporations Act 2001 or the Australian Securities and Investments Commission Act 2001 has potentially expanded the jurisdiction of the FOS to include 'rental properties, antiques and collectibles, estate and structuring advice if a representative of an AFS

---

[23] Banking and Financial Services Ombudsman Limited (March 2008) 'BFSO Bulletin 57', available at: www.bfso.org.au/ABIOWeb/ABIOWebSite.nsf/0/A2502C2CFD46FF46CA2 5741E001713C1/$file/Bulletin+57.pdf [accessed 8 February 2012].

[24] Financial Ombudsman Service, 'Terms of Reference', available at: www.fos.org.au/ centric/home_page/about_us/terms_of_reference_b.jsp [accessed 8 February 2012].

[25] insuranceNEWS.com.au, 'New year, new FOS terms of reference'.

licensee provides advice in relation to them that results in a loss'. The
FOS is also empowered to hear complaints from non-retail clients 'at its
discretion'.

However, an FOS ombudsman cited the jurisdiction of FOS predecessor, the Financial Industry Complaints Service, as also having the same
discretion, which was rarely exercised. Furthermore, the jurisdiction of
the FOS is not limited by the definitions in the Corporations Act 2001.[26] It
should be noted that Australian Securities and Investments Commission
('ASIC') encourages external dispute resolution schemes to 'accept complaints or disputes from a broader range of complainants or disputants
than set out in the retail client definition or those who are provided
with credit or credit services and guarantors under the National Credit
Act'.[27]

The Credit Ombudsman Service Limited – a competing scheme?

In addition to the Financial Ombudsman Service, another external dispute resolution scheme has recently emerged from obscurity in respect of
financial advice and investment-related disputes – the Credit Ombudsman
Service Limited.

The Credit Ombudsman Service Limited was originally incorporated
as the Mortgage Industry Ombudsman Service Limited in 2003, before
adopting its present name in 2004.[28] It provides a free dispute resolution
service for consumer complaints against its members, which include
non-bank lenders, finance brokers, credit unions, building societies, debt
collection firms, financial planners, trustees, servicers, aggregators and
mortgage managers.[29]

It was in the past considered an external dispute resolution scheme only
for the mortgage broking industry, but this was the result of misinforma-
tion and the investment industry's relative ignorance of its existence.[30]

---

[26] L. Egan (2009) 'Criticism of Expanding FOS Jurisdiction', *Money Management*, available at: www.moneymanagement.com.au/news/criticism-of-expanding-fos-jurisdiction
[accessed 8 February 2012].

[27] See RG 139.89 of the Australian Securities and Investments Commission's Regulatory
Guide.

[28] Credit Ombudsman Service, 'COSL's History', available at: www.cosl.com.au/
COSLs-History [accessed 8 February 2012].

[29] Credit Ombudsman Service, 'COSL's Role', available at: www.cosl.com.au/COSLs-Role
[accessed 8 February 2012].

[30] L. Beaman (2010) 'FOS Alternative Emerges', *Money Management*, available at: www.
moneymanagement.com.au/news/fos-alternative-emerges [accessed 8 February 2012].

However, financial advisory and investment groups appear to be taking greater notice of the scheme, which has also had its profile raised by the introduction of the national consumer credit regime in Australia.

Statutory Tribunal

In addition to the two ASIC-approved external dispute resolution schemes, there is also a statutory scheme: the Superannuation Complaints Tribunal, dealing with complaints about the decisions and conduct of superannuation providers (including trustees of regulated superannuation funds and approved deposit funds, retirement savings account providers, and life companies providing annuity policies).[31]

Financial alternative dispute resolution programmes

The Financial Ombudsman Service

The Financial Ombudsman Service is an independent organisation that resolves disputes between consumers and financial service providers.

Range of disputes

The disputes may broadly be separated into: investments (including securities, superannuation, managed investments, derivatives/hedging); insurance (general/domestic insurance, life insurance, small business/farm insurance, professional indemnity insurance, extended warranty); credit (consumer credit, margin loans, business finance, guarantees); payment systems (direct transfer, non-cash); and deposit taking (savings accounts, current accounts, safe custody).[32] It should be noted that it appears that real property finance appears to be excluded from the range of disputes dealt with by the FOS.

Structure

The Financial Ombudsman Service has three divisions: banking and finance, mutuals; investments, life insurance and superannuation; and

---

[31] For more details, please visit the Tribunal's official website at: www.sct.gov.au [accessed 25 April 2012].

[32] Financial Ombudsman Service (2008–2009) *2008–2009 Annual Review*, available at: www.fos.ong.au/centric/home_page/publications/annual_reports_archive.jsp [accessed 25 April 2012].

general insurance. Each division has its own ombudsman, overseen by a Chief Ombudsman.[33]

The Credit Ombudsman Service Limited

The Credit Ombudsman Service Limited also facilitates the resolution of complaints between consumers and members (all within the financial services industry) of its scheme.

Range of disputes

Disputes are categorised as: investment (purchase investment property, refinance investment property, other investment); consumer (first home buyer, personal, purchase home, refinance home); and business (business, refinance business loan).[34] It should be noted that the range of disputes dealt with by COSL as reported in its Annual Report does not appear to be as wide as that of FOS, most notably excluding insurance, payment systems and deposit taking.

Structure

The Credit Ombudsman was, until October 2006, appointed from a panel of qualified and experienced persons, but COSL has since moved to a CEO structure, with a single person acting as both CEO and Ombudsman.[35]

Underlying legal mandate

Under the Corporations Act, financial service licensees must be members of an external dispute resolution scheme approved by ASIC.[36] There is a similar requirement under the National Credit Act in respect of credit licensees.

---

[33] See ibid. p. 10.
[34] See Credit Ombudsman Service, 'Annual Report on Operations 2009–2010', p. 28.
[35] Credit Ombudsman Service, 'COSL's History'.
[36] See Australian Securities & Investments Commission, 'Complaints Resolution Schemes', available at: www.asic.gov.au [accessed 8 February 2012].
       See also RG 165.1 and 165.2 of the Australian Securities and Investments Commission's Regulatory Guide, which provides that:

       RG 165.1 Under the Corporations Act 2001 (Corporations Act), if you are:
       (a) an AFS licensee (s912A(1)(g) and 912A(2)); or
       (b) an unlicensed product issuer or an unlicensed secondary seller (s1017G),

Both the Financial Ombudsman Service and the Credit Ombudsman Service Limited are independent external dispute resolution schemes operated under a corporate entity. The schemes are approved by the Australian Securities and Investments Commission to provide dispute resolution for Financial Services Licence holders, Credit Licence holders and Authorised Representatives of Credit Licence holders.

Under the Corporations Regulations and National Credit Regulations, ASIC is empowered to approve external dispute resolution schemes, taking into account their accessibility, independence, fairness, accountability, efficiency and effectiveness, as well as any other matter ASIC may consider relevant (though at present there are no 'other matters').[37] Of particular relevance are the requirements that:

- there is equitable access by providing services to consumers free of charge;[38]

you must have a dispute resolution system available for your retail clients that meets certain requirements.
RG 165.2 This dispute resolution system must consist of:
(a) IDR procedures that:
    (i) comply with the standards and requirements made or approved by ASIC; and
    (ii) cover complaints made by retail clients in relation to the financial services provided; and
(b) membership of one or more ASIC-approved [external dispute resolution] schemes that covers—or together cover—complaints made by retail clients in relation to the financial services provided (other than complaints that may be dealt with by the Superannuation Complaints Tribunal (SCT)).

[37] For further information, see RG 139.25–139.29, ibid.:
RG 139.25 The Corporations Regulations and National Credit Regulations state that we must take the following into account when considering whether to approve an EDR scheme:
(a) accessibility;
(b) independence;
(c) fairness;
(d) accountability;
(e) efficiency;
(f) effectiveness; and
(g) any other matter we consider relevant.

RG 139.26 The considerations of accessibility, independence, fairness, accountability, efficiency and effectiveness are based on the principles in the Benchmarks for Industry-Based Customer Dispute Resolution Schemes (DIST Benchmarks), published by the then Department of Industry, Science and Tourism in 1997. See the Appendix for further information on the DIST Benchmarks.
[38] See RG 139.52, RG 139.53–139.54, ibid.:

RG 139.52 To promote equitable access, a scheme must provide its EDR procedures free of charge to any complainant or disputant whose complaint or dispute falls within the scheme's jurisdiction.

- the scheme be able to deal with complaints from 'retail clients' per s. 761G of the Corporations Act 2001, including small businesses as defined under that section,[39] or for the purposes of the National Credit Act, handle disputes from persons who have been provided with credit or credit services, or are guarantors under the Act;
- the scheme must report to ASIC any systemic issues and matters involving serious misconduct;[40]
- the scheme must collect and report information to ASIC about complaints and disputes it receives on a quarterly basis and in its annual report, and conduct independent reviews of its operations;[41]
- coverage must be sufficient to deal with the vast majority of types of consumer complaints or disputes in the relevant industry, as well as up to the monetary amounts established for the retail client test in s. 761G

RG 139.53 We consider it a fundamental principle that consumers and investors of financial and credit products and services have free access to the complaint or dispute handling procedures offered by a scheme.

RG 139.54 We understand, however, that charging may be appropriate in some limited cases or special circumstances—for example, where the scheme seeks to extend its jurisdiction to provide its services for a complaint or dispute that is clearly outside the scheme's jurisdiction (e.g. beyond the consideration of 'consumer' or appropriate 'small business' complaints or disputes).

[39] See RG 139.83 of the Australian Securities and Investments Commission's Regulatory Guide: 'RG 139.83 A scheme must, as a minimum, under the Corporations Act, be able to deal with complaints from "retail clients", as defined in s761G and related regulations.'

'Retail clients' is defined in s. 761G of the Corporations Act 2001:

(1) For the purposes of this Chapter, a financial product or a financial service is provided to a person as a retail client unless subsection (5), (6), (6A) or (7), or section 761GA, provides otherwise.

[40] See RG 139.118(a) and RG 139.119, ibid.:

RG 139.118 Requirements that relate to the principle of accountability include that a scheme must:

(a) report to us any systemic issues and matters involving serious misconduct by a scheme member

RG 139.119 A scheme must report any systemic, persistent or deliberate conduct to us. For the purposes of this guide we have classified the types of conduct or issues that might be reported to us into two broad categories:

(a) systemic issues; and

(b) serious misconduct.

[41] See RG 139.118(b) and 139.118(c), ibid.:

RG 139.118 Requirements that relate to the principle of accountability include that a scheme must:

(b) collect and report information to us about complaints and disputes it receives on a quarterly basis and in its annual report; and

(c) conduct independent reviews of its operations.

of the Corporations Act (i.e. AU$500,000). As of 1 January 2012, ASIC requires compensation caps from schemes of at least AU$280,000, except in the case of general insurance brokers, where the compensation cap is at least AU$150,000.[42]

As of 30 June 2010, COSL had 12,724 members,[43] while according to the 2010–2011 Annual Review published by the FOS,[44] FOS had 12,853 members as of 30 June 2011. It is unclear how much overlap there may be between the membership of the two schemes, or if the growth by 5,143 new members in COSL for the year 2009–2010[45] may be related to the [defunct] Financial Co-operative Dispute Resolution Scheme.

Types of dispute

FOS procedure

Complainants are to first make use of the relevant financial services provider's consumer complaints procedure. When this fails to resolve the dispute, it can then be lodged with the FOS – which provides for disputes to be lodged online[46] as well as in writing. The FOS will then contact the financial service provider and ask it to respond to the complainant directly. Disputes will be registered if less than forty-five days have lapsed

---

[42] See RG 139.167, ibid.:

RG 139.167 A scheme's coverage under the Corporations Act and National Credit Act must be sufficient to deal with:

(a) the vast majority of types of consumer complaints or disputes in the relevant industry (or industries); and

(b) for consumer complaints involving monetary amounts up to the value of the retail client test under s761G of the Corporations Act (currently $500,000) or credit disputes involving monetary amounts up to the value of $500,000, the EDR scheme must be able to award compensation up to a capped amount that is consistent with the nature, extent and value of consumer transactions in the relevant industry (or industries):

...

(ii) from 1 January 2012 we require EDR schemes to operate a compensation cap of at least $280,000, unless the EDR scheme covers complaints concerning general insurance brokers, for which a compensation cap of at least $150,000 will apply.

[43] See Credit Ombudsman Service, 'Annual Report on Operations 2009–2010', p. 14.

[44] See Financial Ombudsman Service (2010–2011) *2010–2011 Annual Review*, available at: www2.fos.org.au/annualreview/2010–2011/our-members.html [accessed 2 May 2012].

[45] See Credit Ombudsman Service, 'Annual Report on Operations 2009–2010', p.14.

[46] The online form is available at: https://forms.fos.org.au/OnlineDispute [accessed 25 April 2012].

since the complaint was made to the financial services provider, and the complainant has yet to receive a written response. Where a complainant does not receive a response from the financial services provider within forty-five days, or the response does not resolve the dispute, the complainant should then contact the FOS to progress the dispute.[47]

Jurisdiction

The FOS will then first consider whether or not a given dispute has jurisdiction in accordance with its terms of reference.[48] The jurisdiction of the FOS includes:

- complaints against financial service providers from an individual or individuals, partnerships comprising of individuals, corporate trustees of self-managed superannuation funds or family trust, small businesses, clubs or incorporated associations, policy holders of group life or group general insurance policy where the dispute relates to the payment of benefits under the policy;[49]
- disputes that arise from a contract or obligation under Australian law in respect of the provision of a financial service, provision of a guarantee or security for financial accommodation, entitlement or benefits

---

[47] A different timeframe, however, is used in respect of difficulties in respect of credit facilities: www.fos.org.au/centric/home_page/resolving_disputes/financial_difficulty.jsp [accessed 25 April 2012].

[48] Terms of Reference, available at: www.fos.org.au/public/download.jsp?id=4040 [accessed 8 February 2012].

[49] See para. 4.1 of the Financial Ombudsman Service's Terms of Reference 1 January 2010 (as amended 1 July 2010):

FOS may only consider a Dispute if the Dispute is between a Financial Services Provider and:

   a) an individual or individuals (including those acting as a trustee, legal personal representative or otherwise);

   b) a partnership comprising of individuals – if the partnership carries on a business, the business must be a Small Business;

   c) the corporate trustee of a self managed superannuation fund or a family trust – if the trust carries on a business, the business must be a Small Business;

   d) a Small Business (whether a sole trader or constituted as a company, partnership, trust or otherwise);

   e) a club or incorporated association – if the club or incorporated association carries on a business, the business must be a Small Business;

   f) a body corporate of a strata title or company title building which is wholly occupied for residential or Small Business purposes; or

   g) the policy holder of a group life or group general insurance policy, where the dispute relates to the payment of benefits under that policy.

under life insurance or general insurance policies, legal or beneficial interests arising out of financial investment or a financial risk facility, claims under motor vehicle insurance policies;[50]

and excludes disputes relating to:[51]

- confidentiality or privacy obligations;[52]
- levels of fees, premiums, charges or interest rates;[53]
- assessment of credit risk;[54]

---

[50] See para. 4.2, ibid.:
FOS may only consider a Dispute between a Financial Services Provider and an Applicant:

   a) that arises from a contract or obligation arising under Australian law; and b) that arises from or relates to:

     (i) the provision of a Financial Service by the Financial Services Provider to the Applicant;

     (ii) the provision by the Applicant of a guarantee or security for, or repayment of, financial accommodation provided by the Financial Services Provider to a person or entity of the kind listed in paragraph 4.1;

     (iii) an entitlement or benefit under a Life Insurance Policy ...

[51] While the major types of disputes excluded will be listed below, please refer to para. 5.1, ibid., for the full list.

[52] See para. 5.1(a), ibid.:
about whether a Financial Services Provider has met confidentiality or privacy obligations unless the Dispute about confidentiality or privacy:

     (i) is part of a broader Dispute between the Financial Services Provider and the Applicant; or

     (ii) relates to or arises out of the provision of credit, the collection of a debt, credit reporting and/or the banker-customer relationship

[53] See para. 5.1(b), ibid.:
about the level of a fee, premium, charge or interest rate – unless:

     (i) the Dispute concerns non-disclosure, misrepresentation or incorrect application of the fee, premium, charge or interest rate by the Financial Services Provider having regard to any scale or practices generally applied by that Financial Services Provider or agreed with that Applicant;

     (ii) the Dispute concerns a breach of any legal obligation or duty on the part of the Financial Services Provider; ...

[54] See para. 5.1(c), ibid.:
about the Financial Services Provider's assessment of the credit risk posed by a borrower or the security to be required for a loan – but this does not prevent FOS from considering a Dispute:

     (i) claiming Maladministration in lending, loan management or security matters; or

     (ii) about the variation of a Credit Contract as a result of the Applicant being in financial hardship

- considerations taken into account in respect of life insurance policies offered on non-standard terms;[55]
- decisions to refuse to provide insurance coverage;[56]
- investment performance of a financial investment;[57]
- decisions of trustees of approved deposit funds and regulated superannuation funds;[58]
- relating to the management of a fund or scheme as a whole;[59]
- decisions as to allocation of benefits of financial products between competing claims;[60]
- matters that have already been dealt with by a court of dispute resolution tribunal;[61]
- matters where legal proceedings have already been commenced;[62]
- matters already lodged with and being dealt with by another external dispute resolution scheme approved by ASIC;[63]

---

[55] See para. 5.1(d), ibid.: 'about underwriting or actuarial factors leading to an offer of a Life Insurance Policy on non-standard terms.'

[56] See para. 5.1(f), ibid.:
about a decision to refuse to provide insurance cover except where:

   (i) the Dispute is that the decision was made indiscriminately, maliciously or on the basis of incorrect information; or
   (ii) the Dispute pertains to medical indemnity insurance cover

[57] See para. 5.1(g), ibid.: 'about the investment performance of a financial investment, except a Dispute concerning non-disclosure or misrepresentation.'

[58] See para. 5.1(h), ibid.: 'about decisions of the trustees (in their capacity as trustees) of approved deposit funds and of regulated superannuation funds.'

[59] See para. 5.1(i), ibid.: 'relating to the management of a fund or scheme as a whole.'

[60] See para. 5.1(j), ibid.: 'that relates to a decision by a Financial Services Provider as to how to allocate the benefit of a financial product (such as but not limited to a Life Insurance Policy) between the competing claims of potential beneficiaries.'

[61] See para. 5.1(l), ibid.: 'that has already been dealt with by a court or dispute resolution tribunal established by legislation, or by another external dispute resolution scheme approved by ASIC.'

[62] See para. 5.1(m), ibid.:
in relation to which the Applicant commenced legal proceedings before the Dispute was lodged with FOS except where:

   (i) the legal proceedings have been discontinued; or
   (ii) the relevant statute of limitation period will shortly expire and the Applicant undertakes in writing not to take any further steps in the proceedings while FOS is dealing with the Dispute.

[63] See para. 5.1(n), ibid.: 'that has already been lodged with, and is being dealt with by, another external dispute resolution scheme approved by ASIC.'

- claims in excess of AU$500,000 (though the maximum monetary compensation is below this amount).[64]

Resolution

The FOS will then review and consider the dispute, and try to resolve it through mutual agreement, including conciliation or negotiation methods. Where mutual agreement is not possible, the FOS will conduct a detailed investigation and may offer initial views on the merits of the dispute if it will assist the parties in reaching a resolution. The FOS will often issue a Recommendation, and if the Recommendation is not accepted by either party, a Determination can be made.[65]

The remedies FOS can provide include:

- payment of monies;
- forgiveness or variation of debt, or the release of security for debt;
- repayment, waiver or variation of fees or other amounts paid or owed to a financial service provider;
- reinstatement or rectification of contract;
- variation of the terms of a credit contract in cases of financial hardship; and
- remedies dealing with privacy issues of individuals.[66]

---

[64] See para. 5.1(o), ibid.: 'where the value of the Applicant's claim in the Dispute exceeds $500,000.'

[65] Financial Ombudsman Service, 'Dispute handling process in detail', available at: www. fos.org.au [accessed 8 February 2012].

[66] See para. 9.1 of the Terms of Reference 1 January 2010 (as amended 1 July 2010): 'Subject to paragraphs 9.2 to 9.8, FOS may decide that the Financial Services Provider undertake a course of action to resolve the Dispute including:

a) the payment of a sum of money;
b) the forgiveness or variation of a debt;
c) the release of security for debt;
d) the repayment, waiver or variation of a fee or other amount paid to or owing to the Financial Services Provider or to its representative or agent including the variation in the applicable interest rate on a loan;
e) the reinstatement or rectification of a contract;
f) the variation of the terms of a Credit Contract in cases of financial hardship;
g) the meeting of a claim under an insurance policy by, for example, repairing, reinstating or replacing items of property; and
h) in the case of a Dispute involving a privacy issue with an individual – that the Financial Services Provider should not repeat conduct on the basis that it constitutes an interference with the privacy of an individual or that the Financial Services Provider should correct, add to or delete information pertaining to the Applicant.

Provision is also made for financial compensation on various other bases, including costs and non-financial loss.[67] Provision is also made for the award of interest,[68] but punitive, exemplary or aggravated damages are expressly excluded.[69]

FOS statistics

From 1 July 2008 to 30 June 2009, the FOS received 19,107 new disputes, an increase from 14,359 in the corresponding period in the year before.[70]

In the same period, the FOS closed 17,007 disputes, an increase from 14,333 in the corresponding period in the year before. Of the 17,007 disputes closed for the year 2008–2009, 6,500 were by agreed resolution.[71] A quarter of all disputes for that year were resolved within 30 days, and 63 per cent of all disputes were resolved within 90 days. Close to 90 per cent (88 per cent) of all disputes were resolved within 180 days.[72]

COSL procedure

The COSL procedure is virtually identical to that of the FOS, involving the same steps of receiving complaints, registering the complaints,

---

[67] See paras. 9.3 and 9.4, ibid.:
  a) Subject to paragraph 9.3 c) and paragraph 9.7, FOS may decide that the Financial Services Provider compensate the Applicant for consequential financial loss or damage up to a maximum amount of $3,000 per claim made in the Dispute.
  b) Subject to paragraph 9.3 c) and paragraph 9.7, FOS may decide that the Financial Services Provider compensate the Applicant for non-financial loss but only where:
    (i) an unusual degree or extent of physical inconvenience, time taken to resolve the situation or interference with the Applicant's expectation of enjoyment or peace of mind has occurred; or
    (ii) in the case of a Dispute pertaining to an individual's privacy rights – injury has occurred to the Applicant's feelings or humiliation has been suffered by the Applicant.

  The maximum amount of compensation for non-financial loss will be $3,000 per claim made in the Dispute.

[68] See para. 9.5, ibid.:
  a) Subject to paragraph 9.5 b) FOS may decide that the Financial Services Provider pay interest on a payment to be made by the Financial Services Provider to the Applicant.

[69] See para. 9.6, ibid.: 'Punitive, exemplary or aggravated damages may not be awarded.'
[70] See Financial Ombudsman Service, 2008–2009 Annual Review, p. 19.
[71] See ibid., p. 42.   [72] See ibid., p. 43.

investigation, followed by a conciliation and if necessary, a determination by the Ombudsman that leads to a binding determination award.[73] Complainants must first give the financial service provider an opportunity to address the complaint. Where complainants are dissatisfied with the response or do not receive a response to the complaint within forty-five days, a complaint can be made to COSL.[74]

Jurisdiction

A complaint can only be made to COSL where the complainant is a consumer, and the complaint is about a member providing a financial service.[75] The types of complaint covered by COSL include:[76]

- breaches of Australian law or duties imposed by law;
- failures to give effect to rights provided to complainants by law;
- breaches of applicable codes of practice;
- failures to meet standards of good practice in the financial services industry; or
- where a service provider has acted unfairly towards a complainant. and exclude:[77]
- complainants to whom the relevant financial services do not directly relate;[78]

---

[73] Credit Ombudsman Service, 'Complaints Process', available at: www.cosl.com.au/Complaints-Process [accessed 8 February 2012].

[74] Credit Ombudsman Service, 'Make a Complaint', available at: www.cosl.com.au/Make-a-complaint [accessed 8 February 2012].

[75] See para. 6.1 of the COSL Rules issued by the Credit Ombudsman Service (Seventh Edition, effective as of 1 July 2010):
A Complaint can be made to the Credit Ombudsman Service about a Member if:

   (a) the Complainant is a Consumer; and
   (b) the Complaint is about a Financial Service; and
   (c) the Complaint is otherwise one that COSL can deal with under these Rules.

[76] See para. 7.1, ibid.:
COSL will deal with a Complaint if, in relation to a Financial Service, the Member:

   (a) breached relevant laws (or duties imposed by law) or did not give effect to a right provided by law to the Complainant in relation to the subject matter of the Complaint;
   (b) breached an applicable code of practice;
   (c) did not meet standards of good practice in the Financial Services Industry; or
   (d) acted unfairly towards the Complainant.

[77] Paragraph 10.1, ibid., lists out twenty categories of complaints (from (a) to (t)) that the COSL will decline to handle.

[78] See para. 10.1(k), ibid.: 'the Complainant is not the person to whom the Financial Services directly relate.'

- matters not directly related to financial services;[79]
- non-members of COSL;[80]
- claims in excess of COSL's AU\$500,000 (though compensation is capped at AU\$250,000 at present);[81]
- complaints in respect of fees, charges, commission or interest rates;[82]
- complaints about the service provider's policies or commercial judgments, including assessment of lending risk, commercial criteria and refusals of loan applications;[83]
- complaints about contract or obligations not arising from Australian law;[84]
- claims where the remedies sought are outside the jurisdiction of COSL;[85]
- complaints outside the time limit for claims;[86]

---

[79] See para. 10.1(a), ibid.: 'the Complaint is about a Member's acts or omissions that do not comprise or are not otherwise directly related to the Financial Services.'

[80] See para. 10.1(b), ibid.: 'the Complaint is about someone who is not a Member at the time the Complaint is made.'

[81] See para. 10.1(c), ibid.: 'the Complainant is seeking compensation in an amount in excess of COSL's monetary compensation limit in respect of the Complaint.'

[82] See para. 10.1(d), ibid.:
the Complaint relates to a fee, charge, commission or interest rate, unless:

  (i) the Complaint concerns the non-disclosure, misrepresentation, miscalculation or incorrect application of the fee, charge, commission or interest rate; or

  (ii) the charging of the fee, charge, commission or interest rate is in breach of the law or is unconscionable.

[83] See para. 10.1(e), ibid.:
the Complaint is about something done or not done by, or the policies or commercial judgment of, someone other than the Member the Complainant is complaining about, examples of which are:

  (i) a lender's assessment of lending risk, or of financial or commercial criteria, or of character; or

  (ii) a lender's decision to refuse the Complainant's loan application or the release of part of the security for the loan or to approve either of them subject to conditions; or

  (iii) the loan interest rates and fees charged by a lender; or

  (iv) a lender's policy to require mortgage insurance.

[84] See para. 10.1(g), ibid.: 'the Complaint relates to a contract or obligation not arising under Australian law.'

[85] See para. 10.1(h), ibid.: 'in the case of a secured loan, the security is situated or legally registered outside Australia or is governed by laws other than the laws of Australia.'

[86] See para. 10.1(l), ibid.: 'the time within which a Complainant must make a Complaint to COSL, as prescribed by Rule 10.2, has elapsed.'
In para. 10.2, ibid., 'time limit' is defined as follows:

The times within which a Complaint must be made to COSL are as follows:

  (a) For those aspects of a Complaint that relate to financial hardship applications, unjust transactions or unconscionable interest and other charges under the National Credit Code, the later of either:

- matters that have been dealt with by a court, tribunal, arbitrator or other external dispute resolution scheme;[87]
- matters that are more appropriately dealt with in another forum, such as a court, tribunal or other ASIC-approved external dispute resolution scheme;[88]
- issues which may have important consequences for the business of the financial services provider or financial services industry, or raises an important or new point of law;[89]
- complaints that are not about breaches of law, code or standards of good practice;[90]
- complaints about the performance of an investment product;[91] or

> (i) two years from when the Credit Contract is rescinded, discharged or otherwise comes to an end; or
> (ii) two years from when a final response is given by the Member at IDR; and
> (b) for all other Complaints, six years from the date that the Complainant first became aware (or should reasonably have become aware) that they suffered the loss,
>
> unless the Member agrees to COSL dealing with the Complaint or COSL considers that there are exceptional circumstances that warrant its dealing with the Complaint.

[87] See para. 10.1(n), ibid.:
the Complaint has been dealt with by a court, tribunal, arbitrator or another external dispute resolution scheme, unless:

(i) a decision about the merits of the Complaint has not been made; or
(ii) both the Complainant and the Member consent in writing to the Complaint being considered by COSL

[88] See para. 10.1(p), ibid.: 'it is more appropriate that the Complaint is dealt with in another forum such as a court, tribunal or another ASIC-approved EDR scheme.'

[89] See para. 10.1(q), ibid.: 'the Complaint involves an issue which may have important consequences for the business of the Member or the Financial Services Industry generally, or raises an important or novel point of law, and is dealt with under the special procedures set out in Rule 29.'

[90] See para. 10.1(r), ibid.:
even if the matters set out in the Complaint were found to be true, these matters would not constitute:

(i) a breach of relevant laws (or duties imposed by law) by the Member, or a failure by the Member to give effect to a right provided by law to the Complainant in relation to the subject matter of the Complaint;
(ii) a breach of the applicable code of practice by the Member;
(iii) a failure by the Member to meet standards of good practice in the Financial Services Industry; or
(iv) the Member acting unfairly towards the Complainant

[91] See para. 10.1(s), ibid.: 'the Complaint relates to the investment performance of an investment product, unless the Complaint concerns non-disclosure or misrepresentation or misleading conduct.'

- complaints that lack substance or are being pursued for an improper purpose.[92]

Resolution

At the conciliation stage, COSL will facilitate informal negotiations to try to achieve a fair resolution, prepare a case summary setting out the parties' respective positions, make a recommendation about how the complaint can be resolved, and prepare a settlement agreement where a resolution is reached. If necessary, a conciliation conference may also be held.[93] If no resolution can be reached, the matter can proceed to a determination, by which the Credit Ombudsman will determine the complaint based on the documents provided. The Credit Ombudsman's decision is binding on the relevant financial service provider, but only where the complainant accepts that decision. Complainants are not bound by the Ombudsman's decision and will retain their legal rights for referral to the courts.[94]

The remedies COSL can provide include:

- compensation awards under AU$250,000 (where the claim exceeds this limit, the financial service provider can request that the complainant provide a waiver of liability in respect of matters dealt with by the compensation award – the release must be for the entire claim, even if the amount exceeds the remedy awarded by COSL);[95]
- interest or earnings in addition to the compensation award, even where it may exceed the monetary compensation limit;[96]
- variation of a debt, release of security for a debt, repayment, variation or waiver of fees or other amounts paid or owed to the financial service provider, discontinuing enforcement action against a complainant,

---

[92] See para. 10.1(t), ibid.: 'the Complaint is lacking in substance or is being pursued by the Complainant for an improper purpose.'

[93] Credit Ombudsman Service, 'Complaint FAQs – What happens at the Conciliation Stage?', available at: www.cosl.com.au/Complaint-FAQs [accessed 8 February 2012].

[94] Ibid., 'Complaint FAOs – Am I bound by COSL's decision?'

[95] See para. 9.3 of the COSL Rules:
If the Complainant accepts the compensation awarded by COSL, the Complainant must provide the Member (if the Member so requests) with a binding release of the Member from liability in respect of the matters resolved by the award of compensation. The release must be for the full value of the claim the subject of the Complaint, even if this amount exceeds the amount of the remedy decided upon by COSL.

[96] See para. 9.4, ibid.: 'COSL may also award interest or earnings in addition to any compensation awarded, even if the interest or earnings, when added to the compensation awarded, exceeds the monetary compensation limit.'

non-enforcement of default judgment against a complainant, release of a complainant from a contract, and variation of the terms of a credit contract due to financial hardship.[97]

Punitive, exemplary or aggravated damages cannot be awarded by COSL,[98] but the Credit Ombudsman is empowered to make orders requiring financial service providers to perform or refrain from performing an act in respect of the subject matter of the complaint.[99]

COSL statistics

For the year 2009–2010, COSL received 1,153 complaints.[100] It closed 1,111 complaints, 170 by mutually accepted resolution,[101] and 56 per cent of which were closed within three months of the complaint being received.[102]

Service providers

Per the requirements of ASIC, external dispute resolution schemes provide their services free of charge to consumers.[103] Both FOS and COSL[104] are funded by fees from financial service providers who are members of their external dispute resolution schemes, as well as fees from the resolution of disputes.

Oversight

External dispute resolution schemes approved by ASIC must report to ASIC any systemic issues and matters involving serious misconduct[105]

---

[97] See para. 9.5, ibid.: 'If interest or earnings is awarded, it will be calculated from the date of the cause of action or matter giving rise to the Complainant's claim, but COSL will have regard to any factors it considers relevant, including but not limited to, the extent to which the conduct of either party contributed to any delay.'

[98] See para. 9.8, ibid.: 'Punitive, exemplary or aggravated damages may not be awarded.'

[99] See para. 9.9, ibid.: 'Alternatively or in addition, the Credit Ombudsman can make an Order requiring the Member to do or to refrain from doing some act in relation to the subject matter of the Complaint.'

[100] Credit Ombudsman Service, 'Annual Report on Operations 2009–2010', p. 20.

[101] Ibid., p. 22.   [102] Ibid., p.19.

[103] See RG 139.46 of the Australian Securities and Investments Commission's Regulatory Guide.

[104] Credit Ombudsman Service, 'Member Fees', available at: www.cosl.com.au/Member-Fees [accessed 8 February 2012].

[105] See RG 139.118(a) of the Australian Securities and Investments Commission's Regulatory Guide.

and are also required to collect and report information to ASIC about complaints and disputes it receives on a quarterly basis and in its annual report, and conduct independent reviews of its operations.[106]

Systemic issues are ones that have implications beyond the immediate actions or rights of the parties to the complaint or dispute.[107] Serious misconduct includes fraud, gross negligence or inefficient conduct, or wilful or flagrant breaches of relevant laws.[108] It is the responsibility of the schemes to identify these matters, refer them to the financial service provider for response and action, and report the information to ASIC.[109]

Information is also collected and reported in respect of:

- number of complaints or disputes received;
- demographics of complainants or disputes;
- number of complaints or disputes that fall outside the scheme's Terms of Reference;
- caseload and status of ongoing cases;
- time taken to resolve complaints or disputes;
- profiles of complainants or disputes; and
- number and outcome of disputes closed.[110]

---

[106] See RG 139.118(b) and 139.118(c), ibid.

[107] See RG 139.121 of the Australian Securities and Investments Commission's Regulatory Guide: 'At a broad level, systemic issues relate to issues that have implications beyond the immediate actions and rights of the parties to the complaint or dispute.'

[108] See RG 139.126, ibid.: 'Serious misconduct may include fraudulent conduct, grossly negligent or inefficient conduct, and wilful or flagrant breaches of relevant laws.'

[109] See RG 139.129, ibid.: It is the responsibility of a scheme to:

    (a) identify systemic issues and cases of serious misconduct that arise from the consideration of consumer complaints and disputes;

    (b) refer these matters to the relevant scheme member or members for response and action; and

    (c) report information about the systemic issue or serious misconduct to us, in accordance with these guidelines.

[110] See RG 139.149, ibid.:

To comply with our requirements for reporting, a scheme must collect and record information about:

    (a) the number of complaints (or disputes) and inquiries received;

    (b) the demographics of complainants or disputes (where practicable) who have lodged a complaint or dispute with the scheme;

    (c) the number of complaints or disputes received that fall outside the scheme's Terms of Reference (with reasons);

    (d) the scheme's current caseload, including the age and status of open cases;

    (e) the time taken to resolve complaints or disputes;

Strengths

FOS: rationale for merger

The predecessor schemes of the FOS were merged as the result of the recommendation of the Productivity Commission in the belief that the effectiveness of the services would be improved by consolidating the bodies into a single scheme.[111]

Proponents of the merger cite greater accessibility to cost-effective dispute resolution for more consumers and avoiding US-style sub-prime lending through a lack of regulation of mortgage broking[112] – ironically, however, it appears that COSL and not FOS deals with disputes relating to mortgage lending.

COSL: competing with FOS?

The head of the scheme's operations and corporate affairs has stated that while the way disputes are handled by COSL are similar, if not identical, to FOS, COSL has more members than FOS. The advantages offered by COSL over FOS include: 'significantly lower' membership and complaint resolution costs, 'particularly for smaller operators' and better communication and member relations methods.[113] This is supported by the COSL website, which states that its members receive 'faster, simpler and informal complaints resolution' and 'inexpensive and effective complaint resolution mechanism', as well as 'assistance in maintaining and managing your client relationships'.[114]

(f) the profile of complaints or disputes to enable identification of:
  (i) the type of financial or credit product or service involved;
  (ii) the product or service provider;
  (iii) the purpose for which the financial or credit product or service was obtained;
  (iv) the underlying cause(s) of the complaint or dispute; and
  (v) any systemic issues or other trends; and
(g) the number of complaints or disputes closed, and an indication of the outcome of each closed complaint or dispute.

[111] W. Klijn (2008) 'Govt gives FOS green light', *Investor Daily*, available at www.investordaily.com.au/cps/rde/xchg/id/style/4653.htm?rdeCOQ=SID-OA3D9633-A6FEA22A [accessed 8 February 2012].

[112] A. Sharp (2008) 'One-stop Shop to Help Consumers', *The Age*, available at: www.theage.com.au/business/onestop-shop-to-help-consumers-20080710–3d96.html [accessed 8 February 2012].

[113] L. Beaman, 'FOS Alternative Emerges'.

[114] Credit Ombudsman Service, 'COSL Membership', available at: www.cosl.com.au/Becoming-a-member [accessed 8 February 2012].

Statements such as those cited above and also found in the annual report[115] suggest COSL has taken a competitive approach towards FOS and appears keen to promote the differences between the two schemes and the advantages offered by COSL over FOS, and also to increase the range of disputes it deals with.

Challenges

Both schemes reported significant increases in the number of disputes received as a result of the financial crisis. Due to the continuing recovery of the world economy and recent natural disasters in Australia, it has been anticipated that the number of disputes is likely to continue on an increasing trend.

As a result of this increase in caseload, increased resources were required by COSL's operations, leading to increases in member fees.[116] It remains to be seen whether or not as COSL seeks to compete with FOS, it will continue to be able to offer the advantage of lower costs – at present, application fees for all membership types other than credit representatives is AU$165 at COSL, compared with $220 at FOS. It should be noted from the statistics cited above that the number of disputes dealt with by COSL is far below the number dealt with by FOS, and thus in order to truly compete with FOS, COSL will not only have to be wary of this costs issue, but also continue to increase its expertise in different areas of the financial services industry.

By contrast, in merging five external dispute resolution schemes together, the challenge for FOS is most likely to lie in enhancing efficiency and unifying standards, policies and procedures, which may not be a simple task given the broad range of disputes dealt with by FOS. Furthermore, maintaining its relationships with its members may be another area in which FOS faces challenges, as has been alluded to.[117]

---

[115] 'My Board and I are conscious that COSL is one of only two external dispute resolution schemes operating in Australia with the approval of the Australian Securities and Investments Commission. It is a privilege that we do not take for granted and an acknowledgment that healthy competition in the sector is vital to promote transparency and accountability and to discourage complacency and mediocrity.' See Credit Ombudsman Service, 'The Chairman's Foreword', 'Annual Report on Operations 2009–2010', p. 6.

[116] COSL Member Alert (18 June 2009), available at: www.cosl.com.au/Resources/COSL/Sites/COSL/PDF/News/MemberNews-Issue22.pdf [accessed 8 February 2012]. See also COSL Member News Issue 27 (1 April 2010), available at: www.cosl.com.au/Resources/COSL/Sites/COSL/PDF/News/MemberNews-Issue27.pdf [accessed 8 February 2012].

[117] L. Beaman, 'FOS Alternative Emerges'.

It also remains to be seen whether either scheme will adopt the approach of the FOS in the United Kingdom by reporting on complaints received about individual businesses to the regulators.[118]

Lessons learned

Under RG 139.158, external dispute resolution schemes are required by ASIC to commission independent reviews of their operations and procedures three years after the initial approval by ASIC and every five years thereafter.[119]

Under the review of its predecessor schemes, recommendations that appear to have been implemented by FOS include: public databases on membership;[120] publishing edited sample findings;[121] increasing the monetary limit of its jurisdiction;[122] and further development of its hardship cases policy.[123] Another key lesson appears to have been the implementation of an online complaints channel, which may have increased the number of complaints made to the Banking and Financial Services Ombudsman.[124] The FOS has also launched an e-learning tool to assist with complaint handling for its members to improve educative support.[125]

It remains to be seen whether or not other recommendations from such reviews may be implemented in the future by the FOS. These include:

---

[118] insuranceNEWS.com.au, 'Ombudsman closer to complaints reports', available at: www. insurancenews.com.au [accessed 8 February 2012].

[119] See RG 139.158 of the Australian Securities and Investments Commission's Regulatory Guide:

An EDR scheme must commission an independent review of its operations and procedures:

  (a) three years after its initial approval by us; and

  (b) every five years thereafter, unless we specify a shorter timeframe of less than five years.

[120] Recommendation 3, Independent Review, Banking and Financial Services Ombudsman (November 2004).

[121] Recommendation 13, ibid.; also see Recommendation 18, Independent Review, Credit Union Disputes Resolution Centre (November 2005).

[122] Recommendation 22, ibid.; also see Recommendation 21, Independent Review, Credit Union Disputes Resolution Centre (November 2005).

[123] Recommendation 25, ibid.; also see Recommendation 12, Independent Review, Credit Union Disputes Resolution Centre (November 2005).

[124] Banking Day (11 December 2008) 'Ombudsman an early port of call for banking disputes' available at: www.bankingday.com [accessed 25 April 2012].

[125] M. Pokrajac (20 August 2010) 'FOS upgrades dispute resolution approach', available at: www.moneymanagement.com.au/news/fos-upgrades-dispute-resolution-approach [accessed 8 February 2012].

researching reasons why some inquirers do not pursue their complaints;[126] using external advocates;[127] improving its forum with members[128] and a continuous improvement forum with consumers;[129] developing a fast track for urgent disputes;[130] moving to decision if there are unreasonable delays;[131] and regular surveys of consumers and members in respect of experiences, fairness and satisfaction.[132]

Recommendations adopted following independent review by COSL include: the integration of operations under a CEO;[133] improving the reporting of annual complaints data;[134] providing parties with an early summary of contentions and articulation of key issues;[135] increasing its jurisdictional limit;[136] and increasing the Ombudsman's compensation power.[137]

It remains to be seen whether or not other recommendations from the review may be implemented in future, such as moving to decision if there are unreasonable delays on the part of the financial service provider[138] and establishing closer links with other financial sector complaints schemes to learn from their experiences.[139]

Contribution to consumer confidence and domestic financial performance

The existence of two competing dispute resolution schemes, as noted by the COSL head of operations and chairman, is inherently positive for consumers and financial service providers. Despite complaints in

---

[126] Recommendation 5, Independent Review, Banking and Financial Services Ombudsman (November 2004).

[127] Recommendation 6, ibid.

[128] Recommendation 10, ibid.

[129] Recommendation 24, ibid. Also see Recommendation 11, Independent Review, Credit Union Disputes Resolution Centre (November 2005).

[130] Recommendation 18, ibid. Also see Recommendation 13, Independent Review, Credit Union Disputes Resolution Centre (November 2005).

[131] Recommendation 20, ibid.

[132] 'Review of the Financial Industry Complaints Service 2002 – Final Report', p. ii.

[133] Recommendations 19, 31 and 33, Independent Review of the Credit Ombudsman Service Ltd (May 2006).

[134] Recommendation 21, ibid.

[135] Recommendation 16, ibid.

[136] Recommendation 35, ibid.

[137] Recommendation 36, ibid.

[138] Recommendation 27, ibid.

[139] Recommendation 34, ibid.

respect of the jurisdiction of such schemes[140] and reservations expressed by McClellan J, the broad range of disputes covered by the two schemes can enhance consumer protection in the financial services market of Australia.

The efforts made under these schemes in respect of financial hardship in particular have the potential to alleviate or mitigate some of the effects of the aftermath from the financial crisis, though it remains to be seen whether these measures will be extended to SMEs in future.[141]

---

[140] See discussion above and also Banking Day (3 September 2010) 'Dispute resolution teething troubles', available at: www.bankingday.com [accessed 25 April 2012].

[141] Banking Day (15 April 2010) 'Small business financial disputes on the rise', available at: www.bankingday.com [accessed 25 April 2012].

4

Financial dispute resolution in Japan

Introduction

Japan's newly emerging Financial Alternative Dispute Resolution Service aims at providing accessible, free dispute resolution services for consumer complainants. Primary among its operating principles are efficiency and accessibility. While the total number of claims brought to early financial alternative dispute resolution schemes in Japan have been relatively low, given the overall sound expertise of those appointed to serve on the financial dispute resolution committees, they will continue to provide an alternative means of resolving consumer financial disputes in Japan.

Background

Low levels of litigation in Japan

Civil disputes in Japan are taken to court with less frequency than in other comparably developed countries.[1] Japan has a low litigation rate, the reasons for which are debated by academics. On one side, 'institutionalists' argue that Japan's legal system makes litigation undesirable, while 'culturalists' argue that even if the legal obstacles were removed, Japanese people would tend to resolve their disputes by non-confrontational means.[2]

---

[1] See for example: Glenn P. Hoetker and Tom Ginsburg (8 September 2004) 'The Unreluctant Litigant? An Empirical Analysis of Japan's Turn to Litigation', *U Illinois Law & Economics Research Paper No. LE04–009*, available at: http://papers.ssrn.com/sol3/papers.cfm?abstract_id=608582 [accessed 23 May 2012]; Luke R. Nottage (2005), 'Civil Procedure Reforms in Japan: The Latest Round', *Ritsumeikan University Law Review*, 22, pp. 81–86; Eric A. Feldman (2007), 'Legal Reform in Contemporary Japan', *University of Penn Law School, Public Law Research Paper No. 07–17*, available at: http://papers.ssrn.com/sol3/papers.cfm?abstract_id=980762 [accessed 23 May 2012].

[2] Cole (2007) 'Commercial arbitration in Japan: Contributions to the debate on Japanese non-litigiousness', *NYUJ Int'l L & Pol*, 40, p. 29.

However, while there is a low level of litigation, there also appears to be a low level of usage of alternative dispute resolution ('ADR') processes such as arbitration.[3]

Historical use of ADR

As early as 1890, when Japan's Code of Civil Procedure was based on a German model, a system was put in place that allowed for both in-court mediation before trial and mediation during trial. This followed from the historical practice of *kankai*, a conciliation process based on the French *conciliation preliminaire* adopted in 1875.

Following the Second World War, Japan's legal system was overhauled based on an American model, which consolidated civil and commercial mediation into a single system, as well as creating conciliation commissions within the courts as a means of pre-trial mediation. This emphasis on mediation has expanded, with private enterprises taking a central role in the creation of non-confrontational dispute systems. However, this demonstration of a long history of ADR processes cannot by itself account for the low levels of litigation in the country.[4]

Japan's new financial ombuds system

Japan's Financial ADR System, modelled largely on the United Kingdom Financial Ombuds Service, provides for access to a number of independent ADR providers. The primary source of law for Japan's current new Financial ADR System is derived from an amendment to the Financial Instruments and Exchange Act (the 'FIEA') in June 2009. The 2009 amendment applies to the accreditation system under the Law Concerning the Promotion of the Use of Alternative Dispute Resolution Procedures (the 'ADR Promotion Law') to sixteen business related sectors, including banks, insurance companies, non-bank moneylenders and financial instruments business operators.[5] Under the revised FIEA, each business category may establish a dispute resolution organisation within twelve months of the amendment. Entities in each financial sector can apply to the Financial Services Agency (FSA) for accreditation as designated

---

[3] T. Cole, 'Commercial arbitration in Japan: Contributions to the debate on Japanese non-litigiousness', p. 29.

[4] Ibid.

[5] Financial Instruments and Exchange Act, art. 156.

dispute resolution organisations (*shitei-funso-kaiketsu-kikan*), which are responsible for handling relevant complaints and acting as providers of dispute resolution services for their industries.[6]

In order to initiate the use of the Financial ADR System, a financial institution is required to enter into a master agreement on the implementation of complaint-handling and dispute resolving procedures (*tetsuzuki-jisshi-kihon-keiyaku*) with the designated dispute resolution organisation.[7] The master agreement imposes obligations for mandatory participation by registered financial institutions in the dispute resolution proceedings if it does not have any justifiable grounds for refusing participation when claims are submitted by customers[8] and disclosure of relevant materials for the cases that are raised.[9] The FIEA requires dispute resolution organisations make public announcements of financial institutions that have failed without reasonable justification to participate in proceedings or disclose materials as required.[10] Each financial institution enters into the same agreement with the designated dispute resolution organisation so that there is no discriminatory treatment for any financial institution.[11] If there is more than one designated dispute resolution organisation in the same sector, a financial institution is only obliged to enter into a master agreement with one of them.[12] As the establishment of a designated dispute resolution organisation is not mandatory, some sectors may have no organisation to govern disputes. Financial institutions in such sectors will still have to comply with the relevant laws to provide customers with procedures for dealing with complaints, i.e. providing proper training to employees in charge of handling grievances and providing for the settlement of disputes through a certified ADR organisation.[13]

All general complaints and disputes related to financial instruments or services are covered under the Financial ADR System.[14] As there are

---

[6] Nagashima Ohno and Tsunematsu (2010) 'Japan: Financial Alternative Dispute Resolution', *International Financial Law Review*, available at: www.iflr.com/Article/2713008/Financial-alternative-dispute-resolution.html [accessed 25 April 2012].

[7] Financial Instruments and Exchange Act, art. 37.

[8] Financial Instruments and Exchange Act, art. 156–44.

[9] Financial Instruments and Exchange Act, art. 156–44.

[10] Financial Instruments and Exchange Act, art. 156–45.

[11] Freshfields Bruckhaus Deringer (June 2011), 'Financial Alternative Dispute Resolution System', available at: www.freshfields.com/publications/pdfs/2011/jun11/30588.pdf [accessed 25 April 2012].

[12] Ibid.   [13] Ibid.

[14] Masako Miyatake, T. Andriotis, Nishimura and Asahi. 'Japan's New Financial ADR System' (2010) *Bloomberg Law Reports*, available at: www.hugheshubbard.

no restrictions on the users entitled to bring a claim, both customers and financial institutions can bring a claim to the designated dispute resolution organisation.[15] Furthermore, foreign entities and individuals are allowed to utilise the system, although a foreign financial institution which has not been registered under the FIEA is not required to submit to the jurisdiction of the designated dispute resolution organisations.[16] Frivolous claims or disguised claims with the mere intent of obtaining confidential corporate information will not be entertained.[17]

Upon receiving a petition for dispute resolution, the designated dispute resolution body will investigate the extent to which obligations determined during the settlement are being fulfilled and make recommendations to the financial institution to fulfil its relevant obligations.[18]

The dispute resolution committees are appointed from lawyers, certified judicial scriveners, and individuals with experience in the financial industry as prescribed by the Cabinet Office Ordinance.[19] This includes persons who have been engaged for an aggregate of no less than five years as a lawyer, professor of law, or similar; persons who have been engaged for at least five years as a customer, counsellor or similar; and persons who have been engaged for an aggregate of no less than ten years in the business of customer protection at corporations that conduct grievance services.[20] The designated dispute resolution organisation must also decide on its own process of appointing its dispute resolution committee, the method of elimination of interested persons and the rules by which a dispute is resolved.[21] As the FIEA does not specify any standard by which a dispute resolution committee must rely in settling a dispute, there are concerns that widely different approaches will be adopted and as a result

---

com/files/Publication/e66266f4-0130-4416-ae75-accafffcde78/Presentation/PublicationAttachment/4792b24e-4239-45b5-a62a-b7b03488f6df/Japan's%20New%20Financial%20ADR%20System%20-%20Andriotis%20Bloomberg%20Article.pdf [accessed 25 April 2012]. Originally published by Bloomberg Finance L.P in the Vol. 1, No. 2 edition of the Bloomberg Law Reports – Alternative Dispute Resolution.

[15] Ibid.   [16] Ibid.

[17] Financial Instruments and Exchange Act, art. 156–50.

[18] Financial Services Agency, 'Results of public comments on the draft government ordinance and draft cabinet office ordinance, etc. on the 2009 partial revision of the Financial Instruments and Exchange Act etc., results of the public comments on the draft cabinet office ordinances, etc. regarding disclosure system of information of corporations, etc. pertaining to those parts of the 2009 partial revision of the Financial Instruments and Exchange Act, etc.', *FSA Newsletter No.832010*, available at: www.fsa.go.jp/en/newsletter/2010/02b.html [accessed 25 April 2012].

[19] Ibid.   [20] Ibid.

[21] Financial Instruments and Exchange Act, art. 156–44.

lead to potentially uneven outcomes.[22] There is also particular concern with the degree of independence of the dispute resolution organisations, which are formed from entities within the business sector.[23]

At the close of an ADR session, a settlement proposal or a special mediation proposal will be offered by the dispute resolution committee. A financial institution is not obliged to accept a settlement proposal but the Ministry of Finance may compel acceptance of a special mediation proposal[24] unless the customer does not accept the special mediation proposal, or a customer or a financial institution files a lawsuit, or a settlement is reached between the customer and financial institution.[25]

The operations of designated dispute resolution organisations are funded by contributions by financial institutions in the industry.[26] Customers are not required to pay for dispute resolution proceedings that they initiate with financial entities.

FINMAC

In April 2009, FINMAC (Financial Instruments Mediation Assistance Center: NPO) was established as a new financial ADR organisation for disputes between customers and financial instruments service providers. FINMAC evolved out of the previous 'Securities Mediation and Consultation Center', which was an internal organ of the Japan Securities Dealers Association ('JSDA').

The previous organisation accepted complaints and consultations from customers about operations performed by JSDA member firms and conducted 'mediation' between member firms and their customers to solve disputes concerning securities businesses operated by the members. After migrating to FINMAC, the above mentioned services are being offered

[22] Ibid.
[23] Yokoi-Arai (2004) 'A comparative analysis of the Financial Ombudsman Systems in the UK and Japan', *Journal of Banking Regulation*, 5, pp. 333–357, at p. 348. See also Herbert Smith (16 November 2009) 'ADR for financial sector retail to start soon, but it is still flawed', available at: www.herbertsmith.com/NR/rdonlyres/EA8A230E-9964-48ED-B3E4–7B5E613BDB15/13439/RegulatoryNewsletterNo16ENovember2009.pdf [accessed 25 April 2012].
[24] See Masako Miyatake, T. Andriotis, Nishimura and Asahi. 'Japan's New Financial ADR System' in note 14, which cited Norio Nakazawa and Yasuo Nakajima. 'The summary of alternative dispute resolution system in the financial field (financial adr system)', *Shoji Homu No. 1876*, p. 48.
[25] Ibid.   [26] Ibid.

through contract-based business operators such as members of the Financial Futures Trading Association, Investment Trust Association, JSDA, Japan Commodities Investment Sales Association and to the Specific Business Operators (individually registered Type II financial instruments business operators, etc.).[27]

Lack of involvement of regulators?

While much has been made of alternative dispute resolution in Japan, it bears mention in the context of securities disputes for two reasons. First, the information available belies the conventional wisdom that in resolving private disputes, mediation and conciliation have surpassed or usurped the role of the judiciary. Second, it further illustrates the lack of involvement by regulatory agencies and self-regulatory organisations in the formation of legal standards and remedies.[28]

Low levels of alternative dispute resolution

The Securities and Exchange Surveillance Commission ('SESC') and JSDA both actively refer investor disputes to the JSDA's mediation programme. In doing so, issues related to active investor disputes become not regulatory issues but issues for alternative dispute resolution. In practice, investor disputes generate neither regulatory issues nor ADR cases. Notwithstanding the referrals, investors go elsewhere, and mediation is rare.[29]

Underlying legal mandate

FINMAC was designated the Dispute Settlement Body (for) Financial Instruments under the (Securities) Exchange Law on 1 April 2011.[30] Its jurisdiction appears to apply to financial intermediaries, members of the Japan Securities Dealers Association, the Investment Trusts Association Japan, Japan Securities Investment Advisors Association,

[27] Comparative analysis of Asian securities regulators & SROs and market characteristics (data and information provided by participating organisations in the 6th Asia Securities Forum Tokyo Round Table).

[28] A. M. Pardieck (2001) 'The formation and transformation of securities law in Japan: from the bubble to the big bang', *UCLA PAC. BASIN L.J.*, 19, p. 1.

[29] Ibid.

[30] See www.finmac.or.jp (translated by Google) [accessed 26 April 2012].

the Institute of Financial Futures Association, the Japan Commodities Fund Association, and persons who engage in Type II Financial Instruments Business.[31]

Types of dispute

Range of disputes

FINMAC provides counselling and mediation for disputes in respect of the buying and selling of securities, business asset management and investment advice, financial futures business, investment-related business products, and first-class financial products.[32]

Procedure

Complainants are required to first contact a counsellor at FINMAC, who will provide advice by telephone in respect of a complainant's questions. Where a complaint is made in respect of financial instruments, FINMAC will pass the details of the complaint to the financial service provider and request they carry out an (internal) investigation, the results of which are reported back to the complainant. Where the complainant disagrees with the report, they can contact FINMAC again and submit the matter to mediation. The mediator will then try to assist the parties in reaching a settlement agreement.[33]

Service providers

FINMAC appears to be incorporated as a non-profit corporation.[34] Consultations are free of charge, but mediation costs between 2,000–50,000 yen, depending on the amount of damages in question.[35]

---

[31] See 'Operating rules for mediation and complaint resolution assistance' (translated by Google), available at: www.finmac.or.jp/html/kujyo/pdf/kisoku02.pdf [accessed 8 February 2012].

[32] Ibid.

[33] See 'Flow of Consultation' (translated by Google), available at: www.finmac.or.jp [accessed 8 February 2012].

[34] See www.finmac.or.jp (translated by Google) [accessed 26 April 2012].

[35] See 'Frequently Asked Questions' (translated by Google), available at: www.finmac.or.jp [accessed 8 February 2012].

Consumer financial dispute resolution in Japanese courts

As noted above, civil litigation has generally been viewed as a last resort among most disputants in Japan.[36] This extends to the financial context where the courts adjudicate far fewer business-related cases than in Germany or in the United States.[37]

Commercial cases at the first instance are generally initiated at the District Courts or Summary Court level.[38] There are fifty District Courts in Japan with territorial jurisdiction over an area which is identical to each prefecture and 438 Summary Courts throughout the country with limited jurisdiction over civil cases involving claims not exceeding 1,400,000 yen.[39] Although there is no specialised commercial court within the Japanese legal system to deal with financial disputes, the District Courts normally are divided into departments to handle different kinds of case. The Tokyo District Court has divisions which deal with disputes related to company law and corporate reorganisation law (8th Civil Division), and interim remedies.[40]

The procedures for commercial litigation are governed by the Civil Procedure Law (Law No. 29 in 1890, as amended). An action is commenced by filing a complaint either with the District Court or Summary Court.[41] Filing fees are measured by the value of the claim under the Law on Civil Litigation Costs.[42] A higher amount of claim attracts a higher court filing fee. The complaint must be served on the defendant who then must give an answer to the complaint.[43] Subsequent court proceedings include

[36] Takeyoshi Kawashima (1963) 'Dispute resolution in contemporary Japan', in A. T. von Mehren (ed.) *Law In Japan: The Legal Order In A Changing Society* (Cambridge: Harvard University Press), pp. 41–72.

[37] Harald Baum (2011) *Debating the Japanese Approach to Dispute Resolution. Max Planck Research* (Max Planck Institute for Comparative and International Private Law), available at: www.mpg.de/4379741/W006_Culture-Society_084-091.pdf [accessed 28 May 2012].

[38] C. Platto (1999) *Economic Consequences of Litigation Worldwide* (Kluwer Law International).

[39] Supreme Court of Japan website, at: www.courts.go.jp/english/system/system.html#04 [accessed 19 January 2012].

[40] C. Celnik, and C. Yakura, 'Dispute Resolution Handbook 2011/12 – Japan', *Practical Law Company*, available at: www.practicallaw.com/9-502-0319 [accessed 26 April 2012].

[41] Supreme Court of Japan website, at: www.courts.go.jp/english/proceedings/civil_suit.html#ii_b_2_a [accessed 19 January 2012].

[42] Articles 3 and 4 of the Law on Civil Proceeding Costs (Minji Soshou Hiyou Tou Ni Kansura Houritsu) (Law No. 40 of 1971, amended through 1996), available at: www.houko.com/00/01/S46/040.HTM#s4 [accessed 26 April 2012].

[43] Ibid.

preparatory proceedings, witness examinations and hearings.[44] Preparatory proceedings are conducted to ascertain material issues. Witness examinations or interrogatories are used to clarify the issues in dispute. While preparatory proceedings are generally closed to the public, the hearing is held in open court.[45] A party can prevent a third party from reading or copying litigation records that contain trade secrets or material if a party presents prima facie evidence that it is entitled to such protection.[46]

The judge can intervene at any stage of the proceedings to mediate a settlement before a judgment is given. The court may even require a party to accept a court proposed settlement subject to an adverse judgment with harsher terms.[47] In 2008, about 16.6 per cent of civil litigation cases (in relation to monetary disputes) were settled in the first instance and 32.6 per cent were settled in the second instance.[48] In addition, the judge can also set a date for conciliation (*wakai*). Approximately 36.0 per cent of cases relating to commercial affairs were successfully disposed of through conciliation.[49]

First appeals (*kouso*) may be made to the High Court as of right. There are eight High Courts located in major cities in Japan. The Tokyo High Court has exclusive original jurisdiction over cases to rescind decisions of quasi-judicial agencies such as the Fair Trade Commission.[50] The Supreme Court is the court of final resort for second appeals (*joukoku*). There is a five-year limitation period for commercial claims from the time when the right holder can exercise his rights.[51]

In recent years, there are signs that financial disputes litigation is on an upward trend due to the implementation of law reforms emphasising consumer protection. For example, according to an analysis published in 2009, misrepresentation claims have been on the rise over the past decade.[52] This has been attributed to the amendment of the Securities and

---

[44] Ibid.   [45] Ibid.

[46] Code of Civil Procedure, art. 92.   [47] Code of Civil Procedure, art. 265.

[48] Ministry of Internal Affairs and Communications, Statistics Bureau (2011), '25–11 Cases Newly Receive and Cases Disposed of Litigation Cases and Conciliation Cases by Type (2005–08)', 'Chapter 25 Justice and Police', *Japan Statistical Yearbook 2011*, available at: www.stat.go.jp/english/data/nenkan/back60/1431-25.htm [accessed 26 April 2012].

[49] Ibid.

[50] Supreme Court of Japan website, at: www.courts.go.jp/english/system/system.html#03 [accessed on 19 January 2012].

[51] Commercial Code, art. 522.

[52] M. Ikeya and S. Kishitani (21 July 2009) 'Japan: Trends in Securities Litigation in Japan: 1998–2008 – Damages Litigation Over Misstatements on the Rise', *NERA Economic Consulting*, available at: www.mondaq.com/article.asp?articleid=83300 [accessed 26 April 2012].

Exchange Law in 2004 which provides for estimating damages related to ongoing disclosure, and the implementation of systems of internal control over financial reporting under the Financial Instruments and Exchange Act (FIEA) in 2008 which subject misstatements in such reports to civil liability.[53] The more stringent disclosure environment[54] has brought about high-profile cases such as Livedoor[55] and Seibu Railway.[56]

The most recent statistics published in 2011 show a fall in the number of judgments issued for misstatements. However, at the same time, the number of regulatory actions by the SESC on monetary penalties for misstatement has climbed to a record high of twelve from nine in 2009.[57] As such actions will lower a plaintiff's burden of proving a misstatement, they can develop into potential litigations over misstatements in the future. The number of litigations between financial institutions, including securities companies and their customer investors, was also at its highest level of forty-four in 2010. These litigations include matters such as alleged violation of the suitability of products, failure to provide adequate explanation in soliciting the transaction of bonds, investment trusts and structured bonds.[58]

Lessons learned

The work of the judiciary in fashioning new duties and new rights has instigated new legislation, the Financial Product Sales Act and the Consumer Contract Act. Both pieces of legislation codify positions taken by more conservative courts. The Financial Product Sales Act codifies an objective duty to explain and the Consumer Contract Act limits the basis for rescission. The new legislation, however, breaks with the past in codifying new private rights of action. The role of the judiciary as a central arbiter of

[53] Ibid.
[54] A. Hironaka and J. Katsube (24 June 2010) 'Securities Litigation Picks Up', *International Financial Law Review*, available at: www.iflr.com/Article/2617835/Securities-litigation-picks-up.html [accessed 26 April 2012].
[55] J. Frederick (20 January 2006) 'The Livedoor Scandal: Tribe Versus Tribe', *Time*, available at: www.time.com/time/world/article/0,8599,1151722,00.html [accessed 26 April 2012].
[56] The Japan Times Online (31 March 2005) 'Pension fund group to sue Seibu Railway', available at: www.japantimes.co.jp/text/nn20050331a2.html [accessed 26 April 2012].
[57] M. Ikeya and S. Kishitani (2 August 2011) 'Japan: Trends in Securities Litigation in Japan: 2010 Update', *NERA Economic Consulting*, available at: www.mondaq.com/x/140680/Class+Actions/Trends+in+Securities+Litigation+in+Japan+2010+Update [accessed 26 April 2012].
[58] Ibid.

private rights and duties is codified, rather than legislation being enacted to prevent further action by the courts through government sponsored and mandated mediation and conciliation commissions.

The new legislation applies to almost all financial transactions and ensures the courts will continue to play an active role. The changes suggest that judicial resolution of private disputes and development of legal norms will share equal billing with government application of public law and administrative guidance.[59]

Contribution to consumer confidence

Through 1998, the JSDA offered conciliation and mediation services, but from 1992 to 1998, the JSDA received only nine conciliation and forty-seven mediation cases. In 1998, the JSDA terminated the conciliation programme. With an overall average of eight cases per year, as compared to the hundreds of disputes handled by the courts during the same period, the JSDA has not functioned effectively as a dispute resolution body. Furthermore, even with procedural amendments in 1998, expectations for its role in the future are not high.[60]

Contribution to domestic financial performance

With the Bubble economy and its collapse, the need for effective regulation in Japan, as elsewhere, has been great. The civil justice system in Japan has become the primary forum for the development of legal standards regulating transactions involving the general investor, and has become the primary forum, alongside the newly emerging consumer financial dispute resolution schemes such as FINMAC, for providing restitution and consumer redress.[61]

---

[59] Pardieck, 'The formation and transformation of securities law in Japan: from the bubble to the big bang'.
[60] Ibid.   [61] Ibid.

Part II overview: survey findings regarding the ombuds process

Survey

In order to assess how ombudsmen view the benefits, challenges and suggestions for the improvement of ombuds processes, a survey was conducted between the autumn of 2011 and the summer of 2012. Nearly a hundred survey questionnaires were distributed to practitioners throughout the world. A total of forty-eight arbitrators and ombuds people from East Asia, North America, Europe, the Middle East and Africa responded. The participants represented highly experienced practitioners, members of government regulatory ombuds services and private arbitration commissions. The majority of those surveyed (44 per cent) had worked for institutions involved in consumer financial dispute resolution for more than four years.

Survey design

The survey used in this study contained a quantitative part asking for yes/no answers and numerical responses in the form of percentage estimates or evaluations according to four- and five-point scales.

The first part of the survey asked participants background information on their years of experience, region of practice and primary method of resolving consumer financial disputes (i.e. arbitration, ombuds process or multi-tier process including the use of negotiation and mediation). The second part examined participants' observations regarding what they see as the benefits, challenges and areas for improvement in the resolution of consumer financial disputes using either arbitration or ombuds methods of resolution.

Sample pool and distribution

The sample pool consisted of ombuds people, arbitrators, mediators and members of consumer financial regulatory bodies. The sample group was

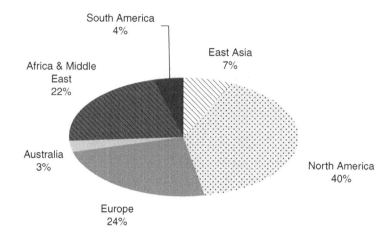

Figure 4.1   Survey participants

selected from contacts made with members of the ABA Section of Dispute Resolution, ADR Resources Group, the Association for International Arbitration, the Commercial and Industry Arbitration and Mediation Group, the Commercial Dispute Resolution Group, CPR Institute, International Arbitration Group, the Ombuds Group, Resolution Systems Institute and participants at the Asia Pacific Mediation Forum in 2011.

Close to a hundred surveys were distributed to arbitrators, ombuds people and dispute resolution practitioners and a total of forty-eight individuals responded. The questions were distributed at ADR conferences in East Asia, online through a web-based survey collection site, and in person with members of arbitration centres in Shenzhen, Hong Kong, Macau, the United States and Europe.

The summary of the findings are as follows: practitioners of consumer financial dispute resolution view ombuds processes as particularly useful in providing an independent and free review service for financial customers. At the same time the service also helps to identify areas of improvement and reform for banks.[62] Perhaps as a result of such benefits, the use of ombuds processes has been increasing in recent years. The majority of respondents (89 per cent) indicated that they had in fact seen an increase in the use of ombuds processes in consumer financial dispute resolution

---

[62] Survey No. 1 (July 2011–March 2012).

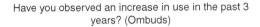

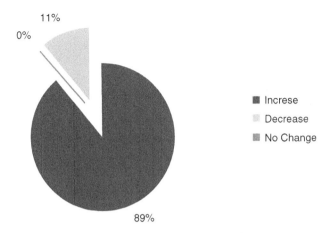

Have you observed an increase in use in the past 3 years? (Ombuds)

11%

0%

89%

■ Increse

▨ Decrease

▨ No Change

Figure 4.2 Perception of increase/decrease in the use of ombuds processes

in recent years. At the same time, practitioners acknowledged areas for continued improvement including the need for greater public education,[63] oversight and quality assurance of ombuds processes.[64]

Benefits of using an ombuds process for consumer financial dispute resolution

The survey identified a number of benefits associated with the ombuds process of consumer financial dispute resolution. Among the benefits include the fact that the process constitutes an 'impartial review service provided free of charge to financial customers'. In addition it helps to 'improve financial literacy of customer[s]' and 'helps to identify areas of improvement for bank[s]'.[65] It also provides 'parties with a sense of self-determination' and a 'platform to be heard'.[66] Avoidance of costly court proceedings was likewise cited as a benefit of the process.[67] Finally the process is 'quick, free and confidential'.[68]

---

[63] Survey No. 1 (July 2011–March 2012).
[64] Survey No. 4 (July 2011–March 2012).
[65] Survey No. 1 (July 2011–March 2012).
[66] Survey No. 2 (July 2011–March 2012).
[67] Survey No. 3 (July 2011–March 2012).
[68] Survey No. 4 (July 2011–March 2012).

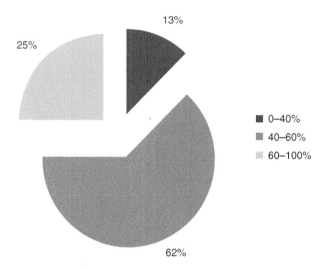

Figure 4.3   Settlement rate – ombuds

Perhaps as a result of such benefits, the use of ombuds processes has been increasing in recent years. In response to the question, 'do you see an increase in the use of ombuds services …', the majority of respondents (89 per cent) indicated that they had in fact seen an increase in the use of ombuds processes in consumer financial dispute resolution in recent years.

In examining the results of the survey regarding the rate of settlement in a multi-tiered ombuds process, over 87 per cent of respondents observed that settlement occurred in 40–100 per cent of cases. This appears to be a positive rate of settlement and provides an indication of the overall effectiveness of the process.

Areas for improvement

At the same time, those surveyed identified a number of areas in which the ombuds processes could be improved in resolving consumer financial disputes. These included 'getting the message out' to financial institutions through increased public information including 'pamphlets, bank web-site and regulator websites' as 'many still don't know about [the] service'.[69]

---

[69] Survey No. 1 (July 2011–March 2012).

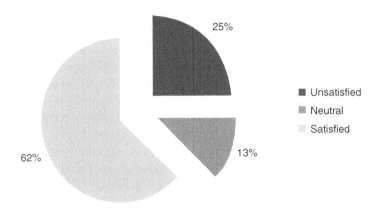

Figure 4.4 Perception of satisfaction with the overall process – ombuds

In addition, some have suggested the need to cultivate greater 'business "buy-in" and cooperation'.[70]

While a number of areas exist for continued improvement in the delivery of consumer financial ombuds services, overall, the majority of respondents (62 per cent) noted general satisfaction on the part of users with the overall ombuds process.

Suggestions for further development

Finally, in response to the question, 'what suggestions do you have for improving the overall process' of consumer financial dispute resolution, participants shared a number of helpful observations. These included 'increased financial literacy of consumers on a whole',[71] 'better mediators',[72] 'more "teeth"' to the process',[73] a system of oversight by which to 'ensure awareness and quality of the interventions'[74] and '[stat]utory requirements to [establish] an ADR system' in those jurisdictions that do not yet have such requirements.[75]

[70] Survey No. 3 (July 2011–March 2012).
[71] Survey No. 1 (July 2011–March 2012).
[72] Survey No. 2 (July 2011–March 2012).
[73] Survey No. 3 (July 2011–March 2012).
[74] Survey No. 4 (July 2011–March 2012).
[75] Survey No. 5 (July 2011–March 2012).

Conclusion

Overall, the findings of the survey indicate that practitioners of consumer financial dispute resolution view ombuds processes as particularly useful in providing an independent and free review service for financial customers. At the same time the service also helps to identify areas of improvement and reform for banks.[76] Perhaps as a result of such benefits, the use of ombuds processes has been increasing in recent years. The majority of respondents (89 per cent) indicated that they had in fact seen an increase in the use of ombuds processes in consumer financial dispute resolution in recent years. At the same time, practitioners acknowledged areas for continued improvement including the need for greater public education,[77] oversight and quality assurance of ombuds processes.[78]

[76] Survey No. 1 (July 2011–March 2012).
[77] Survey No. 1 (July 2011–March 2012).
[78] Survey No. 4 (July 2011–March 2012).

PART III

Arbitration systems

Part III examines the structure and function of arbitration-based consumer financial dispute resolution models in the United States, Singapore and Hong Kong, as well as emerging systems in China. These chapters systematically examine the structural design, policy orientation, complaint procedures, financing and oversight of financial dispute resolution centres as established within each region. Survey findings regarding the benefits, challenges and suggestions for improving the delivery of arbitration services in consumer financial disputes are presented at the end of this Part.

5

Financial dispute resolution in the United States

Introduction

In the United States, several major programmes exist for the resolution of consumer financial disputes. These include both private arbitration and court-annexed programmes for credit card and bank loan complaints. Among the most prominent nationwide programmes in the area of investment disputes is the Financial Industry Regulatory Authority ('FINRA'). What characterises most consumer dispute resolution programmes in the United States is a common concern for efficiency and finality. However, such goals are increasingly being examined in the larger context of principles of equity and transparency as limited opportunities exist for court oversight and no general right of appeal exists on the part of the complainant to pursue claims in court (as in the ombuds model) if the complainant is not satisfied with the final award.

The American Arbitration Association

Among the more prominent alternative financial dispute resolution scheme, the American Arbitration Association ('AAA') provides a special set of rules for financial disputes: the AAA Arbitration Rules for Commercial Financial Disputes, which are applicable to all disputes relating to commercial financial arrangements, products, or other matters, or conduct relating thereto.[1] This would include credit card and bank loan disputes. To meet the financial sector's interest in speedy proceedings, the Rules provide a limited period for arbitration proceedings with

---

[1] See r. 1 of the AAA Arbitration Rules for Commercial Financial Disputes: 'The parties to a dispute involving any commercial financial arrangement, product or other matter or conduct relating thereto, shall be deemed to have made these rules a part of their arbitration agreement whenever they have provided for arbitration by the American Arbitration Association (AAA) or under its Commercial Financial Disputes Arbitration Rules.'

a maximum timeframe of 120 days.[2] For disputes where only a small amount of money is involved (up to $75,000), an expedited procedure applies,[3] according to which a sole arbitrator will decide the dispute, preferably after only one day of hearing. If a second hearing is necessary, the rules provide that it shall take place within seven days of the first hearing. The award has to be rendered within thirty days of the conclusion of the hearing.[4]

However, in a Securities Industry Conference on an Arbitration pilot programme in 2000, in which investors were offered the option to file with

[2] See r. 1, ibid.: 'Consistent with the expedited nature of arbitration, the parties shall make every effort in good faith to conclude the arbitration within 120 days of its commencement.'

[3] See r. 9, ibid.: 'Unless the AAA in its discretion determines otherwise or the parties agree otherwise, the Expedited Procedures shall be applied in any case where no disclosed claim or counterclaim exceeds $75,000, exclusive of interest and arbitration costs.'

[4] S. Kratsch (2010) 'The financial crisis: arbitration as a viable option for European financial institutions', *Arbitration*, 76(4), pp. 680–685.

For details of the expedited procedures, see rr. 51–55, ibid.:

51. The parties shall accept all notices from the AAA by telephone. Such notices by the AAA shall subsequently be confirmed in writing to the parties. Should there be a failure to confirm in writing any notice hereunder, the proceeding shall nonetheless be valid if notice has, in fact, been given by telephone.

52. (a) Where no disclosed claim or counterclaim exceeds $75,000, exclusive of interest and arbitration costs, the AAA shall appoint a single arbitrator, from the National Roster, without submission of lists of proposed arbitrators.

(b) Where all parties request that a list of proposed arbitrators be sent, the AAA shall submit simultaneously to each party an identical list of five proposed arbitrators, drawn from the National Roster of Arbitrators, from which one arbitrator shall be appointed. Each party may strike two names from the list on a peremptory basis. The list is returnable to the AAA within seven days from the date of the AAA's mailing to the parties.

If for any reason the appointment of an arbitrator cannot be made from the list, the AAA may make the appointment from among other members of the National Roster without the submission of additional lists.

(c) The parties will be given notice by telephone by the AAA of the appointment of the arbitrator, who shall be subject to disqualification for the reasons specified in Section 17. Within seven days, the parties shall notify the AAA, by telephone, of any objection to the arbitrator appointed. Any objection by a party to the arbitrator shall be confirmed in writing to the AAA with a copy to the other party or parties.

53. The arbitrator shall set the date, time and place of the hearing. The AAA will notify the parties by telephone, at least seven days in advance of the hearing date. A formal notice of hearing will also be sent by the AAA to the parties.

54. Generally, the hearing shall be completed within one day, unless the dispute is resolved by submission of documents under Section 35. The arbitrator, for good cause shown, may schedule an additional hearing to be held within seven days.

55. Unless otherwise agreed by the parties, the award shall be rendered not later than 30 days from the date of the closing of the hearing.

JAMS or the AAA, investors selected the SRO's arbitration forum (such as FINRA) over non-SRO forums' higher fees and investors' 'general degree of comfort with existing and more familiar SRO procedures'.[5]

Challenges and shortcomings of mandatory consumer credit card arbitration

Mandatory consumer credit card arbitration forums in the United States have been the focus of public litigation in recent years regarding alleged ties to credit card and collection industries. A recent consent decree issued in 2009 between Minnesota Attorney General Lori Swanson and the National Arbitration Forum ('Forum') – the country's largest administrator of credit card and consumer collections arbitrations – brought to light serious systemic issues including lack of impartiality and independence on the part of the National Arbitration Forum. It was found that the National Arbitration Forum 'worked alongside credit card companies to get them to put unfair arbitration clauses in the fine print of their contracts and to appoint the Forum as the arbitrator'.[6]

The Forum, which was named as the arbitrator of consumer disputes in tens of millions of credit card agreements, according to the suit, allegedly hid from the public its extensive ties to the collection industry.[7] The lawsuit alleged that the Forum worked behind the scenes to convince credit card companies and other creditors to insert arbitration provisions in their customer agreements and then appointed the Forum to decide the disputes. It also alleged that the company arbitrated 214,000 consumer arbitration claims in 2006, nearly 60 per cent of which were filed by law firms with which the Forum was linked through ties to a New York hedge fund.[8]

According to the terms of the settlement, the National Arbitration Forum agreed to stop accepting any new consumer arbitrations or in any manner participate in the processing or administering of new consumer arbitrations. The company will permanently stop administering arbitrations involving consumer debt, including credit cards, consumer loans, telecommunications, utilities, health care and consumer leases.[9]

---

[5] W. B. L. Little (2008) 'Fairness is in the eyes of the beholder', *Baylor L. Rev.*, 60, p. 73.
[6] See D. Gupta (20 July 2009) 'Consent Decree in Minnesota v. NAF', *Consumer Law & Policy Blog*, available at: http://pubcit.typepad.com/clpblog/2009/07/consent-decree-in-minnesota-v-naf.html [accessed 26 April 2012].
[7] Ibid.   [8] Ibid.   [9] Ibid.

Such suits have brought to light the potential inequities existing behind the fine print of consumer agreements, including mandatory pre-dispute arbitration clauses, and have sparked US Congressional interest and investigation.[10]

Financial dispute resolution through FINRA

In order to understand the role and function of FINRA, the most prominent nationwide programme for the arbitration of consumer disputes with broker-dealers and financial institutions, it is necessary to examine its legislative and regulatory background.

Arbitration of Securities Disputes: Securities Act 1933

The Securities Act of 1933 was the first major piece of federal legislation governing securities. It combined a full disclosure scheme with antifraud provisions and the end product was federal statutory requirement to file a registration statement (prospectus) with Federal Trade Commission, imposing civil and criminal liabilities for failure to comply.[11]

Although this created government and self-regulatory oversight, the general philosophy of the regulation of the sale of securities is 'buyer-beware', with Federal and state laws requiring that investors receive material information concerning securities being offered for public sale, and prohibit deceit, misrepresentation and other fraud.[12]

Securities Exchange Act 1934

The Securities Exchange Act of 1934 established the Securities Exchange Commission ('SEC') to regulate and enforce securities markets. It also contained disclosure provisions for those who buy and sell securities in the secondary market rather than the company's initial offerings, and creates

---

[10] Ibid.

[11] C. W. Cole (2007–2008) 'Financial Industry Regulatory Authority (FINRA): is the consolidation of NASD and the regulatory arm of NYSE a bull or a bear for US capital markets?', *UMKC L. Rev.*, 76, pp. 251–272.

[12] K. Powell (2008) 'Business law: what Montana lawyers need to know about FINRA', *Montana Lawyer*, 33, p. 31.

remedies for fraud in trading and manipulating secondary markets.[13] The Act also requires stock exchanges to register with the SEC.[14]

The Maloney Act 1938 was an amendment to the 1934 Act, and requires registration by national securities associations of over-the-counter ('OTC') brokers and dealers with the SEC. The National Association of Securities Dealers ('NASD') was the only association to register.[15] The SEC was created by the 1934 Act and has broad regulatory authority to oversee the securities industry.[16]

Self-regulatory organisations: FINRA

Self-regulatory organisations ('SROs') are defined as non-governmental entities responsible for regulating their members through the adoption and enforcement of rules and regulations governing the business conduct of their members.[17]

Securities industry SROs began as private sector membership organisations of securities industry professionals. They set standards of conduct for their members and disciplined errant members. Securities industry SROs existed before the federal securities laws were enacted in 1933 and 1934, and important concepts of federal law were taken from SRO regulation and became an added layer of regulation on top of SRO regulation. Over the last seventy-five years, SROs have grown in membership and become more powerful organisations, but they also have become integrated into the scheme of federal statutory regulation, and now operate subject to SEC oversight of all of their activities. Moreover, as SROs have proliferated, some new SROs have been created by amendments to the securities laws. They are thus a peculiar mix of private sector self-regulation and delegated governmental regulation.[18]

New York Stock Exchange

The New York Stock Exchange ('NYSE') is one of the stock exchanges registered with the SEC that has dominated exchange trading. Stock

---

[13] C. W. Cole, 'Financial Industry Regulatory Authority (FINRA): is the consolidation of NASD and the regulatory arm of NYSE a bull or a bear for US capital markets?'.

[14] Ibid.   [15] Ibid.   [16] Ibid.   [17] Ibid.

[18] R. S. Karmel (2008) 'Should securities industry self-regulatory organizations be considered government agencies?' *Stan. J.L. Bus. & Fin.*, 14, p. 151.

exchanges may be distinguished from the over-the-counter market by their trading floors.[19]

In respect of self-regulation, NYSE established NYSE Regulation to govern exchange and member firms, to investigate and prosecute NYSE and SEC rule violations that occur on or through systems and facilities of the NYSE, and ensures companies listed on NYSE meet financial and corporate governance listing standards.[20]

National Association of Securities Dealers

The National Association of Securities Dealers was formed in 1939 in response to the Maloney Act of 1938, which permitted a national association of securities brokers and dealers to self-regulate over-the-counter markets. It developed the National Association of Securities Dealers Automated Quotations ('NASDAQ') in 1971, which operates and has improved the quality and organisation of the OTC securities market, becoming the second largest stock market in the United States. NASD licensed over 665,000 individuals and oversaw 5,100 firms with over 170,000 branch offices, and set rules for firm and representative behaviour as well as disciplined firms and individuals who do not comply with NASD rules or SEC regulations.[21]

In 1994, the Rudman Committee was formed to review NASDAQ governance and operations, and concluded NASD and NASDAQ should separate to some degree, leading NASD to sell the NASDAQ stock market in 2000 – NASD remains regulator of NASDAQ by contract, and is still the only national securities association to register with SEC, hence retaining regulatory jurisdiction over any security not traded on an exchange.[22]

Financial Industry Regulatory Authority

The Financial Industry Regulatory Authority on its face is simply a consolidation of NASD and the enforcement and arbitration functions of NYSE Regulation. Although it combines the regulatory functions of an exchange with a securities association, many of the different provisions concerning stock exchanges and securities associations in the 1934 Act

---

[19] C. W. Cole, 'Financial Industry Regulatory Authority (FINRA): is the consolidation of NASD and the regulatory arm of NYSE a bull or a bear for US capital markets?'.
[20] Ibid.   [21] Ibid.   [22] Ibid.

are similar, and it is thus feasible for one organisation to carry out the duties of both.[23]

The stated purpose for the consolidation of the NASD and NYSE's regulatory arm is to bring more efficiency to securities industry regulatory efforts by creating a single rule book for broker-dealers. FINRA was designed as a monopoly SRO under the active and direct oversight of the SEC. Although FINRA may not be a government entity, in all or virtually all of its activities, it can be viewed as exercising powers delegated to it by the SEC.[24]

Federal Arbitration Act

The Federal Arbitration Act was passed by Congress in 1925, requiring courts to 'enforce arbitration agreements in the same manner as other contracts'.[25]

Section 2 of the Act[26] declares irrevocable and enforceable written arbitration provisions in all maritime transactions and contracts 'involving commerce'.[27]

Wilko v. Swan 346 U.S. 427 (1953)

In the case of Wilko v. Swan the Supreme Court held that a pre-dispute agreement to arbitrate a claim under the Securities Act 1933 was unenforceable for public policy reasons notwithstanding the existence of the Federal Arbitration Act. The Court felt that since there were risks that arbitrators would misapply law, which the judiciary would not be able to overturn under the Federal Arbitration Act, allowing securities

---

[23] Ibid.

[24] Karmel, 'Should securities industry self-regulatory organizations be considered government agencies?'.

[25] B. B. Zoltowski (2008), 'Restoring investor confidence: providing uniformity in securities arbitration by offering guidelines for arbitrators in deciding motions to dismiss before a hearing on the merits', *Syracuse L. Rev.*, 58(3), pp. 375–396.

[26] Section 2 of the Act states that:

A written provision in any maritime transaction or a contract evidencing a transaction involving commerce to settle by arbitration a controversy thereafter arising out of such contract or transaction, or the refusal to perform the whole or any part thereof, or an agreement in writing to submit to arbitration an existing controversy arising out of such a contract, transaction, or refusal, shall be valid, irrevocable, and enforceable, save upon such grounds as exist at law or in equity for the revocation of any contract.

[27] J. I. Gross (2010) 'The end of mandatory securities arbitration?', *Pace L. Rev.*, 30, p. 1174.

arbitration would in effect allow claimants to waive provisions of the Securities Act.[28]

Shearson/American Express, Inc. *v.* McMahon *482 U.S. 220 (1987)*

In the case of *Shearson/American Express, Inc.* v. *McMahon*, the Supreme Court held that pre-dispute agreements to arbitrate were valid.[29]

The Court stated that *Wilko* v. *Swan* was decided under the Securities Act as opposed to the Exchange Act and that in any event *Wilko* v. *Swan* 'must be read as barring waiver of a judicial forum only where arbitration is inadequate to protect the substantive rights at issue'. The Court interpreted the provision against waiver in the Securities Exchange Act to only prohibit waiver of substantive rights, whereas agreements to arbitrate just waived jurisdiction. Originally designed to provide 'a fast, efficient and cost-effective means of resolving securities disputes', the SEC supported the Court's approval of securities arbitration agreements. The SEC felt arbitration would provide a forum in which investors could resolve small claims that did not justify the expense of litigation.[30]

Since then, virtually all customers' disputes with their broker-dealers and registered representatives are resolved through arbitration in the FINRA (or its predecessors NASD and NYSE) forum.[31]

Rodriguez de Quijas *v.* Shearson/American Express, Inc. *490 U.S. 477 (1989)*

The case of *Rodriguez de Quijas* v. *Shearson/American Express, Inc.* was the Supreme Court case that expressly overruled *Wilko* v. *Swan* following *Shearson/American Express, Inc.* v. *McMahon*.[32]

Subsequent to the *Shearson/American Express, Inc.* v. *McMahon* and *Rodriguez de Quijas* v. *Shearson/American Express, Inc.* decisions, the number of SRO securities arbitrations substantially increased.[33]

---

[28] B. B. Zoltowski, 'Restoring investor confidence: providing uniformity in securities arbitration by offering guidelines for arbitrators in deciding motions to dismiss before a hearing on the merits'.

[29] Ibid.   [30] Ibid.

[31] B. Black (2010) 'How to improve retail investor protection after the Dodd-Frank Wall Street Reform and Consumer Protection Act', *U. Pa. J. Bus. L.*, 13, pp. 59–106.

[32] S. Kratsch, 'The financial crisis: arbitration as a viable option for European financial institutions'.

[33] Little, 'Fairness is in the eyes of the beholder'.

Arbitration Fairness Act 2009

In recent years, academics, media commentators and consumer advocates have questioned the use of pre-dispute arbitration clauses in consumer and employment agreements, which result in class action waivers, inconvenient venue selection, cost-shifting provisions, and process limitations being forced on parties with inferior bargaining power. Courts usually enforce such clauses under the Federal Arbitration Act due to the Supreme Court's mandate that courts ruling on arbitrability questions must apply a presumption of arbitrability. Both the Senate and House introduced nearly identical bills to enact the Arbitration Fairness Act to reflect findings that the Federal Arbitration Act intended to apply to disputes between commercial entities of similar sophistication and bargaining power, but Supreme Court decisions have changed the meaning of the Federal Arbitration Act to extend to disputes between parties of disparate economic power. Furthermore, most consumers and employees have little or no meaningful option regarding whether to submit their claims to arbitration – a process that many argue undermines the development of public law for civil and consumer rights as there is no meaningful judicial review of arbitrator's decisions, and the process is not transparent.[34]

If passed by Congress, this Act would amend the Federal Arbitration Act to invalidate pre-dispute arbitration agreements requiring arbitration of employment, consumer, franchise and civil rights disputes. The Senate version of the Arbitration Fairness Act expressly extends its coverage to securities industry disputes through the definition of consumer disputes. However, Congress' legislative agenda for 2010 has placed the Arbitration Fairness Act on the backburner and focused on financial services regulatory reform.[35]

Dodd-Frank Wall Street Reform and Consumer Protection Act

The Dodd-Frank Wall Street Reform and Consumer Protection Act was a major reform bill that includes a provision that empowers the SEC to prohibit pre-dispute arbitration agreements in customer agreements.[36]

---

[34] J. I. Gross, 'The end of mandatory securities arbitration?'.
[35] Ibid.   [36] Ibid.

Section 921 of the Act[37] grants the SEC authority to limit or prohibit the use of pre-dispute arbitration agreements.[38]

FINRA mandate and function

FINRA is now the largest non-governmental regulator for all securities firms doing business in the United States. It oversees nearly 5,100 broker-age firms, 173,000 branch offices and over 669,000 registered securities representatives.[39] Its role includes market oversight,[40] salesperson regula-tion,[41] investor education, enforcement and arbitration.

---

[37] Section 921 of the Act provides that:

(a) Amendment to Securities Exchange Act of 1934- Section 15 of the Securities Exchange Act of 1934 (15 U.S.C. 78o), as amended by this title, is further amended by adding at the end the following new subsection:
'(o) Authority to Restrict Mandatory Pre-dispute Arbitration- The Commission, by rule, may prohibit, or impose conditions or limitations on the use of, agreements that require customers or clients of any broker, dealer, or municipal securities dealer to arbi-trate any future dispute between them arising under the Federal securities laws, the rules and regulations thereunder, or the rules of a self-regulatory organization if it finds that such prohibition, imposition of conditions, or limitations are in the public interest and for the protection of investors.'
(b) Amendment to Investment Advisers Act of 1940- Section 205 of the Investment Advisers Act of 1940 (15 U.S.C. 80b-5) is amended by adding at the end the following new subsection:
'(f) Authority to Restrict Mandatory Pre-dispute Arbitration- The Commission, by rule, may prohibit, or impose conditions or limitations on the use of, agreements that require customers or clients of any investment adviser to arbitrate any future dispute between them arising under the Federal securities laws, the rules and regulations thereunder, or the rules of a self-regulatory organization if it finds that such prohibition, imposition of conditions, or limitations are in the public interest and for the protection of investors.'

[38] B. Black, 'How to improve retail investor protection after the Dodd-Frank Wall Street Reform and Consumer Protection Act'.

[39] Powell, 'Business law: what Montana lawyers need to know about FINRA'.

[40] Ibid. FINRA oversees and regulates trading on a national level, including NASDAQ, the American Stock Exchange, the International Securities Exchange, the Chicago Climate Exchange in the OTC markets, as well as trades in NYSE and Amex-listed securities reported to NASDAQ. It also regulates trading in the corporate bond markets. Corporate bond transactions are reported to FINRA's Trade Reporting and Compliance Engine ('TRACE') and are disseminated to the public.

[41] Ibid. FINRA oversees background checks, examinations, licensing and oversight of licensed securities salespersons. It also operates a central licensing and registration sys-tem for US securities industry and regulators, contains the registration records of more than 6,800 registered broker-dealers and the qualification, employment, and disclosure histories of more than 660,000 active registered individuals (salespersons).

Investor education, enforcement and arbitration

FINRA provides public educational materials that give a general overview of the securities industry and other basic information on securities intended to be accessible to laypersons.[42]

FINRA has authority to discipline licensed securities firms and registered individuals for breaches of rules and federal securities laws. Jurisdiction works in coordination with the dual federal–state jurisdiction that gives authority to the SEC and the state regulators to regulate the members of the securities industry through administrative, civil and criminal filings.[43]

The majority of contracts between salesperson, broker-dealer firms and customers include an arbitration requirement, and most contractual disputes go through an arbitration process. Though there are several organisations that could handle securities arbitrations, the majority of security disputes are handled by FINRA according to its rules and regulations for arbitration.[44]

Compulsory arbitration between member firms and member firms and their employees has generally been viewed as a matter of private contract, a condition of being a member of an SRO.[45]

Even if a customer agreement does not contain a pre-dispute arbitration clause, the FINRA Code of Arbitration Procedure for Customer Disputes Rule 12200[46] requires broker-dealers to submit to arbitration at the demand of a customer.[47]

In addition to the more formal arbitration procedure, FINRA offers a non-binding mediation programme. During the period 2005–2007,

---

[42] Powell, 'Business law: what Montana lawyers need to know about FINRA'.

[43] Ibid.

[44] Ibid.

[45] Karmel, 'Should securities industry self-regulatory organizations be considered government agencies?'.

[46] Rule 12200 provides that:
Parties must arbitrate a dispute under the Code if:

- Arbitration under the Code is either:
  (1) Required by a written agreement, or
  (2) Requested by the customer;
- The dispute is between a customer and a member or associated person of a member; and
- The dispute arises in connection with the business activities of the member or the associated person, except disputes involving the insurance business activities of a member that is also an insurance company.

[47] J. I. Gross, 'The end of mandatory securities arbitration?'.

according to FINRA's statistics, approximately 70–80 per cent of claims filed were settled or resolved through means other than an arbitrator decision, 3–4 per cent of cases were resolved by arbitrators on the basis of written submissions, and 18–20 per cent of cases were resolved after a formal hearing.[48]

Underlying legal mandate

The primary function of SROs is the regulation of broker-dealers, serving as intermediaries between the SEC and regulated members of the industry. A broker is defined as 'any person engaged in the business of effecting transactions in securities for the account of others', and a dealer as 'any person engaged in the business of buying and selling securities for such person's own account'. Many firms operate as both brokers and dealers. The Securities Exchange Act requires broker-dealers to register with the SEC and join either a registered national securities exchange or an SRO.[49]

The authority granted to FINRA under the Exchange Act allows it to be an effective intermediary between the SEC and its registered broker-dealers. While the SEC does not have the general authority to adopt rules governing the conduct of registered broker-dealers in relation to their customers, FINRA, and other SROs like it, require their members to adopt rules of conduct and to retain the power to enforce these rules (and other supervisory policies and procedures) using designated enforcement and examination staff.[50]

Types of dispute

Procedure

FINRA administers 'the largest [US] dispute resolution forum for investors and registered firms'. FINRA Dispute Resolution ('FINRADR') provides both mediation and arbitration, and suggests, but does not require, that an aggrieved investor first attempt to resolve the conflict with the brokerage firm's management. The FINRA Code of Arbitration Procedure

---

[48] S. Choi, J. E. Fisch and A. C. Pritchard (2010) 'Attorneys as arbitrators', *J. Legal Stud.*, 39, p. 109.

[49] J. T. Koebel (2010) 'Trust and the investment adviser industry: Congress' failure to realize FINRA's potential to restore investor confidence', *Seton Hall Legis. J.*, 35, p. 61.

[50] Ibid.

for Customer Disputes applies to any dispute between a customer and a member that is submitted to arbitration.[51]

Once an investor is compelled to arbitrate a claim, the modern process is akin to litigation with only slight variation. Arbitration, despite being touted as a 'quick, fair, and relatively inexpensive' alternative to litigation, employs similarly formal procedures that can increase costs and cause delays. First, the complainant files an initial statement of claim with the Director of Dispute Resolution, 'specifying the relevant facts and remedies requested'. The respondent then serves an answer including relevant facts, available defences and any counterclaims. A panel, usually consisting of three arbitrators, is appointed to consider the initial statement of claim and all responsive pleadings. Similar to litigation, the parties are subject to a discovery process including depositions, motion hearings on disputed collateral matters, and possible sanctions for failure to comply with any of the FINRA Code requirements. The parties produce witnesses and the arbitrators have the authority to issue subpoenas where necessary to compel production of documents or persons to appear. Except in certain circumstances, parties present their evidence in the form of testimony and documents in a litigation-like hearing before the arbitral panel. Unlike litigation, however, evidence is admissible notwithstanding state or federal evidence rules, although witnesses must testify under oath or affirmation.[52]

Financial Industry Regulatory Authority rules establish two categories of arbitrators – public and non-public (industry). Under the current procedures, claims for less than $25,000 are resolved through a simplified procedure involving a single arbitrator who resolves the case without a formal hearing. Claims for between $25,000 and $50,000 receive a hearing conducted by a single arbitrator, although any party has the right to request a three-person panel. If the claim is heard by a single arbitrator, FINRA rules require that the arbitrator be a public arbitrator unless the parties agree otherwise. Claims for $50,000 or more are resolved by a panel consisting of three arbitrators. If the case is heard by a three-person panel, the rules provide that the panel will be composed of two public arbitrators and one non-public (industry) arbitrator.[53]

[51] C. Alpert (2008) 'Financial Services in the United States and United Kingdom: Comparative Approaches to Securities Regulation and Dispute Resolution', *BYU Int'l L. & Mgmt. Rev.*, 5, p. 75.

[52] Ibid.

[53] S. Choi, J. E. Fisch and A. C. Pritchard, 'Attorneys as arbitrators'.

Current and former professionals in the securities industry and other professionals with substantial industry ties may not be classified as public arbitrators (Uniform Code of Arbitration, FINRA Code r. 10308[a][5][54]). Public arbitrators are thus intended to be industry outsiders or 'neutrals'. Non-public arbitrators, commonly known as industry arbitrators, include current and former brokers, bankers and other securities professionals. The category also includes attorneys, accountants and other professionals who have devoted 20 per cent or more of their professional work to industry clients (Uniform Code of Arbitration, FINRA Code r. 10308[a][4][55]).

Arbitrators for FINRA arbitrations are chosen through a list selection system administered by the director of dispute resolution, termed the Neutral List Selection System ('NLSS'). The lists are generated by a NASD computer program using a rotational method, although the computer eliminates arbitrators with obvious conflicts of interest. Along with the lists, the parties are also provided with background information on

---

[54] FINRA Rule 10308[a][5] states that:

(A) The term 'public arbitrator' means a person who is otherwise qualified to serve as an arbitrator and:
  (i) is not engaged in the conduct or activities described in paragraphs (a)(4)(A) through (D);
  (ii) was not engaged in the conduct or activities described in paragraphs (a)(4)(A) through (D) for a total of 20 years or more;
  (iii) is not an investment adviser;
  (iv) is not an attorney, accountant, or other professional whose firm derived 10 percent or more of its annual revenue in the past 2 years from any persons or entities listed in paragraph (a)(4)(A);
  (v) is not employed by, and is not the spouse or an immediate family member of a person who is employed by, an entity that directly or indirectly controls, is controlled by, or is under common control with, any partnership, corporation, or other organization that is engaged in the securities business;
  (vi) is not a director or officer of, and is not the spouse or an immediate family member of a person who is a director or officer of, an entity that directly or indirectly controls, is controlled by, or is under common control with, any partnership, corporation, or other organization that is engaged in the securities business; and
  (vii) is not the spouse or an immediate family member of a person who is engaged in the conduct or activities described in paragraphs (a)(4)(A) through (D).

[55] FINRA Rule 10308[a][4] states that:

The term 'non-public arbitrator' means a person who is otherwise qualified to serve as an arbitrator and:
  …
  (C) is an attorney, accountant, or other professional who has devoted 20 percent or more of his or her professional work, in the last two years, to clients who are engaged in any of the business activities listed in subparagraph (4)(A); …

each arbitrator, including a copy of that arbitrator's Arbitrator Disclosure Report. Parties are allowed to request additional information about the arbitrators.[56]

The chair of the panel is typically responsible for the overall administration of the proceeding, including the resolution of discovery disputes, ruling on evidentiary issues, etc. Parties have the right, in the first instance, to designate the chair of the panel by agreement, although, according to FINRA, the parties agree on the designation of the chair only 20 per cent of the time. If the parties are unable to agree, the chair is appointed by the director and is to be the public arbitrator who received the highest combined ranking 'as long as the person is not an attorney, accountant, or other professional who has devoted 50 [per cent] or more of his or her professional or business activities, within the last two years, to representing or advising public customers in matters relating to disputed securities or commodities transactions or similar matters' (Uniform Code of Arbitration, FINRA Code, Rule 10308[c][5][A]).

Unlike the United Kingdom or Australia, since FINRA complainants must pay an arbitration fee, a hearing deposit, and attorneys' fees, cost-deterrence serves as a filter, and therefore strict jurisdictional prerequisites for arbitration are unnecessary.[57]

Awards

If the parties proceed to an award, the FINRA Code requires that a majority of arbitrators agree on the rulings and determinations, but it does not require written opinions. 'Awards are subject to judicial review on the merits' only for 'manifest disregard' of the law and 'do not serve as precedent'.[58] This limited judicial review and absence of a required reasoned opinion allows arbitrators to base awards in favour of claimants on 'general equity grounds'.[59]

FINRA Arbitration has no statutory cap on the value of awards, but incorporates a small-claims procedure, by which it diverts claims for $25,000 or less to a Simplified Arbitration Procedure. Unless the customer requests a hearing, such claims are decided solely on the parties' written submissions.[60]

---

[56] S. Choi, J. E. Fisch and A. C. Pritchard, 'Attorneys as arbitrators'.
[57] C. Alpert, 'Financial Services in the United States and United Kingdom: Comparative Approaches to Securities Regulation and Dispute Resolution'.
[58] Ibid.   [59] Ibid.   [60] Ibid.

Fees

FINRADR is administered by FINRA, and is funded by regulatory fees from FINRA members, dispute resolution fees from users, as well as other fees from FINRA's regulatory role.

Oversight

The SEC exercises oversight authority over FINRA as the SRO for broker-dealers, which is the principal regulator.[61]

SROs set rules governing member firms in the financial industry and provide oversight, supplementing that of the SEC. Eight SROs report to the SEC, which subjects SRO rules to an approval process.[62]

The SEC provides little oversight over FINRA arbitration. Little oversight by the SEC combined with the court's grant of nearly limitless power to arbitrators makes investor protection uncertain at best.[63]

Strengths

Benefit of merger

As a result of the merger of NYSE and NASD the regulatory efficiency for firms that were members of both NYSE and NASD has increased.[64] This merger also combines NASD's experience in administering an arbitration forum and NASD's ability to sanction its members.[65]

Lack of legal remedies/alternatives

No consideration is currently being given to amending federal securities legislation to provide an explicit damages remedy for careless and

---

[61] B. Black, 'How to improve retail investor protection after the Dodd-Frank Wall Street Reform and Consumer Protection Act'.

[62] J. T. Koebel, 'Trust and the investment adviser industry: Congress' failure to realize FINRA's potential to restore investor confidence'.

[63] B. B. Zoltowski, 'Restoring investor confidence: providing uniformity in securities arbitration by offering guidelines for arbitrators in deciding motions to dismiss before a hearing on the merits'.

[64] C. W. Cole, 'Financial Industry Regulatory Authority (FINRA): is the consolidation of NASD and the regulatory arm of NYSE a bull or a bear for US capital markets?'.

[65] Little, 'Fairness is in the eyes of the beholder'.

incompetent investment advice. Courts resist investors' efforts to recover damages for losses caused by failure to adhere to standards of care and competence established under federal securities laws and SRO rules, unless the investor can establish fraud because of the suspicion that dissatisfied investors seek to hold their investment advice providers responsible whenever they lose money; courts worry about 'hindsight bias', that fact-finders will find investment advice faulty simply because it turned out to be unsuccessful. The advantage of securities arbitration from a retail investors' perspective is that they may be able to recover damages despite the unavailability of a legal remedy, and emphasis of the FINRA arbitration forum on equity allows arbitrators to fashion a remedy for investors that may not be supported by the law.[66]

The pre-dispute arbitration agreement also provides reasonable notice, the right to retain counsel and to present evidence, a convenient geographical location for the evidentiary hearing, and the right to adequate relief. Arbitration with FINRA generally allows the claimant to have the dispute resolved in a timelier manner than litigation. Moreover, the statutes of limitations in many jurisdictions are substantially shorter than the NASD Customer Code's six-year eligibility rule – an investor claim filed in civil litigation might be more likely dismissed upon these grounds, whereas in arbitration the investor might have been awarded a substantial portion of his or her compensatory damages regardless of the statutes of limitations.[67]

FINRA Arbitration also offers finality benefits for either side when successful.[68]

Challenges

Harmonisation

Following the merger of NASD and NYSE Regulation, there has been the challenge of how the rules of the two organisations should be merged and harmonised, raising the issue of whether FINRA should continue with rules-based regulation or move to a principle-based or tier-based approach.[69]

---

[66] B. Black, 'How to improve retail investor protection after the Dodd-Frank Wall Street Reform and Consumer Protection Act'.

[67] Little, 'Fairness is in the eyes of the beholder'.

[68] C. Alpert, 'Financial Services in the United States and United Kingdom: Comparative Approaches to Securities Regulation and Dispute Resolution'.

[69] C. W. Cole, 'Financial Industry Regulatory Authority (FINRA): is the consolidation of NASD and the regulatory arm of NYSE a bull or a bear for US capital markets?'.

Bank broker-dealers

FINRA recently proposed to adopt a modified version of NASD Rule 2350, known as the 'bank broker-dealer rule'. The proposed rule change seeks to prevent FINRA member firms that offer broker-dealer products and services through contractual 'networking arrangements' with financial institutions – both on and off the premises of those institutions – from undertaking certain business practices that might tend to confuse or harm customers of financial institutions. The proposed rule change also aims to prevent customer confusion by, inter alia, ensuring that certain disclosures are made to customers so they can understand and appreciate the distinction(s) between the products and services sold by a financial institution and those sold by its broker-dealer affiliate.[70]

The proposed rule change protects bank customers who may be solicited for the purchase of investment products and services, but only to a limited extent. It does not rectify sales practices of broker-dealers – affiliated with financial institutions – which tend to confuse, and even mislead, financially unsophisticated investors of modest means who can least afford to be exposed to excessive risk.[71] Additionally, the proposed rule change adds no meaningful surveillance, inspection, enforcement, or punitive mechanisms to prevent and/or redress insidious practices that are akin to 'bait and switch' tactics and are particularly effective against financially unsophisticated investors.[72] In fact, the proposed rule change even rolls back some key regulatory provisions, an especially unsettling retreat when one considers the lack of oversight during the recent market malaise and the contribution that such abridgement may have made to the present economic contraction as a reverse 'wealth effect' impinges upon consumer behaviour. It is arguable that the proposed rule change is inadequate to sufficiently protect investors and promote genuine market integrity.[73]

Challenge to mandatory securities arbitration

As noted above, the passage of the Arbitration Fairness Act would extend to pre-dispute arbitration agreements in the securities industry.

---

[70] J. I. Gross and E. Pekarek (2010) 'Banks and brokers and bricks and clicks: an evaluation of FINRA's proposal to modify the "bank broker-dealer rule"', *Alb. L. Rev.*, 73, p. 465.
[71] Ibid.   [72] Ibid.   [73] Ibid.

Furthermore, the SEC has now been empowered to prohibit such clauses in customer agreements.

Investor advocates argue securities arbitration is unfair, inefficient, expensive and biased towards the securities industry, while the securities industry argues the process works well, is faster and less expensive than litigation, and is fair to all parties involved.[74]

It has been argued that because securities arbitration differs from other forms of consumer arbitration, the power of the SEC should not be exercised and the Arbitration Fairness Act should not be extended to the securities industry. In this regard, it has been pointed out that the SEC robustly exercises its authority to oversee FINRA, including its dispute resolution arm, while no administrative agency reviews consumer or non-securities employment arbitration forums. FINRA Conduct Rule 3110(f) prescribes language that member firms must include in their customer agreements, and precludes brokerage firms from including unfair provisions, or provisions that limit a customer's rights and remedies. FINRA bars brokerage firms from imposing class action waivers, and FINRA Dispute Resolution does not permit class arbitrations, thus freeing investors to pursue class action claims in court. FINRA's Code of Arbitration Procedure for Customer Disputes contains provisions that expressly contradict the types of unfair consumer arbitration provisions that the Arbitration Fairness Act targets, and FINRA actively facilitates forum access by subsidising forum fees and reducing costs to lower levels than consumer arbitration and other measures. It also actively promotes transparency of the process and recently amended its rules to require arbitrators to write an explained decision if all parties jointly request one. FINRA also ensures that where an arbitration panel awards damages, the investor will collect the damages promptly.

Furthermore, in giving investors a choice between arbitration and litigation, investors may face a more hostile environment in court, as well as facing significant procedural hurdles, in contrast with the equitable principles an arbitration panel can employ. Given the high costs of litigation, firms may decline post-dispute requests for arbitration, especially in smaller cases, discouraging customers from pursuing claims altogether. Elimination of mandatory securities arbitration could result in higher transaction costs as firms would need to account for higher costs to litigate rather than arbitrate. There is also empirical evidence to show that investors may not choose their forum of dispute resolution rationally or even

---

[74] J. I. Gross, 'The end of mandatory securities arbitration?'.

make the choice in their best interests. Eliminating mandatory securities arbitration could also lead to the repeal of Rule 12200 of the FINRA Code of Arbitration Procedure for Customer Disputes,[75] which allows customers to demand broker-dealers submit to arbitration. Optional arbitration would also reduce political pressure on FINRA to ensure the fairness of the forum.[76]

Explained decisions

On 15 March 2005, the NASD filed a proposed rule with the SEC to provide written explanations in arbitration awards upon the request of customers, or from a request by associated persons involved in industry controversies. The NASD surprisingly admitted that the lack of an explained decision made it 'all but impossible [for the judiciary] to determine whether [the panel] acted with manifest disregard of the law'. To date, the SEC has not yet ruled upon FINRA's 2005 proposed rule regarding explained decisions. However, given FINRA's recently proposed rule amendments requiring an explanatory decision accompanying an order of dismissal for a dispositive motion filed before the end of a claimant's case, it is clear that the SEC will soon have to address the issue of explained decisions in the context of securities arbitrations.[77]

Non-adherence with procedures

Many practitioners doubt the fairness of the SRO arbitration process, believing that the limited document and information discovery afforded under the NASD Customer Code is difficult to obtain due to the securities industry having little respect for complying with NASD discovery procedures because they simply do not believe that an arbitration panel will be as likely as a sitting judge to sanction them for their discovery violations and related behaviour.[78]

Cost and complexity

Observers have noted that the NASD Code of Arbitration no longer reflects a simple, efficient medium for the economical resolution of securities

---

[75] For Rule 12200, see footnote 46 above.
[76] Ibid.
[77] Little, 'Fairness is in the eyes of the beholder'.
[78] Ibid.

disputes. Instead it exhibits the characteristics of the Federal Rules of Civil Procedure but without the procedural safeguards of full discovery, fair award of costs to the prevailing party, explanatory orders, a sitting judge, and appellate review.[79] The practice of securities arbitration is more contentious than in previous times, arguably due to the lack of judicial oversight. Given the substantial filing fees, pre-hearing and hearing costs levied by the NASD – from a pure cost of recovery perspective – litigation has become a relative bargain.[80] It is not atypical for a four-day arbitration evidentiary hearing, coupled with the costs of pre-hearing conferences, to produce fees and expense billings from the NASD totalling substantially in excess of $10,000. Factoring in the tendency of arbitration panels to 'split the baby', whether it relates to arbitration fees and expenses or to the actual award provided to the 'successful' claimant, the claimant's net recovery may be reduced to a fraction of what may have been awarded in litigation by a judge or a jury strictly adhering to a judge's instructions on the law.[81] This substantial potential expense stands as both a psychological and monetary barrier to the FINRA arbitration forum for many defrauded investors. Although FINRA may waive its fees based on a showing of 'hardship', this waiver is not automatically given and the final determination of hardship is customarily not decided prior to incurring the hearing expenses.

Lessons learned

Congress requested the US General Accountability Office ('GAO') to evaluate SRO arbitration relating to concerns held by Congress, state regulators and investor groups 'about whether industry-sponsored arbitration is fair to investors', with a primary concern that 'arbitration at an industry-sponsored forum may have a pro-industry bias'. The GAO issued an initial study in 1992 (the 1992 GAO Report) finding that there existed no industry bias at industry sponsored forums versus independent forums, but made no finding regarding the overall 'fairness' of the arbitration process due to the limited number of customer disputes being litigated and the inherent differences between the litigation and arbitration processes. The 1992 GAO Report did find that, at the time, the SROs lacked internal controls sufficient to reasonably assure that SRO arbitrators were either independent or competent. In particular, the 1992 GAO Report found that the SROs had no formal standards to qualify arbitrators,

---

[79] Ibid.   [80] Ibid.   [81] Ibid.

performed no background verification regarding information provided by the arbitrators, and had no system to properly train arbitrators to function fairly and appropriately. A subsequent GAO study in 2000 included positive findings regarding the SROs' implementation of the 1992 GAO Report's recommendations allowing arbitration parties a greater role in arbitrator selection, verifying arbitrator background information, and improving arbitrator training.[82]

Securities arbitration has consistently been criticised as favouring the securities industry over the interests of investors. The NASD created the Arbitration Policy Task Force in 1994 to evaluate and respond to a number of criticisms, including claims that the system was biased or industry dominated. Although the NASD's task force found no evidence of bias, a number of its recommendations were designed to improve the perceived and actual fairness of the system, leading to rule changes in 2004 and 2007 including more stringent arbitrator requirements for updating disclosures.[83]

Contribution to consumer confidence

Investor perception

Empirical evidence shows (1) investors have a far more negative perception of securities arbitration than all other participants; (2) investors have a strong negative perception of the bias of arbitrators in the securities arbitration forum; and (3) investors lack knowledge of the securities arbitration process.[84] Gross and Black's 2008 study concluded that 'Despite FINRA's commendable efforts to improve the process, these efforts will likely prove unsuccessful in winning customers' confidence so long as they are required to accept both an industry arbitrator and an unexplained award'. Among the findings of the study included:[85]

---

[82] Ibid.
[83] S. Choi, J. E. Fisch and A. C. Pritchard, 'Attorneys as arbitrators'.
[84] J. I. Gross and B. Black (2008) 'When perception changes reality: an empirical study of investors' views of the fairness of securities arbitration', *J. Disp. Resol.*, 2, p. 349.
[85] Ibid. The findings also included:

    40.58 per cent of the customers who responded either disagreed or strongly disagreed with the proposition that their arbitration panel was impartial.

    55.48 per cent of the customers who responded either agreed or strongly agreed with the proposition that they would be more satisfied if they had an explanation of the award.

- 40.4 per cent of the customers who responded either disagreed or strongly disagreed with the proposition that their arbitration panel was open-minded.
- 70.77 per cent of the customers who responded either disagreed or strongly disagreed with the proposition that they were satisfied with the outcome.
- 49.13 per cent of the customers who responded either agreed or strongly agreed that the arbitration process was too expensive.
- 60 per cent of the customers who responded either disagreed or strongly disagreed with the proposition that they have a favourable view of securities for customer disputes.
- 61.3 per cent of the customers who responded either disagreed or strongly disagreed with the proposition that arbitration was fair for all parties.

However, it has been argued that changes to investor perception of the fairness of the FINRA arbitral process may have been caused by the market itself, and the fact that in a period of market instability, more awards and damages are likely to go in favour of investors than in a period of stability – ironically, what is likely is that in light of the 2008 market crash, investors will receive larger and more frequent awards. Therefore, it is likely that in a follow-up survey inquiring about the securities arbitration forum, an investor survey will likely find that the users of the forum believe the present form of the forum is fair.[86]

Arbitrator conflicts of interest and bias

Empirical evidence shows arbitrators who also represent brokerage firms or brokers in other arbitrations award significantly less compensation to investor-claimants than do other arbitrators.[87]

51.55 per cent of the customers who responded either disagreed or strongly disagreed with the proposition that they would recommend to others that they use arbitration to resolve their securities disputes.

62.62 per cent of the customers who responded either disagreed or strongly disagreed with the proposition that they, as a whole, feel that the arbitration process was fair.

49.2 per cent of the customers who responded either disagreed or strongly disagreed with the proposition that arbitration was without bias for all parties.

[86] S. D. Grannum (2009) 'The faith and face of securities arbitration: after the 2008 crash', in D. E. Robbins (ed.), *Securities Arbitration in the Market Meltdown Era* (New York: Practising Law Institute), Chapter 4.

[87] S. Choi, J. E. Fisch and A. C. Pritchard, 'Attorneys as arbitrators'.

In 1992, the General Accounting Office (1992) published the results of a study of arbitration awards during an eighteen-month period in 1989 and 1990. The GAO found that claimants received an award of monetary damages in 59 per cent of arbitrations and received, on average, 61 per cent of claimed damages. In 2000, the GAO published an updated report that reflected data from 1992 to 1998. That study found that investors' win rates had declined to an average of 51 per cent over the time period but reasoned that this decline might be the result of an increase in settled claims rather than a pro-industry bias. More recent data indicate that the investor win rate has continued to decline. Statistics from FINRA show that investors received an award of monetary damages or other non-monetary relief in 42 per cent of the cases decided in 2006 and in 37 per cent in 2007.[88]

There is a long-held view by many practitioners that arbitrators, after finding the brokerage firm liable to the investor, are prone to 'split the baby' when deciding the amount of compensatory damages to be paid by the securities industry in an effort to placate the industry arbitrator, and to increase the likelihood that industry respondents will not strike arbitrators (public or industry) from serving on future arbitration panels. Moreover, there is the view that arbitration panels judge the securities industry's major broker-dealers with greater leniency than their smaller broker-dealer brethren. These perceptions find a statistical foundation by a study recently released by Edward S. O'Neal, Ph.D, a former Assistant Finance Professor at Wake Forest University's Babcock Graduate School of Management, and investor representative Daniel R. Solin, Esq.[89]

The O'Neal-Solin Report also disclosed that the greater the compensatory dollar amount requested, or the larger the size of the brokerage firm named as the respondent, the smaller the expected recovery percentage for the investor tends to be on average. In fact, the larger size of the broker-dealer and the compensatory amount claimed can dramatically reduce the likelihood for recovery and the percentage amount recovered.[90]

The arbitration selection process may also be subject to the appearance of bias emanating from the mandated industry arbitrator. Efforts by FINRA to alleviate this problem by changing the rules to allow for the option of all-public panels in FINRA arbitrations, however, have been met

---

[88] Ibid.   [89] Little, 'Fairness is in the eyes of the beholder'.
[90] Ibid.

with criticism by industry experts, who cite the potential for increased costs due to reliance on an expert witness rather than the expertise of an industry panellist.[91]

Another characteristic which casts doubt upon the fairness of arbitration is the lack of adequate judicial review resulting from the standard of 'manifest disregard' for the law. In essence, a party must basically prove arbitrator misconduct in order to have the award vacated.[92]

Contribution to domestic financial performance

Securities litigation as a hindrance to economic growth

Along with Canada and Australia, the United States is one of three G20 nations to permit securities class actions. Although originally envisioned as a means to provide relief to aggrieved investors and supplement limited regulatory oversight, securities class-action litigation has become an inefficient means of redress for investors, a costly encumbrance to businesses and a hindrance to capital formation. In one recent study, approximately 41 per cent of the companies listed on the major stock exchanges had been named as defendants in at least one federal securities class action. The total monetary value of securities class-action settlements in 2008 was $3.09 billion. The average settlement value from 2002 to 2008 was $45.6 million, which represents approximately a 175 per cent increase from the average value of $16.6 million from 1996 to 2001. It has been argued that securities class-action lawsuits pose an impediment to economic growth in the United States. The threat of private securities class-action lawsuits is among the primary disincentives to listing on US exchanges. To cope with the cost of securities litigation, companies must raise the price of their goods and services. Doing so, in turn, logically harms the competitiveness of US businesses in a global marketplace dominated by low-cost goods and services in nations where providers do not face such threats. Conversely, a system of securities arbitration as an alternative to securities class-action litigation in federal courts may indirectly facilitate capital

---

[91] L. Konish (1 March 2011) 'All-public Panels Approved For Arbitrations; A step in the right direction-or just a cost increase?', *onwallstreet*, available at: www.onwallstreet. com/ows_issues/2011_3/all-public-panels-approved-for-arbitrations-2671609-1.html [accessed 8 February 2012].

[92] Ibid.

formation, make US markets more competitive on the global stage, and ultimately spur economic growth by reducing the costs of capital.[93]

However, in the context of the perceptions of bias in the arbitral process, it has been argued that the inability of investors to effectively enforce property rights through a more efficient mechanism, whether it be through litigation, arbitration, binding mediation through a neutral third party, or an administrative law judge, leads to market inefficiency, which is detrimental to the health of an economic system. In the short run, market inefficiencies benefit only those few who encourage them while in the long run they are harmful to the overall economy.[94] Often it is the small investor bringing his claim in a court of law or arbitral institution that serves as the early warning system of wide spread wrong-doing. Increased transparency, sensible regulation and the ability of the individual investor to enforce his or her property rights in a court of law are important components of any solution to preventing future economic instability.[95]

---

[93] B. J. Bondi (2010) 'Facilitating economic recovery and sustainable growth through reform of the securities class-action system: exploring arbitration as an alternative to litigation', *Harvard Journal of Law & Public Policy*, 33(2), pp. 607–638.

[94] B. Stark (2009) 'Compulsory arbitration: its impact on the efficiency of markets', in D. E. Robbins (ed.), *Securities Arbitration in the Market Meltdown Era* (New York: Practising Law Institute), Chapter 9.

[95] Ibid.

6

Financial dispute resolution in Singapore

Background

The Financial Industry Disputes Resolution Centre ('FIDReC') in Singapore in many ways reflects a hybrid system of adjudication which functions similarly to the arbitration model in that decisions are made by recognised private industry and legal professionals while it also bears some similarity to the ombuds model in that decisions are rendered without prejudice to the claimant. The system itself reflects the importance placed on principles of fairness, impartiality and efficiency.

Longstanding history of consumer organisations

Consumer bodies have a long history in Singapore – one of the most notable examples is the Consumers Association of Singapore ('CASE'), which was established in 1971 for the protection and promotion of consumer interests. CASE had a role in lobbying for the Consumer Protection (Fair Trading) Act of Singapore, which came into effect in March 2004. CASE provides dispute resolution processes for consumer-to-business disputes through its mediation centre, set up in June 1999, with a 70–80 per cent rate of resolution.

Two predecessor dispute resolution schemes

The banking and insurance sectors of Singapore have in place dispute resolution mechanisms – the Consumer Mediation Unit and the Insurance Disputes Resolution Organisation respectively.

The Consumer Mediation Unit ('CMU') was set up by the Association of Banks in Singapore in January 2003. Where customer complaints were previously referred back to banks, the establishment of the CMU enabled consumers who were dissatisfied with the banks' response to take their complaint to an independent, impartial and structured process to seek redress. The CMU was empowered to deal with complaints on banking business transacted through bank branches, by telephone, through ATM and electronic means, and also included credit card and investment complaints. The panel of mediators of CMU could award compensation of up to S$50,000. This involved a two-stage process: first, within fourteen days of receiving a complaint, the CMU will respond to a complainant with an assessment, free of charge. Where the complainant is dissatisfied with the assessment, on payment of an administrative fee of S$50, he can refer his complaint to a panel of mediators. The complaint is then investigated by a panel comprising a banker (from an institution different to the one complained of), a lawyer and a non-banking professional. The panel is empowered to interview or request further information from the complainant or relevant bank. The decision of the panel is not binding on the complainant, and thus the complainant, if still dissatisfied, could take the matter to the courts or arbitration.[1]

The Insurance Disputes Resolution Organisation ('IDRO') was established in February 2003 by Singapore's insurance industry as an alternative, independent channel for the resolution of insurance disputes between insured and insurers. It replaced the Insurance Ombudsman's Tribunal and the Tribunal for Motor Third Party Property Damage Claims. The scope of IDRO's jurisdiction was increased from these predecessor tribunals to include claims against market conduct and service standards. Claims were restricted to S$100,000 for life and general insurance, S$50,000 for third party claims, and S$10,000 for claims relating to market conduct and service standards.[2] When a complaint within the IDRO's jurisdiction was received, it would be taken up by a case manager, who would take the matter up with the insurer and attempt to facilitate a resolution of the dispute. Where such a resolution could not be reached, the complainant would then take his complaint to an IDRO mediator or panel of mediators. The complainant would pay an administrative fee of S$50, and if his claim was below S$10,000, it would be handled by a single mediator, while a panel of mediators had the jurisdiction to make awards up to the limits of IDRO's jurisdiction. Mediator rulings were final and binding only on the insurance company, but the consumer remained free to reject the ruling and pursue legal proceedings, or mediation or arbitration per most insurance policies.

---

[1] Monetary Authority of Singapore Policy Consultation on the Financial Industry Disputes Resolution Centre (October 2004).
[2] Ibid.

A gap in coverage

There are thus dispute resolution schemes for the banking and insurance industries of Singapore, but not for its capital markets. A working group of capital markets representatives concluded in 2003 that it would be more cost effective to leverage the resources of existing schemes than to establish a new scheme for capital markets given the relatively small number of complaints in the capital markets sector.[3]

In May 2004, the Monetary Authority of Singapore formed an Integration Steering Committee to facilitate the integration of dispute resolution schemes for Singapore's financial sector.[4] This integrated scheme was aimed at providing coverage for most retail consumer complaints in the financial sector. The integrated scheme was officially launched on 31 August 2005.[5]

Financial alternative dispute resolution programmes

Financial Industry Disputes Resolution Centre Ltd ('FIDReC')

Rather than operate the financial dispute resolution scheme under one of the existing schemes, the Steering Committee concluded that the scheme should have a new corporate and brand identity 'in the spirit of starting things fresh'. The Financial Industry Disputes Resolution Centre was set up as an independent company, limited by guarantee under a new name, with a phased approach to the integration of its two predecessor schemes.[6]

Range of disputes

FIDReC's jurisdiction extends over all disputes brought by individuals and sole proprietors against financial institutions who are members of FIDReC, except disputes over commercial decisions (including pricing and other policies, e.g. interest rates and fees), cases under investigation by any law enforcement agency, and cases which have been subjected to

---

[3] Ibid. [4] Ibid.
[5] Financial Industry Disputes Resolution Centre Ltd (2005–2006) *Annual Report 2005/6*.
[6] Monetary Authority of Singapore, Policy Consultation on the Financial Industry Disputes Resolution Centre.

a court hearing, for which a judgment or order is passed.[7] These financial institutions include banks, finance companies, life insurers, general insurers, capital market services licensees, licensed financial advisers and insurance intermediaries.[8] The nature of complaints can broadly be separated into four categories: complaints about service standards, financial institutions' practice/policies, market conduct, and others. Financial institutions against which complaints are made can be separated into five groups: banks and finance companies, life insurers, general insurers, capital markets services licensees, and licensed financial advisers and insurance intermediaries.[9]

Structure

Dispute resolution is handled on three levels within FIDReC. First, FIDReC's Counselling Services carries out a preliminary review, and gives the complainant time to consider whether to proceed to the lodging of a formal complaint against a financial institution.[10]

Second, case managers are employees of FIDReC assigned to assist in the mediation of disputes. Case managers have no jurisdiction to make monetary awards, and can only seek to reach a settlement that parties to the dispute are agreeable with.

Third, adjudicators are experts appointed by the Board of Directors of FIDReC, and will, as required, decide disputes in favour of either the consumer or the financial institution where a case manager has been unable to resolve the dispute through mediation. FIDReC's Panel of Adjudicators comprises highly qualified and credible professionals with relevant experience and expertise. Among FIDReC's adjudicators are retired judges, senior counsel, lawyers and retired industry professionals.[11]

Underlying legal mandate

The Monetary Authority of Singapore (Dispute Resolution Schemes) Regulations 2007 came into operation on 22 August 2007. The

---

[7] Ibid.
[8] Financial Industry Disputes Resolution Centre Ltd, *Annual Report 2005/6*.
[9] Financial Industry Disputes Resolution Centre Ltd (2009–2010) *Annual Report 2009/10*.
[10] Ibid.
[11] Financial Industry Disputes Resolution Centre Ltd, *Annual Report 2005/6*.

Regulations are made under s. 28A of the Monetary Authority of Singapore Act,[12] which was introduced on 30 June 2007 to enable the Monetary Authority of Singapore ('MAS') to approve dispute resolution schemes for resolving disputes relating to the provision of financial services in Singapore. The dispute resolution schemes approved by the MAS are listed in the First Schedule to the Regulations. Currently, the dispute resolution scheme operated by the Financial Industry Disputes Resolution Centre Ltd is the only one listed. The Regulations require the listed financial institutions to be members of an approved dispute resolution scheme.[13]

FIDReC members are required to enter into a subscription agreement, under which they are bound by the Terms of Reference, agree not to take legal action against FIDReC, and to honour payment of subscriptions, levies and fees to FIDReC. Members of FIDReC may be expelled for failure to comply with the Terms of Reference or failure to make full payment of subscriptions, levies or fees. However, members will not be removed from FIDReC without the prior consent of MAS.[14]

---

[12] Section 28A of the Monetary Authority of Singapore Act provides that:

(1) The Authority may approve any dispute resolution scheme for the resolution of disputes arising from or relating to the provision of financial services by financial institutions.

(2) The Authority may by regulations require a financial institution registered, licensed, approved or regulated by the Authority under any written law to be a member of such approved dispute resolution scheme and to comply with such terms of membership of the scheme as may be prescribed.

...

(6) The Authority may make regulations —

(a) to provide for the matters that the Authority may have regard to in determining whether to approve a dispute resolution scheme under subsection (1);

(b) to prescribe a list of dispute resolution schemes approved under subsection (1);

(c) to provide for suspension or cancellation of approvals under subsection (1);

(d) to provide for matters relating to the operations of an operator of an approved dispute resolution scheme, including the standards or requirements of its operations, the fees that may be charged for its dispute resolution services, the records that must be kept, the period of retention of the records, the reports that are to be submitted to the Authority, the time for such submission, the terms of membership with the scheme, the procedure for dispute resolution and other matters relating to the administration of the scheme; and

(e) generally to give effect to or for carrying out the purposes of this section.

[13] E. Wong (2008) 'Singapore: financial regulation – dispute resolution schemes', *J.I.B.L.R.*, 23(1), N10–11.

[14] Monetary Authority of Singapore, Policy Consultation on the Financial Industry Disputes Resolution Centre.

Dispute resolution

Terms of Reference

All types of dispute with a member financial institution may be brought before and dealt with by FIDReC subject to the following conditions:[15]

i) the complainant must be an Eligible Complainant (individual consumers or sole proprietors having a customer relationship with the financial institution; persons with beneficial interests under trust or estate or contract of insurance or collective investment scheme; trustees or personal representatives; insured's; or third parties entitled to bring a claim under third party coverage);[16]

---

[15] See Rule 4, Section 2, FIDReC Terms of Reference:

1) All types of Disputes with a FI may be brought before and dealt with by FIDReC (known as 'Eligible Disputes') subject to the following conditions:
   i) the complainant must be an Eligible Complainant;
   ii) the FI involved in the Dispute must be one which is subject to the jurisdiction of FIDReC by reason of it being a subscriber or by reason of it having consented to submit itself to the jurisdiction of FIDReC;
   iii) save in the case of insurance disputes, the activity or Dispute arises out of matters relevant to the Eligible Complainant being or having been a customer of the FI;
   iv) the activity to which the Complaint relates must be subject to the jurisdiction of FIDReC, and in the case of Complaints relating to activities prior to the setting up of FIDReC, subject to the jurisdiction of the Insurance Disputes Resolution Organisation and / or the Consumer Mediation Unit of the Association of Banks of Singapore;
   v) the FI has failed to resolve the Complaint to the satisfaction of the Eligible Complainant within four weeks of receiving it; and
   vi) the FI about which the Complaint is made must be a Subscriber at the time of the act or omission to which the Complaint relates or has agreed to let FIDReC consider such Complaints, and must not have withdrawn from being a Subscriber at the time when the Complaint is referred to FIDReC.
2) All Disputes which have not first been raised by an Eligible Complainant with the FI so as to provide the FI with an opportunity to resolve the Dispute will be deemed a Complaint and if lodged or attempted to be lodged with FIDReC will be referred back to the FI for its due consideration.
3) The territorial scope of the jurisdiction of FIDReC extends to Complaints about the activities of a FI or its Representative carrying on business in Singapore.

[16] See Rule 6, Section 2, FIDReC Terms of Reference: The following persons (known as 'Eligible Complainants') may bring Complaints before FIDReC:

i) individual consumers having a customer relationship with a FI;
ii) sole proprietors having a customer relationship with a FI;
iii) a person who has a beneficial interest in the activity, including the following persons:

ii) the financial institution involved in the dispute must be one which is subject to the jurisdiction of FIDReC by reason of it being a subscriber or by reason of it having consented to submit itself to the jurisdiction of FIDReC;

iii) save in the case of insurance disputes, the activity or dispute arises out of matters relevant to the Eligible Complainant being or having been a customer of the financial institution;

iv) the activity to which the complaint relates must be subject to the jurisdiction of FIDReC, and in the case of complaints relating to activities prior to the setting up of the FIDReC, subject to the jurisdiction of the Insurance Disputes Resolution Organisation and/or the Consumer Mediation Unit of the Association of Banks of Singapore;

v) the financial institution has failed to resolve the Complaint to the satisfaction of the Eligible Complainant within four weeks of receiving it; and

vi) the financial institutions about which the complaint is made must be a Subscriber at the time of the act or omission to which the Complaint relates or has agreed to let FIDReC consider such Complaints, and must not have withdrawn from being a Subscriber at the time when the Complaint is referred to FIDReC.

The territorial scope of the jurisdiction of FIDReC extends to complaints about the activities of a financial institution or its representative carrying on business in Singapore.[17]

Complaints must be made at the earliest opportunity, upon showing that an attempt has been made to resolve the matter by the financial institution's internal dispute resolution unit, but the matter has not been resolved to the satisfaction of both parties or after at least four weeks from the date the matter was referred to the financial institution, whichever is

a) a person who is a beneficiary under a trust or estate;
b) a person for whose benefit a contract of insurance was taken out or was intended to be taken out;
c) a person on whom the legal right to benefit from a claim under a contract of insurance has devolved by contract, statute or subrogation;
d) a beneficial owner of units in a collective investment scheme and the FI is the operator or depository of the scheme;
iv) a trustee or personal representative;
v) an insured; or
vi) such third parties as are entitled to bring a claim under an insurance contract extending the relevant third-party coverage.

17 See Rule 4(3), Section 2, FIDReC Terms of Reference at footnote 15 above.

earlier, and no later than a period of six months after the financial institution has provided its final reply to the Eligible Complainant.[18]

Cases may be dismissed by a case manager with the approval of FIDReC's CEO if the dispute is frivolous or vexatious; has been previously considered and excluded under FIDReC's predecessor schemes; or if there are other compelling reasons why it is inappropriate for the dispute to be dealt with by FIDReC.[19]

Procedure

All financial institutions will be given the opportunity to resolve a dispute before the FIDReC proceeds with the case. Consumers who approach

---

[18] See Rule 13, section 4.1, FIDReC Terms of Reference:

    1) An application for initiating an investigation can only be made by the Eligible Complainant:
        i) at the earliest, upon showing that an attempt has been made to resolve the matter by the FI's internal dispute resolution unit, but the matter has not been resolved to the satisfaction of both parties or after at least four weeks from the date the matter was referred to the FI, whichever is earlier; and
        ii) no later than a period of six months after the FI has provided its final reply to the Eligible Complainant.
    2) In this Rule, a final reply is a letter or other written document issued by the FI to the Eligible Complainant which expressly states that it is the FI's final reply and which expressly informs the Eligible Complainant that if he/she disagrees with the FI, he/she can contact FIDReC for assistance within six months from the date of the said letter or other written document. There must be no outstanding issues between the FI and the Eligible Complainant and the contact particulars of FIDReC must be provided in the said letter or other written document. For the avoidance of doubt, any dispute as to whether any letter or other written document constitutes the final reply from the FI would be solely determined by FIDReC. FIDReC's determination would be binding on the FI and the Eligible Complainant.

[19] Rule 17(1), section 4.1, FIDReC Terms of Reference:

    1) The Case Manager may, subject to the approval of FIDReC's Chief Executive Officer, dismiss a Dispute where:
        i) the Dispute is in the opinion of the Case Manager frivolous or vexatious;
        ii) the matter has previously been considered or excluded by a Former Scheme, but has not been adjudicated upon under Rule 21 and an award made under Rules 27 to 29 (unless material new evidence likely to affect the outcome has subsequently become available). For the avoidance of doubt, all cases which have been settled as set out in Rule 5(vi) or for which an award has been made by the Adjudicators must be dismissed; or
        iii) there are other compelling reasons why it is inappropriate for the Dispute to be dealt with by FIDReC.

FIDReC without first attempting to resolve the dispute with the financial institution will be referred back to the institution.

There is a three-stage process in the settlement of disputes by FIDReC. First, the Counselling Service assists in a preliminary review of the case based on facts and documents provided by the complainant. FIDReC's officers highlight relevant clauses (in the contract, sales documents or other documents) or issues to the consumer. Second, after the preliminary review, the consumer is provided with a copy of FIDReC's Dispute Resolution Form and allowed time to consider whether to proceed to lodge a formal complaint against the financial institution in question.[20] A case manager will try to mediate a settlement between the consumer and financial institution. Where appropriate, mediation conferences are arranged to allow parties to communicate face to face.[21]

Third, disputes that cannot be resolved by mediation and case management will be graduated to the third stage, where an adjudicator or panel of adjudicators with relevant expertise will decide in favour of either the consumer or the financial institution.[22]

Awards

The maximum monetary award for compensation is S$100,000 for claims against insurance companies, and S$50,000 for all other disputes.[23]

Where an award is made by the adjudicator or Panel, it is binding on the financial institution but not on the complainant. The complainant's rights are thus not prejudiced in any way. He is free to choose whether or not to accept the award. Where the complainant chooses not to accept the award, he is free to pursue other remedies such as legal action or arbitration.[24]

---

[20] Financial Industry Disputes Resolution Centre Ltd, *Annual Report 2009/10*.
[21] Financial Industry Disputes Resolution Centre Ltd, *Annual Report 2005/6*.
[22] Monetary Authority of Singapore, Policy Consultation on the Financial Industry Disputes Resolution Centre.
[23] See Rule 29, Section 5, FIDReC Terms of Reference:

    1) The maximum award which may be made in any Dispute referred to FIDReC shall be as follows:
        i) in the case of a dispute involving insured persons and insurance companies, an award of up to S$100,000 per claim; and
        ii) in the case of any other dispute, an award of up to S$50,000 per claim.

[24] Financial Industry Disputes Resolution Centre Ltd, *Annual Report 2005/6*.

Statistics

For the year 2009–2010, FIDReC dealt with 2,055 cases. Of these, 491 were inquiries, 266 were resolved by case management through the counselling services, 1,277 proceeded to mediation and adjudication, and 21 cases were found to be outside FIDReC's jurisdiction.[25] A total of 2,263 cases were resolved by mediation or adjudication in the same period, a 99.6 per cent increase from the year previous of 1,267 cases resolved.

38.1 per cent of complaints resolved by FIDReC were resolved within three months, while 72.7 per cent of complaints were resolved within six months.

Service providers

Mandatory membership of financial institutions means that FIDReC's funding is shared by all relevant institutions, and therefore sustainable in the long term. Members are required to pay a combination of a general levy[26]

---

[25] Financial Industry Disputes Resolution Centre Ltd, *Annual Report 2009/10*.
[26] Section 4 of Annex 1 – Funding Rules of the FIDReC Terms of Reference provides that:

4.1 A FI must pay FIDReC a general levy towards the costs of operating FIDReC. For the purposes of the general levy, a FI will fall into an industry block ('Block') depending on the license which it holds, as follows:
  i. Block A – Banks and finance companies
  ii. Block B – Life and composite insurers
  iii. Block C – General and composite insurers
  iv. Block D – Capital markets services licensees
  v. Block E – Licensed financial advisers and insurance intermediaries

For the avoidance of any doubt, composite insurers that deal with both life insurance business and general insurance business will be classified under both Block B and Block C. Accordingly, such composite insurers are liable to pay the general levy twice, once each under Block B and Block C respectively.

4.2 FIDReC will determine, following an annual review as provided in Clause 8 of this Annex, the amount to be raised from each Block.

4.3 Without prejudice to Clause 4.2, the proportion of costs to be recovered through the general levy will be shared between the five Blocks on the basis of the amount of resources required to deal with the Eligible Disputes generated by that Block, proxied by the block's share of total number of Eligible Disputes.

4.4 Within a Block, the contribution of a FI shall depend on a number of factors known as funding bases which may include, but are not limited to the following:
  i. the number of FIs in the block;
  ii. a FI's retail market share; and
  iii. a FI's usage of FIDReC's resources, proxied by the FI's share of total Eligible Disputes for the block.

and case fees – case fees are tiered to take into account the level of complexity of cases. FIDReC is thus primarily funded by the financial industry, and takes into account the level of usage of the FIDReC by each member financial institution. The MAS initially provided funding to finance the start-up of FIDReC.

No fees are charged to consumers where the dispute is resolved by case management or mediation. A S$50 fee is charged to consumers where the dispute is escalated to the adjudication stage – the fee is imposed to deter frivolous complaints, but is kept low in order to ensure FIDReC is affordable for consumers. Both parties are afforded adequate opportunity to present their case to the adjudicator or Panel. The complainant is allowed to be accompanied by his nominee, who can assist him/her in the presentation of his/her claim.[27]

Fees

Where a case is not resolved through case management or mediation, it proceeds to adjudication before an adjudicator or Panel of Adjudicators. The consumer is required to pay a nominal administrative fee as follows: For all third party claims:

- The consumer pays S$250 per claim and the Financial Institution pays S$500 per claim.
- If the adjudicator finds in favour of the consumer and awards an amount equivalent to 50 per cent or more of the claim, then the consumer would be refunded S$200 per claim. This effectively means the consumer only pays S$50 per claim at the adjudication stage.

4.5 For the purposes of ascertaining the share of disputes from a FI and collectively for a Block, each FI must provide FIDReC with such information as FIDReC may require to assess its share of total contribution according to the funding bases selected for the block, including but not limited to the information as contained in Annex 2 to the Terms of Reference.

4.6 FIs that become subscribers of FIDReC part way through the financial year will be required to pay the general levy on a pro-rata basis.

4.7 A FI which ceases to be a subscriber partway through the year will be required to pay the general levy on a pro-rata basis, provided the FI has provided FIDReC with three (3) months notice in advance and, in any event, at least three (3) months notice prior to the computation date for the general levy payable. For avoidance of doubt, where the FI ceases to be a subscriber after the computation date for the general levy payable, such FI will continue to be liable for all remaining instalment payments due and owing despite the cessation of its subscription to FIDReC.

27 Financial Industry Disputes Resolution Centre Ltd, *Annual Report 2005/6*.

- If the adjudicator dismisses the claim or awards the consumer less than 50 per cent of the claim, the Financial Institution would be refunded S$200 per claim.

For all non third party claims: The consumer pays a case fee of S$50 per claim and the Financial Institution pays a flat case fee of S$500 per claim. No rebate is given to the consumer or the Financial Institution.

Oversight

The FIDReC has the power to notify and/or to submit such information as is within its knowledge relating to systemic issues and market misconduct to the MAS. It is also required to submit to the MAS on a quarterly basis, and in any event no later than fourteen days from the end of the last day of the quarter, a categorised summary report of all disputes received.[28]

The FIDReC also has full power and absolute discretion, where necessary, to disclose any and all information relating to a complaint, dispute or award to MAS and the courts.[29]

Strengths

The FIDReC is said to have streamlined the dispute resolution processes across the entire financial sector of Singapore.[30] It provides an affordable avenue for consumers who do not have the resources to go to court or who do not want to pay hefty legal fees and is staffed by full-time employees familiar with the relevant laws and practices.

FIDReC's adjudication process is modelled on the one used by the Singapore Courts, so that established safeguards in that model are incorporated to ensure that justice and fairness are done.

---

[28] Rule 11, Section 3, FIDReC Terms of Reference provides that:

1) FIDReC shall have power to notify and/or to submit such information as is within its knowledge relating to systemic issues and market misconduct to the MAS.
2) FIDReC shall be required to submit to the MAS on a quarterly basis, and in any event no later than fourteen days from the end of the last day of the quarter, a categorised summary report of all Disputes received. Such report is to be provided in the form of the template as set out in Annex 2.

[29] Rule 11A, Section 3, FIDReC Terms of Reference provides that: 'FIDReC shall have the full power and absolute discretion, where necessary, to disclose any and all information relating to a Complaint, Dispute or Award to MAS and the Court.'

[30] Financial Industry Disputes Resolution Centre Ltd, *Annual Report 2005/6*.

Challenges

Lehman-related financial products disputes, awards and jurisdictional limits

As at 31 August 2010, the total number of claims involving Credit Linked Notes as a result of the filing for Chapter 11 bankruptcy protection by Lehman Brothers in the United States resolved by FIDReC through mediation and adjudication was 1,845.

The issue of whether or not the FIDReC would be prepared to handle cases beyond its award limits has caused some confusion, as it appears that both the FIDReC and certain financial institutions have published information indicating that it would be possible to do so by agreement or with the consent of the financial institution.[31]

Monopoly status, links to financial industry and transparency

A recent commentary has also questioned whether or not FIDReC is fair. In particular, given the monopoly status of FIDReC as the only approved dispute resolution scheme, its close connection to the financial industry, and the imbalance of information between consumers and financial institutions in respect of settlements raises the issue of whether or not FIDReC is sufficiently transparent in respect of proceedings and outcomes.[32]

Lessons learned

Public profile and network

A key challenge faced by FIDReC following its establishment was to find a cost-efficient yet effective manner to carry out the mandate entrusted to it and to remain accessible by reaching out to the public. In this regard, it adopted a strategy which eschewed traditional expensive mass media advertisements. It focused instead on engaging and forging working partnerships and establishing referral systems with organisations/bodies of

---

[31] The Online Citizen (2 January 2009) 'FIDReC – more symbolism than substance?', available at: http://theonlinecitizen.com/2009/01/fidrec-more-symbolism-than-substance/ [accessed 8 February 2012].

[32] L. Haverkamp (21 January 2011) 'Is FIDReC fair?', *Singapore Business Review*, available at: http://sbr.com.sg/financial-services/commentary/fidrec-fair [accessed 8 February 2012].

first contact with consumers as well as other relevant institutions, namely, the Consumers Association of Singapore (CASE), the Automobile Association of Singapore, the Community Mediation Centres run by the Community Mediation Unit of the Ministry of Law, the Asia Insurance Review, the Law Society of Singapore and the Singapore General Hospital.[33]

Convenience of online subscription

The FIDReC has developed an integrated and comprehensive system that manages subscription by new financial institutions wholly online, which allows subscribers to verify the records, status and outcome of their own cases, compute and collect the general levy and case fees and also allows a host of other functions important to FIDReC's operations, such as case and database management and statistics generation. The development of this integrated system has not only resulted in significant and substantial cost savings but has also improved the efficiency of FIDReC's dispute resolution processes.[34]

Extended opening hours

Twice weekly, FIDReC's operational hours are extended until 7.30 p.m. This is a value-added service to afford greater convenience and accessibility to consumers who are only able to meet up with FIDReC's officers outside of traditional working hours.

Introduction of case management process

FIDReC also experienced a high success rate with its case management process, introduced in 2007. For the 36 months commencing 1 July 2007 to 30 June 2010, FIDReC's Counselling Service amicably resolved 1,634 cases, resulting in savings of time and resources.[35] This measure was designed to further enhance its dispute resolution processes, and is especially suitable for resolving disputes which are simpler in scope and issues by helping the consumer better understand the dispute and relevant issues

---

[33] Financial Industry Disputes Resolution Centre Ltd, *Annual Report 2005/6*.
[34] Financial Industry Disputes Resolution Centre Ltd, *Annual Report 2005/6*.
[35] Financial Industry Disputes Resolution Centre Ltd, *Annual Report 2009/10*.

as well as aiding the consumer in considering any settlement offer made by the financial institution in a more objective light.

Contribution to consumer confidence

Given its efficient and generally effective case management record, combined with its effective pre-hearing case management and online resources, one could argue that the FIDReC has contributed to the enhancement of consumer and industry confidence in Singapore and has contributed to an environment conducive to Singapore's annual 5 per cent growth rate.[36]

---

[36] See Singapore Department of Statistics 'Key Annual Indicators', available at: www.singstat.gov.sg/stats/keyind.html [accessed 26 April 2012].

7

Financial dispute resolution in Hong Kong

Background

Hong Kong's centralised dispute resolution scheme for the financial industry, the Financial Dispute Resolution Centre ('FDRC'), opened in 2012 with the aim of 'provid[ing] a platform that helps resolve monetary disputes between an individual consumer and a financial institution in a speedy, affordable, independent and impartial way'.[1] A number of principles appear to be central to the development of the Centre including independence, impartiality, accessibility and efficiency.

Incorporation of mediation in the civil justice reform

While historically, litigation has often been pursued by individuals and commercial enterprises in Hong Kong seeking authoritative legal precedent (and thus binding on similar cases),[2] Hong Kong's FDRC will provide an alternative venue for the resolution of consumer financial disputes.

Driven by its incorporation into Hong Kong civil court procedure during the Civil Justice Reform, alternative dispute resolution and mediation in particular has now received much greater attention. Success in existing court-annexed mediation schemes, such as the pilot scheme for family mediation[3] and construction disputes,[4] has led to the extension of such schemes into various facets of civil procedure. This includes:

---

[1] See Financial Services and the Treasury Bureau (February 2010) 'Proposed Establishment of an Investor Education Council and a Financial Dispute Resolution Centre: Consultation Paper'. Available at www.gov.hk/en/residents/government/publication/consultation/docs/2010/consult_iec_fdrc_e.pdf

[2] G. Soo, Y. Zhao, D. Cai (2010) 'Better ways of resolving disputes in Hong Kong – some insights from the Lehman-Brothers related investment product dispute mediation and arbitration scheme', *J. Int'l Bus. & L.*, 9, p. 137.

[3] Paragraph 630 of the Interim Report of the Chief Justice's Working Party on Civil Justice Reform.

[4] Paragragh 797 of the Final Report of the Chief Justice's Working Party on Civil Justice Reform.

Court's duty to manage cases

...

(2) Active case management includes –

...

(e) encouraging the parties to use an alternative dispute resolution procedure if the Court considers that appropriate, and facilitating the use of such a procedure.[5]

Alternative dispute resolution is explicitly incorporated under Order 25 of the Rules of the High Court (Cap 4A). Order 25 deals with Case Management Summons and Conference, the means by which the Court sets out the details of proceedings prior to their commencement. Among the requirements in Order 25 is the mandatory completion of the Timetabling Questionnaire that is filed by the parties on the close of pleadings.[6] The first section of the Questionnaire deals with Alternative Dispute Resolution ('ADR'), and requires the parties to either (1) confirm they have attempted to settle the case by ADR but were not successful, or

---

[5] See Order 1A, Rule 4(2)(e), Rules of the High Court.
[6] See Order 25, Rule 1, Rules of the High Court:

(1) For the purpose of facilitating the giving of directions for the management of a case, each party shall, within 28 days after the pleadings in an action to which this rule applies are deemed to be closed:
  (a) complete a questionnaire prescribed in a practice direction issued for that purpose by providing the information requested in the manner specified in the questionnaire; and
  (b) serve it on all other parties and file it with the Court in the manner specified in the practice direction.
  ...
(2) This rule applies to all actions begun by writ except-
  (a) actions in which the plaintiff or defendant has applied for judgment under Order 14, or in which the plaintiff has applied for judgment under Order 86, and directions have been given under the relevant Order;
  (b) actions in which the plaintiff or defendant has applied under Order 18, rule 21, for trial without pleadings or further pleadings and directions have been given under that rule;
  (c) actions in which an order has been made under Order 24, rule 4, for the trial of an issue or question before discovery;
  (d) actions in which directions have been given under Order 29, rule 7;
  (e) actions in which an order for the taking of an account has been made under Order 43, rule 1;
  (f) actions in which an application for transfer to the commercial list is pending;
  ...
  (h) actions for the infringement of a patent; and
  ...
  (j) actions for personal injuries for which automatic directions are provided by rule 8.
  ...

that they have no intention of settling the case, or that they are willing to try to settle the case by ADR or other means and thus request a stay of the proceedings; (2) confirm they have filed a Mediation Certificate; or (3) confirm they have filed a Mediation Notice/Response.[7] The Mediation Certificate sets out whether or not parties are willing to attempt mediation to settle the proceedings, and the reasons if the party is not willing.[8] Where parties wish to attempt mediation, they should file a Mediation Notice,[9] and in response, the other party to the proceedings will file a Mediation Response.[10] Under Practice Direction 31 on Mediation,[11] the Court may make adverse costs orders against parties who unreasonably fail to engage in mediation.[12]

Lack of provision for dispute resolution in financial regulation

While alternative dispute resolution procedures, particularly mediation, have been incorporated as an integral component of civil court procedure in Hong Kong, they have yet to become incorporated into the provision of financial services. As was noted in an early review of banking consumer protection by the Hong Kong Monetary Authority ('HKMA'),[13]

> (4) If the plaintiff does not file the questionnaire in accordance with paragraph (1)(b) or take out a case management summons in accordance with paragraph (1B)(b), the defendant or any defendant may-
> (a) take out a case management summons; or
> (b) apply for an order to dismiss the action. (L.N. 152 of 2008)
> ...
> (7) Notwithstanding anything in paragraph (1B), any party to an action to which this rule applies may take out a case management summons at any time after the defendant has given notice of intention to defend, or, if there are two or more defendants, at least one of them has given such notice.

[7] See Annex A, Practice Direction 5.2.
[8] See Appendix B, Practice Direction 31.
[9] See Appendix C, Practice Direction 31.
[10] See Appendix D, Practice Direction 31.
[11] Paragraph 4 of Practice Direction 31 states that: 'In exercising its discretion on costs, the Court takes into account all relevant circumstances. These would include any unreasonable failure of a party to engage in mediation where this can be established by admissible materials. Legal representatives should advise their clients of the possibility of the Court making an adverse costs order where a party unreasonably fails to engage in mediation.'
[12] Bar Circular 097/10 (27 September 2010) has, however, suggested that some practitioners were approaching Court-mandated mediation processes as a mere formality preceding litigation rather than making genuine efforts to reach settlement.
[13] HKMA Information Note for the LegCo Panel on Financial Affairs, 'Comparative Study on Banking Consumer Protection and Competition Arrangements in the UK, Australia and Hong Kong: An Introductory Note', 2001.

a key difference between Hong Kong, the United Kingdom and Australia is that the regulators in both jurisdictions have been given an explicit mandate in relation to the protection of consumers of financial and banking services. In the case of Hong Kong, the HKMA only has a general duty to 'provide a measure of protection to depositors' under the Banking Ordinance. There is no explicit mandate with respect to consumer protection.[14]

This was noted and expanded upon in the Consultation Paper for the Proposed Establishment of an Investor Education Council and a Financial Dispute Resolution Centre:[15]

> The regulators' role is primarily to ensure that the process by which the complaints are handled by the financial services providers is fair and efficient. The regulators do not have the power to mediate or adjudicate on the settlement of a monetary dispute between the regulatees and their clients.
>
> At present, outside of the courts, there is no mechanism in place that can achieve the outcome of a dispute resolution where a consumer and a financial services provider are unable to achieve a bilateral agreement.[16]

Two pertinent examples

This is not, however, to say that no such dispute resolution schemes exist in Hong Kong. Two pertinent examples come to mind. First, since 2007, the Hong Kong Federation of Insurers has funded a pilot mediation project, the New Insurance Mediation Pilot Scheme. The scheme is operated by the Hong Kong Mediation Council, and settles work-related personal injuries claims.[17] Second, in 2008, the Hong Kong Monetary Authority engaged the Hong Kong International Arbitration Centre in respect of the Lehman Brothers-related Investment Products Dispute Mediation and Arbitration Scheme to resolve disputes between investors and banks and securities firms.

The New Insurance Mediation Pilot Scheme mediates claims between parties (with insurers as a third party) rather than disputes between consumers and financial service providers in respect of financial services. Thus, the analysis below will focus on the Lehman Brothers-related Scheme.

---

[14] Paragraph 3, ibid.
[15] Financial Services and the Treasury Bureau, 'Proposed Establishment of an Investor Education Council and a Financial Dispute Resolution Centre'.
[16] Ibid., paragraphs 2.3–2.4, p. 28.
[17] Hong Kong International Arbitration Centre (HKIAC) Annual Report 2009, p. 23.

Financial alternative dispute resolution programmes – Minibonds and the scheme

The causes and effects of the financial crisis of 2008–2009 have been written about extensively in many publications.[18] One key consequence of the filing for bankruptcy of Lehman Brothers was the unwinding of credit-linked notes, marketed as 'Minibonds', arranged by a subsidiary of Lehman Brothers Holdings, which were sold to approximately 34,000 retail investors.[19] As a result of the unwinding, the value of the notes fell to a small fraction of the principal amounts paid for them. In late September and early October 2008, hundreds of Minibond investors took to the streets in protest, and also staged demonstrations at the offices and branches of distributing banks.

At the heart of the Minibonds crisis was whether or not the risks associated with these complex products were fully disclosed and communicated to the retail investors who purchased them. This gave rise to two complaints in particular: first, the way in which Minibonds had been sold to the retail market, particularly by the banks carrying on securities business; and second, their suitability for particular customers given their complexity.

Options for aggrieved consumers

The avenues of complaint open to investors at the time were filing with the Securities and Futures Commission ('SFC') and the HKMA, the Consumer Council, the Small Claims Tribunal and the Courts of Hong Kong.

The Securities and Futures Commission

From September 2008 to December 2009, the SFC received around 8,900 complaints in respect of the mis-selling of Lehman Minibonds-related products. As the statutory regulator of the securities and futures markets of Hong Kong, the SFC receives complaints from investors about unlicensed activities, misconduct by its licensees and in the market, the

---

[18] For a full discussion of the financial crisis' effects in Hong Kong, please see Arner, Hsu and Da Roza, 'Financial Regulation in Hong Kong: Time for a Change'.

[19] 'Securities Futures Commission (December 2008) Issues Raised by the Lehman Minibonds Crisis: Report to the Financial Secretary', paras. 13.3–13.4.

sale of unauthorised investment products, and so on. The SFC has an internal Complaints Control Committee which conducts assessments of complaints to determine whether or not they warrant further action by way of investigation, prosecution or discipline of licensees. Furthermore, the SFC's Code of Conduct for Licensed Persons by or registered with the Securities and Futures Commission requires that such persons have a complaint-handling mechanism, that complaints are handled in a timely and appropriate manner, that steps are taken to investigate and respond promptly to complaints, and that complainants are given advice as to further steps if complaints are not remedied promptly.[20] However, the SFC is not empowered to order wrongdoers to pay compensation to complainants.

The Hong Kong Monetary Authority

Similarly, the HKMA received a large number of complaints from Lehman investors, with the total number of complaints in 2008 being 21,000, up from only 469 in 2007. Under the Banking Ordinance,[21] the HKMA does not have the power to arbitrate or intervene in customer disputes, or require banks to pay compensation. It has a limited role in monitoring the handling of customer complaints by banks – its focus is to ensure banks handle customer complaints fairly and efficiently.[22] The HKMA follows up on complaints that raise supervisory concerns, i.e. complaints indicating that a bank has breached a Code of Banking practice or other guidelines or regulations, and will pursue supervisory concerns and require remedial action by the bank. It is important to note that its power to disclose to the complainant the outcome of the investigation and measures

---

[20] See para.12.3 of the SFC's Code of Conduct for Licensed Persons by or Registered with the Securities and Futures Commission:

A licensed or registered person should ensure that:

(a) complaints from clients relating to its business are handled in a timely and appropriate manner;

(b) steps are taken to investigate and respond promptly to the complaints; and

(c) where a complaint is not remedied promptly, the client is advised of any further steps which may be available to the client under the regulatory system.

[21] Cap. 155.

[22] See also, Hong Kong Monetary Authority, 'What to do if you have a complaint about banking products or services', available at: www.hkma.gov.hk/eng/other-information/consumer-information/complaint_handling_leaflet_b.shtml [accessed 8 February 2012].

taken against the bank is constrained by confidentiality provisions of the Banking Ordinance. In 2002, the HKMA issued a guideline for banks to put in place internal procedures for handling customer complaints – banks should have systems that ensure customer complaints are fully and promptly investigated and resolved in a satisfactory manner. The Banking Services Complaint Unit within HKMA reviews all complaints received to decide if and how they can be taken further – but the focus of the Unit's work is on whether banks' complaint handling procedures are working properly. In respect of complaints relating to the securities and futures business of banks, the HKMA only assesses if the complaints relate to misconduct or non-compliance with rules and guidelines set by the SFC.

The Consumer Council

Established in 1974, the Consumer Council provides consumer complaint and inquiry services – it has no powers of adjudication or investigation itself. Complaints about the Minibonds were also made to the Consumer Council, leading, on 30 October 2008, to the creation of a special workforce to handle Lehman Brothers cases. The workforce was tasked with identifying cases for consideration of financial assistance for legal action under the Consumer Legal Action Fund ('CLAF'). According to the press release issued by the Consumer Council, the criteria for financial assistance included: vulnerability of the complainants; cogency of evidence on untoward sales tactics; inadequate risk disclosure; and misrepresentation. The process involved interviewing selected complainants, a preliminary legal analysis and reporting to the CLAF Management Committee for recommendation to the Board of Administrators for approval. A portion of the work was commissioned out to barristers in private practice in order to expedite the process. By the end of 2008, the Consumer Council reported it had received some 8,274 complaints in respect of Minibonds, which contributed to a tenfold increase in complaints against financial services for that year. At the end of 2009, the number of complaints received by the Consumer Council against financial services was 4,968.

The Small Claims Tribunal

The Small Claims Tribunal is a court that deals quickly, informally and inexpensively with claims not exceeding HK$50,000. Rules and procedures are less strict than other courts, and no legal representation is allowed. Some 135 Minibond investors whose claims did not exceed HK$50,000 sought to recover money against banks in the Tribunal. The adjudicator, having heard all the cases, came to the conclusion that the claims should be referred to the District Court, as the cases concerned banks' responsibilities and risks to consumers, involving new and complicated legal points which would have an impact on the public banking sector.[23] The lack of a precedent case and the fact that the Tribunal may not have had the legal power to handle such cases also contributed to the decision to refer the cases to the District Court.

Litigation in the Courts

Civil litigation was reported to have been initiated by Minibond investors in several cases between December 2008 and January 2009, the first lawsuits of their type. Complainants were also involved in a class action suit started in the United States. However, the high costs of litigation and the lack of a class-action suit in Hong Kong made for high hurdles for Minibond complainants.[24]

Litigation on the matter has not been limited to civil litigation. In January 2010, a former Dah Sing Bank employee was charged with forging a customer's signature to buy Minibonds from the bank. In April 2010, two staff members of the Bank of China (Hong Kong) were charged by the Commercial Crimes Bureau for misleading and inducing customers to purchase structured products such as the Minibonds. In the event of conviction in such criminal cases, the Court may order compensation to be paid as part of the sentence.

Assisted negotiations

Furthermore, on 10 December, the Democratic Party announced that it had assisted over sixty investors to reach settlements totalling HK$30 million in compensation from fourteen of the distributing banks.[25] These assisted negotiations were not part of any formal scheme – the range

---

[23] See Shahla F. Ali and J. K. W. Kwok (2011) 'After Lehman: international response to financial disputes – a focus on Hong Kong', *Richmond Journal of Global Law and Business*, 10(2), available at: http://papers.ssrn.com/sol3/papers.cfm?abstract_id=1903591 [accessed 26 April 2012].

[24] Ibid.

[25] *South China Morning Post* (10 December 2008) '60 investors get HK$30m from banks on minibonds'.

of compensation was described as 'wide' and the average percentage of principal received in compensation was described as 'high', but was not disclosed. The settlements were attributed to the fact that the cases all involved regulation violations. One party member involved was quoted as saying 'Resolutions are going at a snail's pace' in respect of the fact that the resolved cases represented less than 1 per cent of the total number of complaints at the time.

The establishment of the scheme

The primary concern for the aggrieved consumers in respect of the Minibonds was the recovery of the lost principal as quickly as possible. In its report to the Financial Secretary, the SFC noted 'the absence of any simple and quick dispute resolution procedures for aggrieved investors'.[26] In response, on 31 October 2008, the HKMA announced a mediation and arbitration scheme administered by the Hong Kong International Arbitration Centre ('HKIAC') for complainants in respect of Lehman-related investment products distributed by banks, the Lehman Brothers-related Investment Products Dispute Mediation and Arbitration Scheme.[27]

Underlying legal mandate

The Scheme was developed in order to facilitate dispute settlement, and was purely voluntary – hence, the consent of both complainants and the relevant bank was required. There was no statutory backing for the Scheme, which was initiated by the HKMA and the HKIAC.

Types of dispute

The Scheme applied to issues of compensation between investors in Lehman Brothers-related products and banks licensed by the HKMA, and was specifically limited to investors who had made complaints to the HKMA, and whose complaints were referred to the SFC, or if there had been a finding against a relevant individual or executive officer of a bank against whom a complaint was made. The HKMA informed such eligible

---

[26] SFC, Issues Raised by the Lehman Minibonds Crisis: Report to the Financial Secretary, para. 35.1.

[27] Ibid.

investors in writing, and would pay half the fee of the service, with the other half being borne by the relevant bank.[28]

However, the HKIAC also offered a similar service, using the same procedures as those applicable to the Scheme, to investors who were not eligible under the above criteria, if the relevant bank consented to take part, though the costs would have to be borne by the parties themselves.

Preparatory meetings

Prior to the initiation of the resolution process, parties attend preparatory meetings to familiarise the parties with mediation, explore settlement options, and exchange information and documents.[29]

The mediation procedure

The first step in the scheme involved mediation, in which the mediator would attempt to assist the parties in reaching a negotiated settlement, or, if that was not possible, to narrow the issues in dispute, in particular to agree on common facts that may be used in subsequent arbitration or litigation.

The arbitration procedure

In the event that the mediation was not successful, the parties could then elect to arbitrate, which would be binding on both parties. Another person (i.e. not the mediator) would be appointed as arbitrator, and conduct a documents-only arbitration (to the extent possible). The arbitrator's decision would be final.

This procedure, however, was not intended to be used for all disputes, in particular, those involving complex issues or requiring the examination of witnesses.[30]

---

[28] Hong Kong Monetary Authority, 'Explanatory Note on the Scheme', available at: www. hkma.gov.hk/eng/other-information/lehman/explanatory_b.shtml [accessed 8 February 2012].

[29] Soo, Zhao, Cai, 'Better ways of resolving disputes in Hong Kong – some insights from the Lehman-Brothers related investment product dispute mediation and arbitration scheme'.

[30] Ibid.

Statistics

As of 31 December 2009, eighty-six cases went through mediation with seventy-six achieving settlement. Thirty-seven cases were settled by direct negotiation. No cases were referred to arbitration.

Service providers

The HKIAC was the administrator of the Scheme. The HKIAC established panels of mediators and arbitrators for the Scheme, and claimants and respondents could agree on the appointment of a mediator or arbitrator from the Lists, or request the HKIAC appoint one. The HKMA provided the Scheme with an office, staff and venue, including a special hotline for inquiries.

Oversight

The HKIAC established Mediation and Arbitration Rules for the Scheme. Mediators and the HKMA and HKIAC were indemnified from liability 'whether involving negligence or not, from any act or omission in connection with or arising out of or relating in any way to any Mediation and Arbitration conducted under these Rules, save for the consequences of fraud or dishonesty'.

The issue of appeals has not yet arisen. Furthermore, due to the voluntary settlement between the banks and the regulators (see below), the issue of disparity in mediated settlements also did not arise.

Strengths

The high success rate and speedy resolution of Lehman disputes have been cited as the primary strengths of the Scheme.[31] The advantages the Scheme offered to the banks included its speedy and informal nature, which meant that banks could maintain amicable relationships with customers as well as avoid disruption to operations due to long and drawn out disputes and maintain privacy.

These strengths are generally characteristic of all mediation processes. As the resolution process never passed beyond the mediation stage, the potential conflict between the confidentiality of the mediation process

---

[31] Ibid.

and the use of information disclosed during that process in later arbitral or court proceedings, whether agreed upon or not, also was not put to the test.

Challenges

The need for regulator intervention to achieve broad-base settlements

Ultimately, it was the intervention of the regulators that proved the most effective in respect of driving Minibonds settlement forward. In early 2009, Sun Hung Kai Investment Services and KGI Asia voluntarily offered to repurchase Minibonds after the SFC raised a number of concerns in respect of the Minibond sales practices, which formed the basis of reprimands from the SFC. The repurchases were completed on 2 July 2009, and clients of both securities broker distributors recovered the principal amounts invested.

On 22 July 2009, an agreement was reached between the SFC, HKMA and sixteen of the distributing banks, whereby the banks offered to repurchase the Minibonds at a price equal to 60 per cent of the original investment amount for their customers below the age of sixty-five, and at 70 per cent for those above sixty-five. Investors who had previously reached settlements with the banks would also receive *ex gratia* payments to bring their settlement amounts in line with the agreed settlement rate. In exchange, the distributing banks admitted no liability, and furthermore, the SFC discontinued its investigations into the sale and distribution of Minibonds by the banks. The HKMA also informed the banks of its intention not to take any enforcement action in respect of the banks whose customers accepted the offer.

Some 24,168 Minibond investors accepted the repurchase scheme, for which approximately 97 per cent qualified. A further 4,800 Minibond investors who reached settlements before the offer was made in July also received top-up payments.

Thereafter, an agreement on the same terms in respect of compensation was reached between the SFC and Grand Cathay Securities on 17 December 2009, bringing an end to investigations of all nineteen Minibond distributors.

Several days later on 23 December 2009, the SFC, HKMA and Dah Sing Bank and Mevas Bank reached an agreement in respect of Equity-Linked Fixed Coupon Principal Protected Notes issued by Lehman Brothers, whereby the two banks would repurchase the Notes at 80 per cent of the principal amount and also bring earlier settlements in line with that amount. Both the SFC and the HKMA agreed not to take any enforcement action against the two banks.

On 13 January 2010, the SFC reached an agreement with Karl Thomson Investment Consultants – who were not distributors of Minibonds but had purchased and sold them on to eleven clients. Karl Thomson agreed to repurchase the Minibonds on the same terms agreed upon by the banks, the SFC and the HKMA under the 22 July 2009 settlement. This may be contrasted with the voluntary repurchases offered by SHK Investment Services and KGI Asia.

The high numbers involved in the voluntary settlement must be contrasted with the low numbers involved in the Scheme. The low uptake of the Scheme was noted in 'Better ways of Resolving Disputes in Hong Kong', which was attributed to limited understanding of mediation by users as well as the low number of complainants (246) referred by the HKMA.

The suitability of mediation for the Minibonds crisis

Mediation being a dispute resolution process based less upon disputed issues and more on achieving a negotiated outcome is often measured on the basis of whether an agreement was reached rather than on the amount of compensation that was achieved for the aggrieved party. Such an approach may leave complainants at a disadvantage as the balance of bargaining power and information is not on their side. The mediator represents neither side, and complainants without the assistance of legal representation or other advisers will again be placed at a severe informational deficiency, which could disadvantage them greatly as negotiation no longer takes place on equal footing.

Nor is mediation well suited to situations involving high numbers of individuals with complaints, as the relevant factors to be considered for the purposes of negotiation may differ from complainant to complainant.

The use of mediation in the Scheme also raises a fundamental issue as to whether or not it is appropriate to mediate disputes between consumers and financial service providers, particularly where the dispute appears, as was the case with the Minibonds, systemic. In the case of the Minibonds, investigations by the regulators were also ongoing – investigations which may have been highly relevant to addressing the informational deficiency noted above. This deficiency was particularly pertinent in respect of the Minibonds as the key issue involved in the dispute was that the financial service providers were at fault for misleading consumers, a key consideration in reaching equitable settlement.

As noted above, even where the dispute is not one which arises out of a systemic issue, where it affects large numbers of consumers, the confidentiality requirements of the mediation process may interfere with achieving parity between settlements in cases with similar circumstances.

The suitability of arbitration

In respect of the arbitration aspect of the Scheme, though not deployed, given the complexity of the issues in this context, there may have been difficulty in finding arbitrators who were capable of dealing with the interacting regimes of civil law, the bank–customer relationship, and the regulatory regime, as well as understanding the Minibonds themselves. The invitation of the HKIAC to members of the Bar[32] (emphasising prior mediation experience in particular but without reference to knowledge of the relevant issues, laws, codes or regulatory regimes) to apply to join the Scheme on 17 November 2008 seems to highlight this challenge. Moreover, given the similarities between arbitration and litigation, it may prove difficult for a class of complainants to arbitrate their complaints simultaneously, necessitating an individual, case-by-case approach which is liable to be both time-consuming and to produce inconsistent awards – indeed, the Notes to the Scheme emphasise the individual nature of the claims.[33] As representation by legal professionals or other representatives is not a prerequisite of arbitration, the information gap between distributors and complainants is potentially significantly widened. The private nature of arbitration means that decisions and awards may not be disclosed, leaving complainants and the regulatory authorities in the dark as to reasoning and the range of compensation.

Of particular concern in the arbitral process is the fact-finding exercise, which is adversarial and places the onus of proof upon the party that is likely to be at the greatest informational disadvantage. Moreover, the use of arbitration raises the issue of arbitrability – arbitration traditionally not being intended as a method of dispute resolution where there may be regulatory issues involved.

---

[32] Hong Kong Bar Association Circular No. 118/08.
[33] Hong Kong Monetary Authority, 'Notes, Lehman-Brothers-related Investment Products Dispute Mediation and Arbitration Scheme', Paragraph 2.

Lessons learned

The need for dispute resolution processes in the financial industry

In their reports to the Financial Secretary on the Minibonds issue, both the SFC and the HKMA recommended the creation of a dispute resolution process for the financial industry. In particular, the SFC recommended that its Code of Conduct be amended to require client agreements specify a right for clients to have their grievances resolved by a dispute resolution procedure, and further, that the government should hold a consultation on whether there is a need for the creation of a financial ombudsman with powers to order compensation. The HKMA took into account international practice and the desirability of an organisation with the powers to adjudicate or settle disputes between investors and intermediaries, and recommended that consideration should be given to establishing a dispute resolution mechanism for the financial industry.

The recommendations made by the SFC and HKMA in their respective reports gave rise to a proposal in February 2010 by the Financial Services and the Treasury Bureau in respect of the establishment of a Financial Dispute Resolution Centre.

The key features of the proposal are:

- the creation of a financial dispute resolution centre to administer a financial dispute resolution scheme;
- a two-tiered financial dispute resolution scheme whereby disputes are first mediated, and failing mediation, arbitrated;
- participation in the scheme by financial institutions regulated or licensed by the SFC or the HKMA;
- a HK$500,000 cap on claims under the scheme;
- a 'pay-as-you-use' charge to both claimants and institutions, with higher fees payable by financial institutions; and
- that the FDRC would not be empowered with any investigatory or disciplinary powers.

The need for a dispute resolution mechanism has been recognised by the majority of respondents to the public consultation on the proposal.[34]

---

[34] Financial services and the Treasury Bureau (13 December 2010) 'Consultation Conclusions on Proposed Establishment of an Investor Education Council and a Financial Dispute Resolution Centre', para.24, available at: www.fstb.gov.hk/fsb/ppr/consult/doc/consult_iec_fdrc_conslusion_e.pdf [accessed 14 December 2012].

While the proposal bears some resemblance to the Scheme, key differences include a ceiling on claims, charges to complainants as well as service providers, the exclusion of Manditory Provident Fund (MPF) and insurance disputes, and systemic concerns being referred back to the regulators.

Information gathering

The importance of the hotline and the preparatory meetings in gathering information before the dispute resolution process began has been emphasised as one of the lessons to be learned from the Scheme.[35]

Controlling costs

Under the proposal for the establishment of a Financial Dispute Resolution Centre, costs of the procedure will be borne by the parties, though the financial services provider will bear the larger proportion of those costs.

Preventing abuse

One of the challenges the Scheme had to overcome,[36] which has also been mentioned above in respect of the Civil Justice Reform, is the abuse of the dispute resolution process, particularly where parties or one party does not approach the dispute resolution process with a real intent to resolve the dispute.

While abuses may have been prevented during the preparatory meeting stage in the Scheme, the proposal for the establishment of a Financial Dispute Resolution Centre involves a process of preliminary assessment and screening to weed out complaints that lack merit and other abuses that would be a drain on resources.

Disclosure of summary information

As part of the proposal to establish a Financial Dispute Resolution Centre, summary information about cases on an unnamed basis will be published

---

[35] Soo, Zhao, Cai, 'Better ways of resolving disputes in Hong Kong – some insights from the Lehman-Brothers related investment product dispute mediation and arbitration scheme'.
[36] Ibid.

in order to educate consumers, provide information in respect of common problems and alert regulators to issues with wider implications.

Contribution to domestic financial performance and consumer confidence

It remains to be seen whether the proposal to establish a Financial Dispute Resolution Centre, along with proposals to increase regulator scrutiny on retail practices of securities firms and banks engaged in securities business, will restore or improve local confidence. The effects of the Minibonds crisis, having received much international as well as local coverage, continue to be felt through the ongoing protests as well as through the efforts of community groups.[37]

While Hong Kong was not at the epicentre of the financial crisis, the effect on the financial industry and consumer protection in particular is an important one, as Hong Kong's financial markets remain characterised by a relatively high proportion of individual retail investors.

Hong Kong's Financial Dispute Resolution Centre aims to provide retail consumers with a clear route for resolving disputes with banks and financial institutions. A clear avenue of resolution will arguably contribute to greater confidence in market-redress mechanisms and ideally reduce the cost of complaint handling through the courts. Such costs savings could get passed back to consumers in the form of lower fees for financial services, thus spurring greater market dynamism.

---

[37] For further information on the group, please see www.lbv.org.hk/ [accessed 26 April 2012].

Part III overview: survey findings regarding the arbitration process

Survey

In order to assess how arbitrators view the benefits, challenges and suggestions for improving the arbitration process, a survey was conducted between the autumn of 2011 and the summer of 2012. Nearly a hundred survey questionnaires were distributed to practitioners throughout the world. A total of forty-eight dispute resolution practitioners from East Asia, North America, Europe, the Middle East and Africa responded. The participants represented highly experienced practitioners, members of government regulatory ombuds services and private arbitration commissions. Many of those surveyed (44 per cent) had worked for institutions involved in consumer financial dispute resolution for more than four years.

The survey questions were distributed at ADR conferences in East Asia, online through a web-based survey collection site, and in person with members of arbitration centres in Shenzhen, Hong Kong, Macau, the United States and Europe.

The summary of the findings in relation to the arbitration process are as follows: arbitration practitioners viewed the benefits of arbitration services in consumer financial disputes as providing disputants with technical expertise 'where the parties are not arguing over the law, but application of financial/accounting principles'.[38] In addition, respondents noted the 'speed, reduced expense and expertise of the neutral'. Among the challenges include 'proof issues, imbalance of power and information and lack of full discovery options/rights'.[39] Concerns about such disparities were echoed by other participants who noted the prevalence of perceptions that 'large institutions have "repeat-user" advantage'.[40] Practitioners noted suggestions for improvement including the need for '[g]ood program design [including] exit evaluations [and a] grievance

[38] Survey No. 8 (July 2011–March 2012).
[39] Survey No. 10 (July 2011–March 2012).
[40] Survey No. 14 (July 2011–March 2012).

Survey Participants

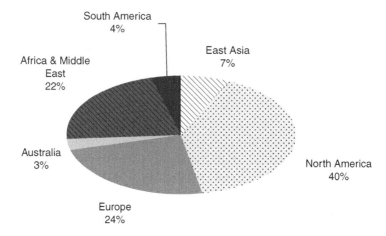

Figure 7.1 Survey participants

process to allow parties to file complaints against neutrals who do not perform well'. In addition, 'a code of ethics for neutrals' was suggested along with 'anything that supports procedural due process'.[41]

Benefits of using an arbitration process for consumer financial disputes

Practitioners were asked about what they saw as the benefits of using arbitration to resolve consumer financial disputes. The responses ranged from, 'speed; reduced expense; expertise of the neutral',[42] to technical expertise, 'where the parties are not arguing over the law, but application of financial/accounting principles, it makes sense for the parties to hire a firm ... to act as the "judge" (arbitrator) to settle the dispute'.[43] This view is echoed by other survey respondents who observed that the process is 'more expeditious [because the] resolution [is performed] by neutrals who understand finance'.[44] Others noted that the process is 'cost effective'[45] in that it helps parties to 'avoid costly litigation, especially in light of the new

[41] Survey No. 10 (July 2011–March 2012).
[42] Survey No. 7 (July 2011–March 2012).
[43] Survey No. 8 (July 2011–March 2012).
[44] Survey No. 13 (July 2011–March 2012).
[45] Survey No. 9 (July 2011–March 2012).

Have you observed an increase in use in the past 3 years? (Arbitration)

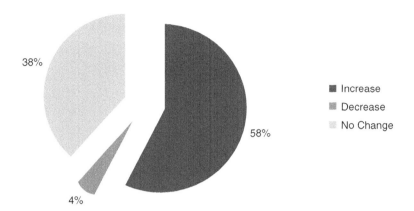

Figure 7.2   Increase or decrease in the use of arbitration for consumer financial disputes

United States Supreme Court decision governing class actions. [It] can offer procedural justice, if [a] program is properly designed.'[46] Finally, respondents noted that the process relies on 'established, court-tested Rules, and … arbitrators with financial dispute experience'.[47]

In addition to the direct benefits of the arbitration processes, those involved in the delivery of a multi-tier process of arbitration preceded by mediation or negotiation noted a number of additional benefits. These include 'cost–time saving[s]',[48] 'bringing about resolution and peace to stakeholders in conflict',[49] 'give[ing] parties [the] opportunity to avoid stress associated with [court] proceedings',[50] 'provid[ing] a mechanism for dialogue'[51] and 'keeping friendships between main contractors and subcontractors looking forward to working together again on the next project'.[52]

Perhaps as a result of such benefits, the use of the arbitration processes has been slightly increasing in recent years. In response to the question,

[46] Survey No. 10 (July 2011–March 2012).
[47] Survey No. 14 (July 2011-March 2012).
[48] Survey Nos. 15, 21, 22, 24, 25 (July 2011–March 2012).
[49] Survey No. 18 (July 2011–March 2012).
[50] Survey No. 20 (July 2011–March 2012).
[51] Survey No. 23 (July 2011–March 2012).
[52] Survey No. 26 (July 2011–March 2012).

Settlement Rate – Arbitration

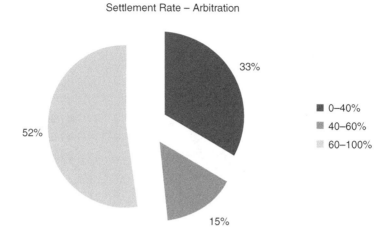

Figure 7.3   Settlement rate – arbitration

'do you see an increase in the use of arbitration services ...' the majority of respondents (58 per cent) indicated that they had in fact seen an increase in the use of arbitration processes in consumer financial dispute resolution in recent years.

In examining the results of the survey regarding the rate of settlement in a multi-tiered arbitration process, over 67 per cent of respondents observed that settlement occurred in 40–100 per cent of cases.

Challenges in implementing the use of arbitration in consumer financial disputes

Among the challenges practitioners observed in the use of arbitration to resolve consumer financial disputes included difficulties with 'administration',[53] limited numbers of cases (i.e. 'unfortunately some will only arbitrate a few cases during their careers') while others may routinely arbitrate '10–20 [cases] a year'.[54] In addition, some have noted limitations in the extent to which 'bankers have incorporated ... arbitration clause[s] into their contracts'.[55] Others have noted that the process involves 'essentially tough distributive bargaining' and that often there are 'proof issues, imbalance of power and information, lack of full discovery options/

[53] Survey No. 7 (July 2011–March 2012).
[54] Survey No. 8 (July 2011–March 2012).
[55] Survey No. 9 (July 2011–March 2012).

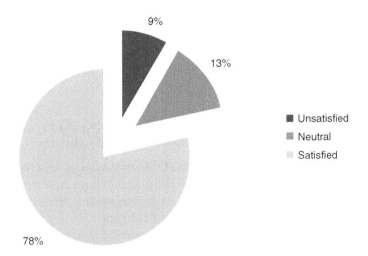

Figure 7.4   Perception of satisfaction with arbitration in resolving consumer financial disputes

rights'.[56] Concerns about such disparities were echoed by other participants who noted the prevalence of perceptions that 'large institutions have "repeat-user" advantage'.[57] In addition, some arbitrators noted that they faced difficulty in 'bring[ing] the parties together'.[58] In addition, in some cases, there were challenges with '[i]mpleading ... other necessary parties who are not party to the arbitration agreement' alongside 'reluctance in judicial assistance' and at times 'unwarranted judicial intervention in the process'.[59]

In addition to the direct challenges associated with the arbitration processes, those involved in the delivery of a multi-tier process of arbitration preceded by mediation or negotiation noted a number of unique challenges. These include lack of 'knowledge of ADR [and] willingness to participate',[60] including the need to educate 'people in conflict that there are cost effective and humane alternatives to litigation',[61] 'difficulties in

---

[56] Survey No. 10 (July 2011–March 2012).
[57] Survey No. 14 (July 2011–March 2012).
[58] Survey No. 11 (July 2011–March 2012).
[59] Survey No. 13 (July 2011–March 2012).
[60] Survey Nos. 15, 23 (July 2011–March 2012).
[61] Survey No. 18 (July 2011–March 2012).

enforcing judgments ... (in some settings)',[62] government cuts in funding[63] and assisting parties to come to agreement[64] particularly in the context of 'lawyers wanting to make fees by taking matters to full litigation'.[65]

While a number of areas exist for continued improvement in the delivery of consumer financial arbitration services, the large majority of practitioners (78 per cent) perceived that claimants were satisfied overall with the process.

Suggestions for improving overall efficacy of the arbitration process in consumer financial disputes

Arbitration practitioners were also asked about what suggestions they have for improving the overall efficacy of the process. Suggestions included the need for parties to include arbitration provisions in their contracts and the utility of hiring subject-matter specialists including those with expertise in accounting.[66] Further, 'parties should be more open to the mediation process to try and resolve some, if not all, items'.[67] In addition, improved training for neutrals was highlighted. One respondent noted the need for '[g]ood program design [including] exit evaluations [and a] grievance process to allow parties to file complaints against neutrals who do not perform well'. In addition, 'a code of ethics for neutrals' was suggested along with 'anything that supports procedural due process'.[68] Along these lines, one participant noted the need for 'early and vigorous case- and discovery-management'.[69] A number of individuals suggested more 'public information' about the arbitration process[70] including 'public educational campaign[s] about the process and better judicial cooperation in appropriate cases and non-intervention'.[71]

In addition to the specific suggestions associated with the arbitration processes, those involved in the delivery of a multi-tier process of arbitration preceded by mediation or negotiation noted a number of specific

---

[62] Survey No. 16 (July 2011–March 2012).

[63] Survey Nos. 17, 21, 22 (July 2011–March 2012).

[64] Survey No. 19 (July 2011–March 2012).

[65] Survey No. 24 (July 2011–March 2012).

[66] See for example, Steven Brams, 'Two-Person Cake-Cutting: The Optimal Number of Cuts' (with Julius B. Barbanel).

[67] Survey No. 8 (July 2011–March 2012).

[68] Survey No. 10 (July 2011–March 2012).

[69] Survey No. 14 (July 2011–March 2012).

[70] Survey No. 12 (July 2011–March 2012).

[71] Survey No. 13 (July 2011–March 2012).

suggestions for improving its overall efficacy. These included greater public 'education about the process',[72] and 'effort to expedite the process and control costs ... [as] arbitration used to be an effective alternative to litigation but now it has also become very expensive'.[73] In this light, some have suggested a 'move toward binding mediation'.[74] Finally, a number of respondents suggested the need for greater 'training, workshops and meet-up[s] for neutrals'.[75]

Conclusion

Largely reflecting many of the benefits as well as some of the challenges facing consumer financial arbitration, the use of arbitration in resolving consumer financial disputes has expanded at a moderate rate. Recent legislation in the United States, for example, has sought to limit the obligation to submit to some mandatory consumer credit card arbitration schemes. The development of arbitration in the context of Hong Kong's Financial Dispute Resolution Centre will provide an opportunity to further examine how principles of fairness and equity are effectively reconciled with objectives of efficacy, independence and accessibility.

[72] Survey Nos. 15, 19 (July 2011–March 2012).
[73] Survey No. 16 (July 2011–March 2012).
[74] Survey No. 16 (July 2011–March 2012).
[75] Survey No. 18 (July 2011–March 2012).

8

Emerging systems: financial dispute resolution in China

Background

At present, the resolution of consumer financial disputes in China operate at a number of levels. This can include direct negotiations with banks, mediation by specialised self-regulatory organisations, arbitration through the China International Economic and Trade Arbitration Commission ('CIETAC') or provincial arbitral bodies such as the Beijing Arbitration Commission or the Shenzhen Arbitration Commission, or adjudication through specialised court programmes.[1] China's centralised programmes of consumer financial dispute resolution include the Securities Association of China's mediation programme as well as the Financial Arbitration rules of CIETAC. Such programmes seek to operate on the basis of principles of equity, efficiency and speed. Consultation is currently underway regarding the establishment of a comprehensive consumer financial dispute resolution programme in China.

The resolution of securities disputes

Under the Securities Law, the main regulator of the securities industry of China is the China Securities Regulatory Commission ('CSRC'). Its functions are comparable to the Securities and Exchange Commission of the United States.

Under the regulation of the CSRC is the Securities Association of China ('SAC'), a nationwide self-regulatory organisation for the Chinese securities industry. One of the functions of the SAC is to 'mediate securities business related disputes among members or among members and their clients'.

---

[1] See S. Ali and H. R. Huang (2012) 'Financial Dispute Resolution in China: Arbitration or Court Litigation?', *Arbitration International* 28(1), pp. 77–100.

Underlying legal mandate

In 2004, the Legal Affairs Office of the State Council and the China Securities Regulatory Commission jointly issued a notice on the arbitration of securities and futures contractual disputes (Securities and Futures Disputes Arbitration Notice). The Securities and Futures Disputes Arbitration Notice promotes arbitration in securities contractual dispute resolution with an aim to make full use of the advantages of arbitration (expediency, flexibility, low cost and confidentiality). The two issues of greatest importance in the notice are the scope of arbitration in securities and futures contractual disputes, and the use of an arbitration clause in securities and futures contracts. It stipulates a wide range of securities contractual disputes that fall into the scope of arbitration. Furthermore, securities and futures model contracts are required to have an arbitration clause and parties have the right to choose an arbitration organisation.[2]

However, while one of the functions of the SAC is to mediate disputes, specific regulations governing the process appear to be under development at present. Rules have been established under the China Futures Association, China's national futures SRO, for mediation, under the authority of the CSRC.[3]

Financial alternative dispute resolution programmes

In addition to the mediation and arbitration of China's securities disputes, CIETAC established its Financial Dispute Arbitration Rules on 8 May 2003, with the aim of filling the demand for quick, expert and objective resolution of disputes over financial transactions.[4] It also takes a conciliation-arbitration approach more generally.

---

[2] S. Zhu (2009) 'Legal aspects of the commodity and financial futures market in China', *The Brooklyn Journal Of Corporate, Financial & Commercial Law*, 3, pp. 377–430. In addition, The Arbitration Law was promulgated on 31 August 1994, and unified arbitration practices across the country. It also harmonised China's arbitration system with internationally accepted practices, principles and systems.

[3] See art. 16 of the Provisional Measures on the Administration of the Members of the China Futures Association (promulgated 29 December 2000), available at: www.csrc.gov. cn/n575458/n4239016/n6634558/n9768113/10011976 [accessed 8 February 2012].

[4] F. Cheung (July/August 2003) 'CIETAC opens doors to financial arbitration', *China Law and Practice*.

Types of disputes

The Financial Disputes Arbitration Rules can be invoked for disputes involving financial transactions on the currency market, capital market, foreign exchange market, gold market and insurance market. The concept of financial transactions is defined very broadly and includes local or foreign currency financing, assignment or sale of local or foreign currency financial instruments and documents, among other things.[5] Disputes that may be submitted under the Financial Disputes Arbitration Rules include disputes solely between financial institutions or between financial institutions and other legal persons or natural persons.[6]

Although the scope of the Financial Disputes Arbitration Rules covers the banking, securities and insurance sectors, the principal target seems to be banking transactions as is suggested by the non-exhaustive list of financial transactions mentioned in the Rules. The list includes loans, deposit certificates, guarantees, letters of credit, negotiable

---

[5] See Articles 1 and 2 of the CIETAC Financial Disputes Arbitration Rules:

Article 1 These Rules are formulated for the purpose of impartial and prompt resolution of disputes arising from financial transactions between the parties.

Article 2 The China International Economic and Trade Arbitration Commission (also known as the Arbitration Court of the China Chamber of International Commerce and hereinafter referred to as the 'CIETAC') independently and impartially resolves, by means of arbitration, disputes arising from, or in connection with, financial transactions between the parties.

The term 'financial transactions' shall refer to transactions arising between financial institutions inter se, or arising between financial institutions and other natural or legal persons in the currency, capital, foreign exchange, gold and insurance markets that relate to financing in both domestic and foreign currencies, and the assignment and sale of financial instruments and documents denominated in both domestic and foreign currencies, including but not limited to:

1. Loans;
2. Deposit certificates;
3. Guarantees;
4. Letters of credit;
5. Negotiable instruments;
6. Fund transactions and fund trusts;
7. Bonds;
8. Collection and remittance of foreign currencies;
9. Factoring;
10. Reimbursement agreements between banks; and
11. Securities and futures.

[6] See Article 2 of the CIETAC Financial Disputes Arbitration Rules at footnote 5 above.

instruments, fund transactions, fund trusts, bonds, foreign exchange collection and remittance, factoring and reimbursement agreements between banks.[7]

There are several indications that insurance disputes are considered a less important area for financial arbitration under the Financial Disputes Arbitration Rules than banking or securities disputes. No insurance-related transactions are included in the exemplary list of financial transactions. There are seven insurance law experts included in the list of arbitrators attached to the Financial Disputes Arbitration Rules, thus offering the parties a limited choice of arbitrators in this area. This is remedied to a certain extent by CIETAC's discretion to permit selection of arbitrators from another arbitration panel designated by it. It remains to be seen whether all or only certain types of insurance transactions will be deemed as open for arbitration under the Financial Disputes Arbitration Rules.

The decision on whether a dispute is a financial dispute that can utilise arbitration under the Financial Disputes Arbitration Rules lies ultimately with CIETAC. Securities-related disputes also do not seem to be the prime target of the Financial Disputes Arbitration Rules. This may be due to the fact that CIETAC might have plans to issue a separate set of rules to govern arbitration in this area.[8]

Procedure

When parties choose to submit their dispute to CIETAC for arbitration, the Financial Disputes Arbitration Rules will only be applied if the parties have agreed to the use of the Financial Disputes Arbitration Rules. Such agreement may have been reached by the parties prior to the dispute or after the dispute arose. In the absence of an agreement, CIETAC will use the CIETAC Arbitration Rules.[9]

The Financial Disputes Arbitration Rules provide that in the event of a discrepancy between the Financial Disputes Arbitration Rules and the CIETAC Arbitration Rules, the Financial Disputes Arbitration Rules will

---

[7] See Article 2 of the CIETAC Financial Disputes Arbitration Rules at footnote 5 above.

[8] F. Cheung, 'CIETAC opens doors to financial arbitration'.

[9] See art. 3 of the CIETAC Financial Disputes Arbitration Rules: 'These Rules shall apply to any financial dispute accepted by the CIETAC for arbitration where the parties have agreed upon the application thereof. Failing such agreement, the Arbitration Rules of the CIETAC shall apply.'

prevail. Matters not addressed in the Financial Arbitration Disputes Rules must be handled in accordance with the CIETAC Arbitration Rules.[10]

The arbitration tribunal hearing a dispute under the Financial Disputes Arbitration Rules must comprise one or three arbitrators. If the parties fail to agree on the number of arbitrators who are to make up the tribunal, the Chairman of CIETAC will make the decision. The procedures for appointment of arbitrators are similar to those found in the CIETAC Arbitration Rules except that the Financial Disputes Arbitration Rules require all arbitrators to be appointed within ten working days after the parties have received the notice of arbitration.[11]

When the parties or the Chairman of CIETAC select arbitrators, they may do so from CIETAC's list of financial arbitrators or from other lists of arbitrators designated by CIETAC.[12] The arbitrators appointed by the parties will be confirmed by CIETAC and CIETAC is not required to provide grounds for its decision to grant or refuse confirmation of these arbitrators.[13] A list of financial arbitrators who are experts in various areas of finance is attached to the Rules.

---

[10] See art. 26 of the CIETAC Financial Disputes Arbitration Rules: 'In the event of any inconsistency between these Rules and the Arbitration Rules of the CIETAC, these Rules shall prevail. For matters not covered in these Rules, the Arbitration Rules of the CIETAC shall apply.'

[11] See art. 12 of the CIETAC Financial Disputes Arbitration Rules:

The arbitral tribunal shall be composed of one or three arbitrators. Where the parties have not agreed upon the number of arbitrators, the Chairman of the CIETAC shall decide whether the arbitral tribunal shall be composed of one or three arbitrators.

Unless otherwise agreed by the parties, where the arbitral tribunal is composed of one arbitrator, the Claimant and the Respondent shall, within ten (10) working days from the date of receipt of the Notice of Arbitration by the party who last receives it, jointly appoint a sole arbitrator or entrust the Chairman of the CIETAC to effect such appointment.

Unless otherwise agreed by the parties, where the arbitral tribunal is composed of three arbitrators, the Claimant and the Respondent shall, within ten (10) working days from the date of receipt of the Notice of Arbitration, respectively appoint an arbitrator or entrust the Chairman of the CIETAC to effect such appointment, and shall, within ten (10) working days from the date of receipt of the Notice of Arbitration by the party who last receives it, jointly appoint a third arbitrator, or alternatively, shall entrust the Chairman of the CIETAC to effect such appointment. The third arbitrator shall be the presiding arbitrator.

[12] See para. 3 of art. 6 of the CIETAC Financial Disputes Arbitration Rules: 'Where the appointment of an arbitrator is to be made by the Chairman of the CIETAC, the Chairman may, unless otherwise agreed by the parties, appoint such arbitrator from the Panel of Arbitrators in Financial Industry or from other Panel of Arbitrators of the CIETAC.'

[13] See paras. 1–2 of art. 6 of the CIETAC Financial Disputes Arbitration Rules:

The parties may appoint arbitrators from the Panel of Arbitrators in Financial Industry of the CIETAC, or from such Panel of Arbitrators as may be designated by the CIETAC.

The provisions of the Financial Disputes Arbitration Rules with respect to the locus and governing law are the same as provided under the CIETAC Arbitration Rules. Unless the parties have agreed otherwise, the site for the arbitration will be the place where CIETAC or its sub-commission is located.[14] In principle, the parties may agree that the venue of the hearing be overseas.

Unless there are mandatory requirements under the law, the parties may agree on the substantive law applicable to the dispute if the case involves a foreign element. In the absence of an agreement between the parties, the arbitration tribunal will decide on the proper substantive law in light of the contractual terms, the practice in the relevant industry and the standards of the trade.[15]

Financial arbitration under the Financial Disputes Arbitration Rules does not necessarily require hearings as is standard under the CIETAC Arbitration Rules. Whether a hearing is held will depend on the agreement between the parties or the decision of the arbitration tribunal. If a hearing is held, the CIETAC Secretariat must advise the parties ten working days prior to the hearing.[16]

The appointment of the arbitrators by the parties shall be subject to the confirmation by the Chairman of the CIETAC. Such confirmation shall be made, or not made, without stating the reasons therefor.

Where the parties have agreed to appoint arbitrators from outside of the CIETAC's Panels of Arbitrators, the arbitrators so appointed by the parties or nominated according to the agreement of the parties may act as arbitrator if the appointment is confirmed by the Chairman of the CIETAC in accordance with the law. Such confirmation shall be made, or not made, without stating the reasons therefor.

[14] See art. 20 of the CIETAC Financial Disputes Arbitration Rules:

Where the parties have agreed on the place of arbitration in writing, their agreement shall prevail. Failing such agreement, the place of arbitration shall be the domicile of the CIETAC or its Sub-Commission. The arbitral award shall be deemed as being made at the place of arbitration.

Unless otherwise agreed by the parties, the arbitral tribunal may conduct oral hearings or other activities at any place it deems appropriate.

[15] See art. 21 of the CIETAC Financial Disputes Arbitration Rules:

Subject to mandatory provisions of law, the parties to any case involving a foreign-related element may agree upon the law to be applied to the merits of the dispute. Failing such agreement, the arbitral tribunal shall apply the law that it determines to be appropriate. In all cases, the arbitral tribunal shall take into account the terms of the contract, the general usages and standard practices of specific business sectors, and abide by the principles of fairness and reasonableness.

[16] See art. 18 of the CIETAC Financial Disputes Arbitration Rules:

The fact that arbitration under the Financial Disputes Arbitration Rules may not always involve a hearing makes the preparation of accurate and complete written submissions all the more crucial for the parties to a financial arbitration. Coupled with the significant tightening of time limits for the submission of a defence and counterclaim (although extensions may be granted) under the Financial Disputes Arbitration Rules, parties may find it difficult to fully present their case. It remains to be seen whether, as a result of this, parties may only elect to arbitrate under the Financial Disputes Arbitration Rules when the matter at issue is well documented from the start and does not require the preparation of extensive documentary evidence. It should be noted that the time problem may be remedied, however, if the parties can agree to a longer time limit for submitting documents.[17]

Fees

CIETAC used to have two sets of standards for arbitration fees: one for arbitration cases involving a foreign element and one for domestic cases. With the enactment of the Financial Disputes Arbitration Rules there is now a third arbitration fee schedule that applies solely to the arbitration of financial disputes. The fees under the new schedule are lower than those charged by CIETAC for the arbitration of disputes involving a foreign element under the CIETAC Arbitration Rules. When compared with CIETAC's domestic case fee schedule, the size of the claim will determine which fee schedule is less costly. For example, the cost for a claim involving an amount of RMB10 million would amount to RMB102,500 under the Financial Disputes Arbitration Rules; under the international and domestic fee schedules of CIETAC the cost would total RMB220,000 and RMB121,550, respectively. For cases involving higher amounts, the fees under the Financial Disputes Arbitration Rules may actually be more advantageous than those under the domestic arbitration fee schedule. This cost advantage may be one of the factors attracting local and foreign

---

The arbitral tribunal shall hold an oral hearing when examining the case. However, the oral hearing may be omitted and the case shall be examined on the basis of documents only if the parties so request or agree and the arbitral tribunal also deems that the oral hearing is unnecessary. If the oral hearing is to be held, the Secretariat of the CIETAC shall serve a Notice of Oral Hearing on each party at least ten (10) working days in advance of the oral hearing date.

[17] F. Cheung, 'CIETAC opens doors to financial arbitration'.

parties to choose arbitration under the Financial Disputes Arbitration Rules rather than under the CIETAC Arbitration Rules.

Strengths

Shortened timeline for financial arbitrations

The goal of quick resolution will mainly be achieved by imposing stricter deadlines and allowing more flexibility in the proceedings than are provided under the ordinary CIETAC Arbitration Rules. A financial arbitration under the Financial Disputes Arbitration Rules can be completed within forty-five days of the formation of the arbitration tribunal, as opposed to the nine months usually required to complete an arbitration under the CIETAC Arbitration Rules.[18]

Flexibility of proceedings

The Financial Disputes Arbitration Rules do not prescribe detailed rules for how the arbitration should be conducted, but rather leave the arbitration tribunal free to conduct the arbitration proceedings in a manner it deems fit. This is only subject to the requirements that the tribunal ensure that the parties are treated fairly and are given a reasonable opportunity to present their cases.

The parties may agree, or the arbitration tribunal may determine, a time limit for presenting evidence. In the absence of such a time limit, the parties must present all evidence to the Secretariat at least three working days prior to the first hearing of the case.

Catering to foreign parties

Many foreign parties or foreign-invested parties may be interested in ensuring a quick resolution of disputes arising out of their financial transactions in China. This would include parties to letters of credit, foreign-invested banks, fund managers and, to a lesser extent, insurance companies in China. The advantages of financial arbitration referred to earlier may be an important factor for such parties to decide to include a financial arbitration clause in their agreements.

---

[18] F. Cheung, 'CIETAC opens doors to financial arbitration'.

The Financial Disputes Arbitration Rules are clearly drafted to achieve the aim of quick and flexible proceedings. That the venue of the hearing may be overseas and that foreign law may serve as the governing law to resolve the disputes should be attractive to foreign parties. It could be argued that the list of eighty-nine arbitrators sitting on the financial arbitration panel is fairly limited and that a foreign bank or insurer in China would probably prefer to choose from a wider list in order to ensure that there are no conflicts of interest. This is in contrast to the list of arbitrators under the CIETAC Arbitration Rules that allows parties to an international dispute to choose from about 500 arbitrators, a third of which are Hong Kong and foreign lawyers. However, the Financial Disputes Arbitration Rules explicitly allow CIETAC to designate other lists of arbitrators from which the parties may appoint arbitrators. This apparently means that arbitrators on CIETAC's general list of arbitrators may also be appointed to serve on an arbitration tribunal hearing a case under the Rules. It is not clear from the Financial Disputes Arbitration Rules whether there are any situations in which CIETAC would not allow parties to choose arbitrators from another arbitration panel.

Moreover, foreign parties choosing arbitration under the Financial Disputes Arbitration Rules may still be confronted with the challenges pertaining to the enforcement of foreign-related arbitration awards in China. However, in recent years the Supreme People's Court has stepped up control over the enforcement of foreign-related awards by allowing only courts of a certain level to hear cases related to the validity of foreign-related arbitration awards and by imposing reporting requirements on the courts hearing such cases. Moreover, it is clear that despite the possibility of an overseas venue, in most cases it can be expected that the arbitration venue will be in China because the other party may withhold its agreement to arbitration outside China.

Challenges

Among the challenges facing CIETAC arbitration of financial disputes is the limited use of its programme.

In China there is a strong urgency to establish a special forum for the resolution of financial disputes. The country's financial sector is changing rapidly and the increasing number and complexity of transactions is proving a fertile breeding ground for disputes. Many of the complex disputes that are arising in the financial sector are being heard by courts that are gradually developing the necessary expertise to deal with the issues involved. As experience continues to be gained, in the short term, litigants will often be required to brief the court on the technicalities of the financial products involved.[19]

It is apparent that the number of financial disputes taken to the courts is on the rise.[20] The Shanghai No.1 Intermediate People's Court held a news conference in December 2010 regarding disputes relating to bank investment products.[21] The Court shared that it had dealt with a total of eighty relevant cases in the past year. The main issues revolved around (i) misleading or fraudulent practices; (ii) unfair standard agreement contracts; and (iii) inaccurate or dishonest disclosure of bank financial statements. The Court also expressed that it faced considerable difficulties in the adjudication of such cases due to the technicality of financial products and the lack of developed laws in this area. The Court suggested that the general public increase its awareness of the risks involved in investing in new financial products and closely inspect the terms of such products to prevent the occurrence of future disputes.

Contribution to domestic financial performance

The Financial Disputes Arbitration Rules offer domestic and foreign parties entering into financial transactions in China the opportunity to choose an efficient alternative to litigation or arbitration under standard rules. The greater flexibility and swiftness in the proceedings may be a strong reason for banks, securities houses, insurance companies and other parties to consider including an arbitration clause in their financial agreements that refers disputes for arbitration under the Financial Disputes Arbitration Rules.[22]

---

[19] F. Cheung, 'CIETAC opens doors to financial arbitration'.

[20] See S. Ali and H.R. Huang, 'Financial Dispute Resolution in China: Arbitration or Court Litigation?'.

[21] ChinaNews (28 December 2010) 'Shanghai No.1 Intermediate People's Court warns against risks of disputes over bank investment products (上海法院: 银行理财产品纠纷多发 吁加强风险防范)', available at www.chinanews.com/fortune/2010/12-28/2752939. shtml [Chinese].

[22] F. Cheung, 'CIETAC opens doors to financial arbitration'.

PART IV

Practice

9

Synthesising lessons learned and policy recommendations

Background

At the end of 2008, the world experienced what is considered to be the worst financial crisis since the Great Depression of the 1930s.

The effects of the crisis manifested in financial centres throughout the world. This crisis gave rise to the search for effective means of resolving financial related disputes. This chapter examines the lessons learned, and based on a comparative cross-jurisdictional analysis, offers recommendations for consumer financial dispute resolution systems design.

The conclusions and policy recommendations contained in this chapter arise from a comparison of dispute resolution schemes for the financial industries of six schemes: the Financial Ombudsman Service of the UK ('FOS (UK)'); the Financial Ombudsman Service of Australia ('FOS (Aus)'); the Japan Financial Ombuds Service; the Financial Industry Dispute Resolution Centre ('FIDReC') of Singapore; the Financial Dispute Resolution Centre ('FDRC') of Hong Kong;[1] and the Financial Industry Regulatory Authority ('FINRA') of the United States respectively.

Several areas of comparison between ombuds and arbitration models are examined in this chapter. These include analysis of jurisdiction, procedure, costs, handling of systemic issues and parallel jurisdiction and mass complaints. Comparisons and recommendations between schemes are made in light of international principles relevant to the adjudication of consumer financial disputes including the need for accessible grievance mechanisms, accountability, efficiency, impartiality and fairness and consideration of the role and function of such schemes in light of regulatory oversight.

---

[1] See generally: Ali, Shahla F. and Da Roza, A. M. (19 July 2011) 'Alternative Dispute Resolution in Financial Markets – Some More Equal than Others: Hong Kong's Proposed Financial Dispute Resolution Centre in the Context of Experience in the UK, US, Australia and Singapore', *Pacific Rim Law & Policy Journal*, Vol. 21, No. 3, 2012; University of Hong Kong Faculty of Law Research Paper No. 2012/20.

In comparing the key elements of the dispute resolution schemes for financial markets in the context of emerging global standards in the jurisdictions studied, two related issues arise: first, what is the role of dispute resolution in financial markets and their regulation? Second, which alternative dispute resolution techniques are most appropriate for use in financial markets and what is their level of appropriateness, not only in resolving disputes but in light of the role dispute resolution plays in financial markets and their regulation?

The financial crisis has demonstrated the limits of the existing methods of dispute resolution. Calls for the establishment of an affordable and efficient method of financial dispute resolution arising from the crisis thus address themselves towards the first issue: dispute resolution is necessary for financial markets not only in providing assurance that disputes over financial rights and legal obligations can be determined by an independent arbiter, and give rise to enforceable remedies, but beyond that is a greater need for accessibility – particularly for consumers. Financial markets are increasingly characterised by high numbers and high levels of participation by private individual investors at the retail level. It is these private investors at the retail level which the study addresses – disputes between consumers and financial service providers. Improving accessibility to justice or the ease with which investors may protect their own rights in financial markets not only serves to enhance market participation and capitalisation via increased consumer confidence, but also arguably serves to enhance market efficiency by lowering the amount of resources that need to be dedicated to the resolution of disputes. This in turn could potentially lead to a redistribution of those resources back into capitalisation of the financial market.

More specifically, in the context of the regulation of financial markets, the introduction of alternative dispute resolution, i.e. alternative to the judicial system, while clearly furthering market efficiency by lowering the resource-intensiveness of resolving financial disputes, raises the issue of whether or not alternative forms of dispute resolution necessarily play the same role as the courts in standard-setting and norms for consumer protection. In every jurisdiction, the role of alternative dispute resolution in a regulatory context seems to differ, leading to the question of whether or not it is desirable for alternative dispute resolution in financial markets to have an ad hoc regulatory role in trying to achieve consistency of outcomes and awards.

With regards to market efficiency, determining an appropriate method of dispute resolution thus becomes doubly important, as the shortcomings of an ineffective dispute resolution method could well lead to an adverse effect not just on consumer confidence, but market efficiency, as well as an increase in the amount of resources dedicated to and associated with dispute resolution.

As will be seen below, the ombuds and arbitration models of consumer financial dispute resolution implement global principles including accessibility, impartiality, equity, accountability and fairness to varying degrees, based on the unique mandate, regulatory function and objectives of each mechanism. For example, as will be seen in the examination of the ombuds models of consumer financial dispute resolution, the principles of accessibility, accountability and fairness may be given greater importance, while in the arbitration model, principles of efficiency may take precedence.

The findings indicate that the appropriateness of a dispute resolution method may be informed by the extent to which it takes on a regulatory role. Regulatory dispute resolution modes such as the ombudsman model that take on inquisitorial elements may be preferred when displacing the judicial function as they incorporate safeguards for disputants against third party discretion. But even for non-regulatory schemes, inquisitorial elements aimed at addressing the power/knowledge gap including suggesting the provision of information regarding relevant standards and rules, at least as touchstones, may still be incorporated into consensual models of dispute resolution, in order to ensure a de minimis level of fairness and confidence in the process.

Jurisdiction

Not every dispute may be submitted to a particular financial dispute resolution scheme. It is often the case that restrictions are imposed to exclude certain types of complainant or certain types of dispute.[2] Recommendations on proposed jurisdiction including limitations imposed on who may bring disputes, and the types of dispute they may bring, must thus be looked at in light of the principles of access to justice.

---

[2] Financial Services and the Treasury Bureau, 'Proposed Establishment of an Investor Education Council and a Financial Dispute Resolution Centre: Consultation Paper, para. 3.4 of Part II.

Eligible parties and access to justice

Financial dispute resolution services all have restrictions in some form on eligible complainants. In most cases, eligibility requirements serve as jurisdictional filters to ensure the relevance of complaints and to ensure that resources are not allocated to frivolous complaints. Such concerns must be counterbalanced with the broader principle of access to justice. In comparing eligibility requirements under the ombuds and the arbitration services, a number of distinctions are apparent. Under the ombuds service, eligibility can be viewed from a broad perspective, with the ultimate aim of ensuring that all eligible complainants have access to an appropriate grievance mechanism. In contrast, under the arbitration model, eligibility requirements are more narrow, which to a certain extent, serves as a jurisdictional filter.

A.   Ombuds model

In general, when viewing jurisdictional access to ombuds schemes across jurisdictions, one can generally conclude that a claimant's eligibility for service is broader than many arbitration-based schemes, as will be examined below.

In the United Kingdom, the Financial Ombudsman Scheme offers coverage for a person who is a consumer, a micro-enterprise, a charity with an annual income of less than £1 million, or a trustee of a trust with a net asset value of less than £1 million.[3] The complainant must be a customer, payment service user, holder or beneficial owner of a collective investment scheme, beneficiary of a personal pension scheme or stakeholder pension scheme, provided a guarantee or security for a mortgage or loan, a beneficiary of a trust or estate of the establishment complained against.[4]

Similarly, jurisdiction under the Australian Financial Ombudsman Service is extended to 'retail clients' per s. 761G of the Corporations Act 2001, including small businesses as defined under that section[5] – which includes individuals, partnerships comprising of individuals, corporate

---

[3] Financial Services Authority *FSA Handbook*, available at: http://fsahandbook.info/FSA/html/handbook/DISP/2/7 [accessed 1 September 2011], DISP 2.7.3.

[4] Ibid., DISP 2.7.6.

[5] Australian Securities and Investments Commission (April 2011) *Regulatory Guide 139*, available at: www.asic.gov.au/asic/pdflib.nsf/LookupByFileName/rg139-published-20-4-2011.pdf/$file/rg139-published-20-4-2011.pdf [accessed 1 September 2011], RG 139.75.

trustees of self-managed superannuation funds or family trust, small businesses, clubs or incorporated associations, policy holders of group life or group general insurance policy.

Finally, under the Japan Financial Ombuds Service, no restrictions exist on the users entitled to bring a claim, as both customers and financial institutions are permitted to bring claims to the designated dispute resolution organisation.[6]

In all schemes examined above, a claimant's eligibility for service is broader than most arbitration-based schemes, as will be examined below.

B.   Arbitration model

In general, examining the arbitration schemes under review in this study, the jurisdictional scope of arbitral schemes appears to be somewhat narrower than the ombuds-based schemes.

As can be seen from the example of the United States in Table 9.1, because the FINRA arbitration process is entirely paid for by complainants and securities firms, jurisdictional filters are unnecessary, though the process is confined by mandate to disputes involving member broker-dealers. Under the FINRA arbitration model, few of FINRA's resources are taken up by the dispute resolution process – by contrast, the dispute resolution schemes in other common law jurisdictions are heavily subsidised, giving rise to a need to limit eligible complainants to ensure that subsidies are taken up by those with the greatest need for them.

The FDRC of Hong Kong[7] and FIDReC of Singapore both have similar jurisdictional restrictions. Both services are reserved for most retail consumer complaints in the financial sector, including individual investors and sole-proprietors.[8] However, in general, these services do not currently include jurisdiction for mid-sized businesses. The restriction on eligible complainants is perhaps unsurprising given that both the FIDReC and the FDRC are entirely new schemes. Equally, however, it should come as no surprise that observers have raised the issue of allowing small corporate

---

[6] M. Miyatake, T. Andriotis (2010). Japan's New Financial ADR System. *Bloomberg Law Reports*. Retrieved from www.hugheshubbard.com/files/Publication/e66266f4-013 0-4416-ae75-accafffcde78/Presentation/PublicationAttachment/4792b24e-4239-45 b5-a62a-b7b03488f6df/Japan's%20New%20Financial%20ADR%20System%20-%20 Andriotis%20Bloomberg%20Article.pdf.

[7] Financial Services and the Treasury Bureau, 'Proposed Establishment of an Investor Education Council and a Financial Dispute Resolution Centre', para. 3.2(a) of Part II.

[8] Ibid.

Table 9.1 *Eligible complainants for consumer financial dispute resolution services*

Type	Service	Eligible parties
Ombuds	FOS (UK)	A person who is a consumer, a micro-enterprise, a charity with an annual income of less than £1 million, or a trustee of a trust with a net asset value of less than £1 million.[a] The complainant must be a customer, payment service user, holder or beneficial owner of a collective investment scheme, beneficiary of a personal pension scheme or stakeholder pension scheme, provided a guarantee or security for a mortgage or loan, a beneficiary of a trust or estate of the establishment complained against.[b] Certain types of complainant are expressly excluded under the Rules.[c]
	FOS (Aus)	'Retail clients' per s. 761G of the Corporations Act 2001, including small businesses as defined under that section[d] – which includes individuals, partnerships comprising of individuals, corporate trustees of self-managed superannuation funds or family trust, small businesses, clubs or incorporated associations, policy holders of group life or group general insurance policy.
	JFOS (Japan)	No restrictions on the users entitled to bring a claim; both customers and financial institutions can bring a claim to the designated dispute resolution organisation.[e]

Arbitration	FIDReC (Singapore)	FIDReC's services are available to all consumers who are individuals or sole-proprietors.[f]
	FDRC (HK)	Available only to individuals and sole proprietors in the initial years of implementation. The government has not ruled out the possibility of extending the scope in the future.[g]
	FINRA (US)	Since FINRA complainants must pay an arbitration fee, a hearing deposit and attorneys' fees, cost-deterrence serves as a filter, and strict jurisdictional prerequisites for arbitration are unnecessary.[h]

[a] Financial Services Authority, *FSA Handbook*, DISP 2.7.3.

[b] Ibid., DISP 2.7.6.

[c] Ibid., DISP 2.7.9.

[d] Australian Securities and Investments Commission, *Regulatory Guide 139*, RG 139.75.

[e] Masako Miyatake, T. Andriotis, Nishimura and Asahi. (2010). Japan's New Financial ADR System. *Bloomberg Law Reports*. Retrieved from www.hugheshubbard.com/files/Publication/e66266f4-0130-4416-ae75-accafffcde78/Presentation/PublicationAttachment/47 92b24e-4239-45b5-a62a-b7b03488f6df/Japan's%20New%20Financial%20ADR%20System%20-%20Andriotis%20Bloomberg%20 Article.pdf.

[f] Financial Industry Disputes Resolution Centre Ltd, 'The Jurisdiction of FIDReC', available at: www.fidrec.com.sg/website/jurisdiction.html [accessed 1 September 2011].

[g] Financial Services and the Treasury Bureau, 'Consultation Conclusions on Proposed Establishment of an Investor Education Council and a Financial Dispute Resolution Centre', p. 9.

[h] C. Alpert, 'Financial Services in the United States and United Kingdom: Comparative Approaches to Securities Regulation and Dispute Resolution', p. 75.

bodies to also be included in the scheme – it has long been an issue that the expense of civil litigation restricts the access to justice of small- and medium-sized enterprises, described as part of the 'sandwich' class by the Judiciary in addressing concerns about access to justice in civil litigation due to high costs.[9] In addition, some concerns have been raised regarding the potential misallocation of resource due to coverage of high-net-worth individuals within the scheme in Hong Kong rather than using a criteria based on those who fall outside of the 'professional investor' class.[10] From recent discussions regarding the FDRC, it is clear that the possibility of expanding the scope of coverage remains open.[11]

Assessment and recommendations

Given that an important principle of consumer financial dispute resolution is access to justice tempered by judicious allocation of resources, both models have different mechanisms in place to balance these complementary requirements. While the ombuds model provides for a broad base of jurisdiction, intake officers, as will be discussed below, are empowered with discretion to determine whether a given dispute falls within the services jurisdiction. At the same time, the arbitration model provides for a narrower scope of jurisdiction. In particular, mid-sized firms, traditionally viewed as constituting a 'sandwich class' – above the threshold for legal aid but vulnerable to the high costs of civil litigation – could benefit from an expanded base of access to consumer financial dispute resolution services in jurisdictions such as Hong Kong and Singapore. At the same time, various classes of users such as professional investors, who comparatively have the benefit of more abundant resources, may be given a scaled charge for services to prevent the potential misallocation of resources.

Dispute type

In comparing the types of disputes complainants are permitted to submit to consumer financial dispute resolution services, in general the ombuds

---

[9] This has been commented upon by the former Chief Justice, Andrew Li, in his final speech at the Opening of the Legal Year Ceremony in 2010, and has been remarked upon by him in previous speeches also.

[10] See Part 1, Sch.1 of the Securities and Futures Ordinance (Cap. 571).

[11] Financial Services and the Treasury Bureau, 'Consultation Conclusions on Proposed Establishment of an Investor Education Council and a Financial Dispute Resolution Centre', paras. 33 and 34.

models tend to handle a wider array of disputes than most arbitration services. This is due to a number of reasons, including the fact that most ombuds schemes represent mergers of pre-existing sectoral schemes that handled a broad range of disputes, as will be discussed below.

A.   Ombuds model

In the United Kingdom, which developed its Financial Ombudsman Service as a consolidation of eight pre-existing independent ombudsmen and complaint-handling schemes[12] including the Insurance Ombudsman Bureau (as the insurance division of the FOS), the Personal Investment Authority and the Securities and Futures Authority Complaints Bureau (as the investment division of the FOS (UK)), and the Banking Ombudsman and the Building Societies Ombudsman (as the banking and loans division of the FOS (UK)),[13] as a result, the UK Financial Ombudsman Service handles a broad range of issues on a compulsory basis arising from payment services, consumer credit activities, lending money, paying money by plastic card, providing ancillary banking services and any ancillary activities including advice.[14] Individuals may voluntarily agree to FOS jurisdiction by contract[15] for matters relating to the activities of an establishment in the United Kingdom or elsewhere in the European Economic Area if the activity is directed at the United Kingdom.[16]

As for Australia, in July 2008, three of the largest existing complaints schemes in the financial services industry were consolidated into a centralised financial dispute resolution scheme approved by ASIC.[17] The Banking and Financial Services Ombudsman, the Insurance Ombudsman Service and the Financial Industry Complaints Service were merged into a single external dispute resolution service under a newly created company – the Financial Ombudsman Service. As a result, the jurisdiction

---

[12] Under Part XVI and Sch. 17 of the Financial Services and Markets Act 2000, and s. 59 of the Consumer Credit Act 2006, the FOS (UK) is set up as the statutory dispute-resolution scheme.

[13] Financial Ombudsman Service, *Annual Report 1999/2000*, p. 19.

[14] Financial Services Authority, *FSA Handbook*, DISP 2.3.1.

[15] Ibid., DISP 2.5.1.

[16] Ibid., DISP 2.6.4.

[17] Financial Ombudsman Service, 'Submission: inquiry into collapses in the financial services industry', available at: www.aph.gov.au/senate/committee/corporations_ctte/fps/submissions/sub353.pdf [accessed 31 August 2011].

of the FOS includes[18] complaints against financial service providers from individual or individuals and holders of group life or group general insurance policy where the dispute relates to the payment of benefits under the policy.

In Japan, the Financial Ombuds Service will hear complaints regarding financial instruments or services. In particular, the service applies to a number of relevant financial sub-sectors, including financial instruments,[19] investment advisory or investment management, and disputes involving financial institutions.[20]

It should be noted that even in jurisdictions where there is a single financial dispute resolution scheme, such as Australia, separate limits remain for insurance complaints.

B. Arbitration model

In examining the arbitration models under study, while most arbitration services specifically exclude insurance complaints, most such schemes hear disputes involving financial institutions and require a prior arbitration agreement.

FINRA, among the largest non-governmental regulators for securities firms doing business in the United States,[21] carries out market oversight, salesperson regulation, investor education, enforcement and arbitration. This differs from the ombudsmen used in the three common law jurisdictions, as an ombudsman exists only to provide an extra-judicial route to resolving disputes, whereas FINRA has a much wider range of regulatory functions in respect of its members, of which dispute resolution may only be a small part. As a result, FINRA[22] will hear any dispute between a customer and a member of FINRA that is submitted to arbitration. Since

---

[18] Financial Ombudsman Service, 'ASIC-approved Terms of Reference effective from 1 January 2010', amended 1 July 2010, available at: www.fos.org.au/centric/home_page/about_us/terms_of_reference_b.jsp [accessed 1 September 2011], para. 4 of section B.

[19] For definitions of Type 1 and Type 2 Financial Instrument Businesses, see Financial Instruments and Exchange Act (Act No. 25 of 1949), art. 28.

[20] M. Yokoi-Arai, 'A comparative analysis of the Financial Ombudsman Systems in the UK and Japan', p. 348.

[21] Powell, 'Business law: what Montana lawyers need to know about FINRA', p. 31.

[22] Financial Industry Regulatory Authority (29 July 2011) 'Code of Arbitration Procedures for Customer Disputes', available at: www.finra.org/web/groups/arbitrationmediation/@arbmed/@arbrul/documents/arbmed/p117546.pdf [accessed 1 September 2011].

FINRA members are primarily broker-dealers, eligible disputes will be those involving a broker-dealer.

Singapore's FIDReC's jurisdiction extends over all disputes brought by individuals and sole proprietors against financial institutions who are members of FIDReC, except disputes over commercial decisions (including pricing and other policies, e.g. interest rates and fees), cases under investigation by any law enforcement agency, and cases which have been subjected to a court hearing, for which a judgment or order is passed.[23]

The FDRC will handle disputes arising out of services provided by financial institutions which are licensees or regulatees of the HKMA or SFC that are 'monetary' in nature.[24] Specifically excluded from jurisdiction are: commercial decisions, such as the provision of credit or margin facilities; pricing-related disputes, such as the setting of fees and interest rates; and cases that have already been the subject of court proceedings.[25] These exclusions are largely in line with those in Australia and Singapore, and also those excluded in the United Kingdom.

Also explicitly excluded from the jurisdiction of the FDRC are insurance matters and Mandatory Provident (i.e. retirement) Fund matters, due to the existence of a dispute resolution scheme for the insurance sector, the Insurance Claims Complaints Bureau, and the absence of disputes characterised as 'monetary' in nature in the MPF system.[26] However, the FSTB clarified in the consultation conclusions that where there are complaints relating to insurance and MPF products sold by financial institutions within the jurisdiction of the FDRC, those complaints will fall within the jurisdiction of the FDRC – similar to the HKMA, the jurisdiction of the FDRC is institutional, rather than sectoral. The ultimate aim is that FDRC's scope be comprehensive, and thus the coverage of the FDRC will be reviewed from time to time.[27]

---

[23] Monetary Authority of Singapore, 'Policy Consultation on the Financial Industry Disputes Resolution Centre'.

[24] Financial Services and the Treasury Bureau, 'Proposed Establishment of an Investor Education Council and a Financial Dispute Resolution Centre', para. 3.2 of Part II.

[25] Ibid., para. 3.8.   [26] Ibid., para. 3.5.

[27] Financial Services and the Treasury Bureau, 'Consultation Conclusions on Proposed Establishment of an Investor Education Council and a Financial Dispute Resolution Centre', paras. 37–39.

Table 9.2 *Dispute types across ombuds and arbitration services*

Type	Service	Disputes
Ombuds	FOS (UK)	The activities to which the compulsory jurisdiction of the FOS applies are regulated activities (see s. 22 of the Financial Services and Markets Act 2000), payment services, consumer credit activities, lending money secured by a charge on land, lending money, paying money by plastic card, providing ancillary banking services or any ancillary activities including advice.[a] The territorial scope of the compulsory jurisdiction is restricted to activities carried on from an establishment in the UK.[b] The voluntary jurisdiction applies to a list of activities similar to those listed under the compulsory jurisdiction, but are not covered by either the compulsory jurisdiction or the consumer credit jurisdiction. The person carrying on the activities must be subject to the voluntary jurisdiction by contract.[c] The voluntary jurisdiction covers the activities of an establishment in the UK or elsewhere in the European Economic Area if the activity is directed at the UK, the contracts governing the activity are made under UK law, and the relevant establishment has notified appropriate regulators in its home state of its intention to participate in the voluntary jurisdiction.[d]
	FOS (Aus)	The jurisdiction of the FOS includes:[e] complaints against financial service providers from individual or individuals, partnerships comprising of individuals, corporate trustees of self-managed superannuation funds or family trust, small businesses, clubs or incorporated associations, policy holders of group life or group general insurance policy where the dispute relates to the payment of benefits under the policy; disputes that arise from a contract or obligation under Australian law in respect of the provision of a financial service, provision of a guarantee or security for financial accommodation, entitlement or benefits under life insurance or general insurance policies, legal or beneficial interests arising out of financial investment or a financial risk facility, claims under motor vehicle insurance policies;

		and excludes disputes relating to:[f] confidentiality or privacy obligations; levels of fees, premiums, charges or interest rates; assessment of credit risk; considerations taken into account in respect of life insurance policies offered on non-standard terms; decisions to refuse to provide insurance coverage; investment performance of a financial investment; decisions of trustees of approved deposit funds and regulated superannuation funds; relating to the management of a fund or scheme as a whole; decisions as to allocation of benefits of financial products between competing claims; matters that have already been dealt with by a court of dispute resolution tribunal; matters where legal proceedings have already been commenced; matters already lodged with and being dealt with by another external dispute resolution scheme approved by ASUC; claims in excess of AU$500,000 (though the maximum monetary compensation is below this amount).[g]
	JFOS (Japan)	All general complaints and disputes related to financial instruments or services are covered under the Financial ADR System. The Law on Partial Revision of the Financial Instruments and Exchange Law for 2009 (Law No 58) promulgated on 24 June 2009 applies the ombudsman service system to 16 relevant financial sub-sectors, including: Type 1 and Type 2 Financial Instrument Businesses[h] Investment Advisory and Agency Business or Investment Management Business; Registered Financial Institutions; and Securities Finance Companies.[i]
Arbitration	FDRC (HK)	Includes disputes involving a monetary elements arising from the dealing with financial institutions which are licensees or regulatees of the Hong Kong Monetary Authority (HKMA) and Securities and Futures Commission (SFC).[j]

Table 9.2 (*cont.*)

Type	Service	Disputes
	FIDReC (Singapore)	FIDReC's jurisdiction extends over all disputes brought by individuals and sole proprietors against financial institutions who are members of FIDReC, except disputes over commercial decisions (including pricing and other policies, e.g. interest rates and fees), cases under investigation by any law enforcement agency, and cases which have been subjected to a court hearing, for which a judgment or order is passed.[k]
	FINRA (US)	The FINRA Code of Arbitration Procedures for Customer Disputes[l] applies to any dispute between a customer and a member of FINRA that is submitted to arbitration.

[a] Financial Services Authority, *FSA Handbook*, DISP 2.3.1.

[b] Ibid., DISP 2.6.1.

[c] Ibid., DISP 2.5.1.

[d] Ibid., DISP 2.6.4.

[e] Financial Ombudsman Service, 'ASIC-approved Terms of Reference effective from 1 January 2010', para. 4 of section B.

[f] Ibid., para. 5 of section B.

[g] Ibid., para. 9.7.

[h] For definitions of Type 1 and Type 2 Financial Instrument Businesses, see Financial Instruments and Exchange Act (Act No. 25 of 1949), art. 28.

[i] Yokoi-Arai, 'A comparative analysis of the Financial Ombudsman Systems in the UK and Japan'.

[j] See Financial Services and the Treasury Bureau, 'Consultation Conclusions on Proposed Establishment of an Investor Education Council and a Financial Dispute Resolution Centre', pp. 9–10.

[k] Monetary Authority of Singapore, 'Policy Consultation on the Financial Industry Disputes Resolution Centre'.

[l] Financial Industry Regulatory Authority, 'Code of Arbitration Procedures for Customer Disputes'.

Assessment and recommendations

While the financial dispute resolution schemes of the United Kingdom and Australia were mergers of pre-existing sectoral schemes and therefore include broad coverage for insurance and pension related disputes, for emergent systems such as those in Hong Kong, Japan and Singapore, it is probably preferable that insurance and pension related disputes remain outside of the jurisdiction of such dispute resolution services at the outset. Insurance products in particular, often having their own dispute resolution scheme, could potentially give rise to confusion. Moreover, there is potential for overlapping jurisdictions to give rise to disparity of awards, which would lead to consumer dissatisfaction.

In light of principles of consistency, it is also recommended that newly emergent schemes consider having a sectoral basis in the short term and an institutional basis in the long term. A sectoral basis would help to avoid the issues of inconsistency, confusion and forum-shopping by eligible complainants in the short run and reflect the underlying regulatory regime that applies to the services that are the subject of resolution. Hence, pension and insurance disputes should be referred back to the relevant dispute resolution/complaint scheme. In the long term, given the increasing integration of financial products, uniform handling processes of such disputes must be developed in conjunction with such schemes in order to ensure that such disputes are dealt with in the same way.

Procedural models

In examining procedural models of consumer financial dispute resolution, a number of similarities, as well as some unique distinctions, can be drawn between schemes. Most, if not all schemes, operate on a three-stage tiered process. First, there is a preliminary stage at which complaints will be assessed for whether or not they fall within the jurisdiction of the service. Often parties at this stage are encouraged to engage in direct settlement talks with the responsible financial institution. Following this step and where the complaint falls within the relevant jurisdictional parameters of the dispute resolution service, it will either be negotiated or mediated. Finally, if mediation or negotiation fails to resolve the dispute, it will be referred to either an ombudsperson or an arbitrator.[28] Each stage of these procedural steps will be examined in greater detail below.

[28] Financial Services and the Treasury Bureau, 'Proposed Establishment of an Investor Education Council and a Financial Dispute Resolution Centre', para. 3.9 of Part II.

Table 9.3 *Comparative features of the preliminary stage*

Type	Service	Preliminary Stage
Ombuds	FOS (UK)	The approach of the FOS (UK) will depend on the facts of the complaint, but generally, at the preliminary stage the FOS (UK) will first gather facts regarding the nature of the complaint. A complaint may be dismissed without having its merits considered where it is considered that the complainant is unlikely to suffer financial loss, material distress or inconvenience, the complaint is frivolous or vexatious, or has no reasonable prospect of success, the establishment complained against has already made an offer of compensation or goodwill payment that is fair and reasonable in the circumstances and still open for acceptance, the subject matter of the complaint has been or is being dealt with by court proceedings, or is more suitably dealt with by the court or other arbitration or complaints scheme.[a]
	FOS (Aus)	The FOS (Aus) will review and consider the dispute, and try to resolve the dispute through mutual agreement.[b]
	JFOS (Japan)	Following initial intake by the JFOS,[c] parties seek a negotiated settlement with the relevant financial institution.[d]
Arbitration	FDRC (HK)	The claimant initiates a proceeding by submitting a claim form to the FDRC listing out the issues under dispute, the claimed amount of financial loss, and the relevant correspondence with the financial institution. Intake officers will gather information from both parties and invite the implicated financial institution to respond.[e]

| FIDReC (Singapore) | First, the Counselling Service assists in a preliminary review of the case based on facts and documents provided by the complainant. FIDReC's officer highlights relevant clauses (in the contract, sales documents or other documents) or issues to the consumer. After the preliminary review, the consumer is provided with a copy of FIDReC's Dispute Resolution Form and allowed time to consider whether to proceed to lodge a formal complaint against the financial institution in question.[f] |
| FINRA (US) | FINRA Dispute Resolution ('FINRADR') is generally initiated following the submission of a claim by claimant who is subject to a prior FINRA arbitration clause. |

[a] Financial Services Authority, *FSA Handbook*, DISP 3.3.4.

[b] Financial Ombudsman Service, 'Dispute handling process in detail'.

[c] Financial Instruments and Exchange Act, art. 144–56.

[d] Financial Instruments and Exchange Act, art. 145–56.

[e] Financial Services and the Treasury Bureau, 'Consultation Paper on the Proposed Establishment of an Investor Education Council and a Financial Dispute Resolution Centre'.

[f] Financial Industry Disputes Resolution Centre Ltd Annual Report 2009/10.

The preliminary stage

In assessing the preliminary stage a number of similarities can be found as well as some unique distinctions between schemes. For the most part, all preliminary stages include a process of fact finding to determine whether the complaint falls within the jurisdiction of the service. However, variation exists as to the extent to which intake officers are empowered to advise potential claimants on the merits of their claim.

A.   Ombuds model

The effort to weed out complaints that lack merit and other abuses that could be a drain on resources at the early stage is not unusual. In common law jurisdictions, it is not unusual for complaints falling outside the jurisdiction of a tribunal to be excluded without a hearing, but in the United Kingdom, it is the Ombudsman who is empowered to dismiss a complaint without a hearing on its merits for a number of well-defined reasons.[29] Such a determination is of course made on the basis of the ombudsman's relevant expertise and experience. This decision is significant in that it ultimately impacts the claimant's ability to access justice. Therefore it is imperative that if intake officers are empowered with this authority, they be trained not only with mediation knowledge but also knowledge about the financial industry, and either be subject to review or reviewed following an application by the relevant financial institution on clearly established grounds. The prospect of dismissal without hearing or review at such an early stage is an area for potential abuse and therefore safeguards and oversight will be necessary.

Given the limits of available resources, a balance must be struck between access to justice and preventing abuses of process. Weeding out complaints at such an early stage may not be appropriate in some cases given the lack of evidence at this stage. Care must also be taken that the intake officer's mandate to explore settlement and his power to exercise final discretion over vexatious or frivolous claims not impose improper pressure on complainants to settle.

---

[29] Financial Services Authority, *FSA Handbook*, DISP 3.3.4.

B.   Arbitration model

The preliminary stage[30] of the Hong Kong FDRC dispute resolution process involves an intake officer, who is trained with mediation knowledge. Complainants make an enquiry, and it is then up to the intake officer to address the enquiry and decide whether or not the dispute raised by the complainant is within the jurisdiction of the FDRC. Where that dispute falls within the jurisdiction of the FDRC, the complainant will complete a claim form, upon receipt of which the intake officer will conduct a fact-finding exercise and also invite a response from the relevant financial institution. The intake officers at this stage explore the possible settlement of the dispute before it enters the mediation stage, and have discretion not to process a dispute where it appears frivolous or vexatious.

The preliminary stage of the Hong Kong FDRC bears some resemblance to the preliminary review of Singaporean FIDReC, though the proposed exploration of an early settlement does not appear to go as far as to highlight relevant clauses and issues for the complainant. The experience in Singapore reflects a high success rate with its case management process, introduced in 2007. For the thirty-six months commencing 1 July 2007 to 30 June 2010, FIDReC's Counselling Service amicably resolved 1,634 cases, saving time and resources.[31] This measure was designed to further enhance its dispute resolution processes, and is especially suitable for resolving disputes which are simple in scope. It does this by helping the consumer better understand the relevant issues in dispute as well as aid the consumer to consider any settlement offer made by the financial institution in a more objective light.

Assessment and recommendations

Relevant principles including access to justice, transparency, efficiency and accountability have relevance when considering the design of the preliminary stage.

In light of the high rate of success in Singapore, consideration may be given to examining some of its effective settlement practices including

---

[30] Financial Services and the Treasury Bureau, 'Proposed Establishment of an Investor Education Council and a Financial Dispute Resolution Centre', paras. 3.10–3.12 of Part II.

[31] Financial Industry Disputes Resolution Centre Ltd, *Annual Report 2009/10.*

early clarification of issues between parties. This would help to make the entire dispute resolution process more efficient, and indeed, such early reviews may help a high number of cases reach an early settlement.

Care must be taken, however, when considering the degree to which intake officers should have discretion over the exclusion of complaints thought to be frivolous or vexatious. In general, processes against frivolous or vexatious complainants are usually initiated by the respondent rather than the arbiter.

Second stage: mediation/conciliation

All leading jurisdictions have come to rely primarily on mediation as the preferred process for the resolution of disputes, given mediation's speed and simplicity. All jurisdictions studied show that the vast majority of cases are concluded at the mediation stage. The criticisms that have been levelled against alternative dispute resolution processes, such as the lack of an independent and impartial third party during negotiations, and the capacity for such processes to mask inbuilt power inequalities between the parties[32] are real concerns that must be examined alongside considerations of efficiency.[33]

Forms of mediation

Generally speaking, among the numerous modes of mediation processes, there are two general modes of mediation relevant to the resolution of consumer financial disputes: facilitative, which is interest based; and evaluative, or rights based.

In interest-based mediation, the mediator assists or facilitates communications between the parties and negotiations generally. The role of the mediator is to help the parties reach a settlement via exploration of the parties' underlying interests and needs.[34]

On the other hand, evaluative mediation involves a mediator making an assessment of and expressing a view on the merits of the dispute, albeit

---

[32] The Hon McClellan J, 'Civil Justice in Australia – Changes in the Trial Process', p. 65.

[33] H. Genn (2009) *Judging Civil Justice*. The Hameline Lectures 2008, Cambridge University Press.

[34] See for example: L. P. Love (2000) 'Images of justice', *Pepperdine Dispute Resolution Law Journal*, available at: http://papers.ssrn.com/sol3/papers.cfm?abstract_id=229990 [accessed 26 April 2012].

Table 9.4 *Comparative features of the mediation/conciliation stage*

Type	Service	Mediation/Conciliation Stage
Ombuds	FOS (UK)	The approach of the FOS (UK) will depend on the facts of the complaint, but generally, the FOS (UK) will attempt to settle the complaint informally through mediation or conciliation.[a]
	FOS (Aus)	The FOS (Aus) will review and consider the dispute, and try to resolve the dispute through mutual agreement, including conciliation or negotiation methods.[b]
	JFOS (Japan)	Following initial intake by the JFOS,[c] parties seek a negotiated settlement with the relevant financial institution.[d]
Arbitration	FDRC (HK)	Following case intake, the FDRC will decide whether it is able to accept the case for mediation. A mediation session will take place after both parties agree on the appointment of a mediator.[e]
	FIDReC (Singapore)	Following initial consultation and case submission, a case manager will try to mediate a settlement between the consumer and financial institution. Where appropriate, mediation conferences are arranged to allow parties to communicate face to face.[f]
	FINRA (US)	FINRA Dispute Resolution ('FINRADR') provides a non-binding mediation programme that can be used at the agreement of both parties.

[a] Financial Services Authority, *FSA Handbook*, DISP 3.3.4.
[b] Financial Ombudsman Service, 'Dispute handling process in detail'.
[c] Financial Instruments and Exchange Act, art. 144–56.
[d] Financial Instruments and Exchange Act, art. 145–56.
[e] Financial Services and the Treasury Bureau, 'Proposed Establishment of an Investor Education Council and a Financial Dispute Resolution Centre'.
[f] Financial Industry Disputes Resolution Centre Ltd, *Annual Report 2005/6*.

a non-binding view.[35] This form of mediation is more common to the Ombudsman process in other jurisdictions, and is closer to the command model of dispute resolution (i.e. where a third party is empowered to suggest a resolution of the dispute) than a consensual model (i.e. where the power to resolve the dispute rests with the parties).

What form of mediation is to be deployed has implications for consideration of what type of dispute resolution methods are most appropriate for use in the context of financial regulation, and how the aims of financial regulation inform the choice of method.

Challenges associated with the mediation process

Despite the success mediation has enjoyed in terms of high rates of settlement, it is a form of alternative dispute resolution that is not without its critics. The risk of mediation, being an unregulated form of 'informal justice' – enjoying a quasi-regulatory authority without the safeguards that are built into litigation – is that it can mask power imbalances in the relationship between parties. This in turn could lead to consumer dissatisfaction. For conservative litigators, alternative dispute resolution techniques raise concerns when compared to the operation of the courts in that there is a lack of scrutiny of the third party during negotiations. Such critics may also point to the heavier cost consequences in the event that alternative dispute resolution processes break down and necessitate court intervention.[36]

Appropriateness of mediation in consumer financial dispute resolution

One key issue in the facilitative model of mediation is that the solution is negotiated, but not required to be principled. This limits the role that the substantive law plays in the settlement of a dispute – as the positive law norm enforcement is subordinated to the dispute resolution process. In the context of financial markets, this may not be desirable for consumers, whose complaints or grievances are likely to arise from a sense of wrongdoing on the part of financial service providers and thus parties may have expectations about the protection of the consumers' rights and principled

---

[35] See L. L. Riskin (1997) 'Understanding mediators' orientations, strategies, and techniques: a grid for the perplexed', *Harvard Negotiation Law Review*, 1(7), available at: http://ssrn.com/abstract=1506684 [accessed 26 April 2012].

[36] The Hon McClellan J, 'Civil Justice in Australia – Changes in the Trial Process'.

settlements to reflect those rights. For example, in many instances, complainants are not in a position to unravel the complex structure of these instruments in order to quantify the risk they potentially represent, and thus know the true value of their own claims. This could place complainants at an enormous disadvantage when trying to resolve their disputes with relevant financial institutions, in not being fully aware of what their rights against the financial institutions are. Overcoming this issue requires the integration of legal norms to enhance transparency and consistency of settlements. While this does not necessarily require the use of judicial procedures such as discovery or the availability of judicial scrutiny over the process, the examination of merits such as in evaluative mediation may potentially lend itself towards a more satisfactory experience for consumers than interest-based mediation.

Where there is a large imbalance of power between the two parties to a dispute, third parties may be called upon in order to redress that balance. The power imbalance to be addressed in the financial industry between consumers and financial service providers is based on the assumption that the financial institution is in the best position of knowledge in respect of products, services and risks – arguably even better than regulators. Therefore, safeguards, such as regulatory and legal guidelines and external oversight, may be required to effectively address such imbalances.

Assessment and recommendations

In examining best practices for the mediation stage of a consumer financial dispute resolution mechanism, consideration may be given to the possible incorporation of information sharing regarding relevant standards and regulation in the context of mediation, in line with the practices of ombudsmen in other jurisdictions. The relevant power imbalances that consumer financial dispute resolution services will primarily be called upon to address involve the state of knowledge between the financial service provider and the consumer. An approach to dispute resolution that integrates regulatory standards or uses them as touchstones appears to be more consistent with the aims of financial oversight, which is largely disclosure based.

Third step: a fork in the road – ombuds or arbitration process

The distinction between the ombuds and arbitration models can be seen most distinctly at the third stage of the resolution process. Most

Table 9.5 *Third stage: ombuds or arbitration procedure*

Type	Service	Third Stage Procedure
Ombuds	FOS (UK)	Where one side is unhappy with the adjudicator's view, they can ask for a review and final decision by an ombudsman. At this stage, the ombudsman will perform an independent review of the complaint. The ombudsman will determine complaints by reference to what is fair and reasonable in the circumstances.[a] In determining what is fair and reasonable, the ombudsman will have regard for the relevant laws and regulations, regulators' rules, guidance and standards, codes of practice, and what the ombudsman considers to be good industry practice at the time.[b]
	FOS (Aus)	Where mutual agreement is not possible, the FOS (Aus) will conduct a detailed investigation and may offer initial views on the merits of the dispute. The FOS (Aus) will often issue a Recommendation, and if the Recommendation is not accepted by either party, a Determination can be made.[c]
	JFOS (Japan)	A settlement proposal or a special mediation proposal will be offered by the dispute resolution committee in each dispute. A financial institution is not obliged to accept a settlement proposal but the Ministry of Finance may compel acceptance of a special mediation proposal[d] unless a customer does not accept a special mediation proposal; a customer or a financial institution files a lawsuit or does not withdraw a lawsuit that has already been filed; or a settlement is reached between a customer and financial institution.[e]
Arbitration	FDRC (HK)	If mediation is unsuccessful, claimants can choose to bring the case further to arbitration. The arbitration awards are final and binding on both sides. The claimant will not be able to pursue the case in court even if he does not agree with the arbitration award.[f]

FIDReC (Singapore)	Disputes that cannot be resolved by mediation and case management will be graduated to the third stage, where an adjudicator or panel of adjudicators with relevant expertise will decide in favour of either the consumer or the financial institution.[g]
FINRA (US)	The majority of contracts between salespersons, broker-dealer firms and customers of the securities industry include arbitration requirements – even if a customer agreement does not contain a pre-dispute arbitration clause, FINRA Code of Arbitration Procedure for Customer Disputes Rule 12200 requires broker-dealers to submit to arbitration on the demand of a customer.[h]

[a] Financial Services Authority, *FSA Handbook*, DISP 3.6.1. See also s. 228 of the Financial Services and Markets Act 2000.

[b] Financial Services Authority, *FSA Handbook*, DISP 3.6.4.

[c] Financial Ombudsman Service, 'Dispute handling process in detail'. Masako *et al.* (2010).

[d] Masako *et al.* (2010).

[e] Freshfields Bruckhaus Deringer, 'Financial Alternative Dispute Resolution System'.

[f] Financial Services and the Treasury Bureau, 'Proposed Establishment of an Investor Education Council and a Financial Dispute Resolution Centre'.

[g] Monetary Authority of Singapore (October 2004) 'Policy Consultation on the Financial Industry Disputes Resolution Centre'.

[h] J. I. Gross, 'The end of mandatory securities arbitration?', 30, p. 1174.

significantly, the ombuds determination is made without prejudice to the complainant, while the arbitrators' decision is binding on both parties. These distinctions will be examined in greater detail below.

A.   Ombuds model perceptions of ombudsmen

In exploring the application of principles of fairness, one comparative article has noted the relatively higher perception of fairness among consumers who have used the ombuds process in comparison with the arbitration process due to the adoption of an inquisitorial approach.[37]

While the majority of disputes resolved by the FOS are resolved at the conciliation and adjudication stage, the multi-tiered structure involving adjudicators and ombudsmen provides the benefit of what has been described as 'effectively an internal right of appeal in FOS procedures'.[38]

The internal review of initial assessments of the merits is of particular importance in the context of the statutory power to resolve disputes with reference to what is fair and reasonable. While the determinations of the Ombudsmen are subject to judicial review, they 'thus far ha[ve] a narrow focus in terms of intervention being confined to instances of irrationality rather than the courts substituting their opinion on the merits for that of an ombudsman'.[39] The policy of non-intervention from the courts serves to strengthen the authority of the determinations of the Ombudsmen and enhances the finality of their decisions, particularly as against financial services firms. At the same time, consumers can have the benefit of the merits of their complaints being reviewed by both an adjudicator and an ombudsman.

The work of ombudsmen

Studies have also demonstrated the ombudsman model offers a more level playing field to consumers than litigation.[40] Previous studies in respect of litigation tend to suggest that 'haves', i.e. government units, large businesses, high socio-economic status groups, tend to fare better in courts

---

[37]   A. Samuel, 'With arbitration facing restrictions, it's time to look at a UK solution for consumer disputes', pp. 111–113.

[38]   Ibid.   [39]   Ibid.

[40]   S. Gilad, 'Why the "haves" do not necessarily come out ahead in informal dispute resolution', p. 307.

than 'have nots'.[41] An explanation for this is the fact that 'repeat players' tend to fare better than individuals or 'one shotters' in court as a result of structural advantages and institutional limitations of the adversarial court system.[42] Repeat players, such as financial service providers in the context of financial disputes, tend to have enhanced access to specialised resources and expertise devoted to handling similar, recurrent disputes; are likely to develop informal relationships with courts and other dispute resolution forums; and can be strategic in the management of individual disputes since each individual case is of lower relative importance to them.[43]

A study which applied these hypotheses to the FOS (UK) to determine whether 'repeat players' fare better than 'one shotters' in ombuds processes, however, found that larger or more experienced firms are not necessarily more successful in defending complaints against them, which may be explained by the informal and ad hoc nature of FOS adjudications – large firms were less capable of playing for rules.[44] Furthermore, professionally represented complainants were less likely to win, perhaps because of the perception on the part of an adjudicator that legally represented complainants might have weaker complaints, and rather than strengthening the complainant's position, a legal representative might equally attempt to play for the rules.[45] The study also found that there was no higher success rate at the FOS for complaints filed by more financially resourced socio-economic groups.[46]

One conclusion that may be drawn is that the informal dispute resolution as carried out by the FOS is explicitly designed to offset some of the advantages enjoyed by repeat players in court litigation, thus providing consumers with a level playing field.[47] Whether or not those advantages would also be applicable in comparison with arbitration, which, as noted above, is a process relatively similar to litigation, is arguable.

Another empirical study has shown that the approach of adjudicators at the FOS and their own perception of their role is not only to adjudicate complaints, but also to manage expectations of consumers – to bridge the gap between a professional analysis of retail-finance complaints and the

---

[41] M. Galanter, 'Why the "haves" come out ahead: speculations on the limits of legal change', pp. 95–160.

[42] Ibid.

[43] Ibid., p. 284.   [44] Ibid., pp. 301–302.   [45] Ibid., p. 303.

[46] Ibid., p. 305.   [47] Ibid., p. 307.

complainant's perception of mistreatment and expectation for redress.[48] In this way, the FOS process does not merely involve holding service providers to account but also shifting consumer expectation and attitudes.[49] While this may appear to be contradictory to the role of accountability the FOS plays, it is arguable that such management is necessary to deal with excessive expectation on the part of consumers as well as the engendering of confidence in the complaint-handling process even if the outcome is adverse for the consumer.

B.   Arbitration

Where a mediation is unsuccessful, a complainant may proceed to arbitrate his claim. Arbitration will generally take the form of a documents-only arbitration, before a single arbitrator, unless the issues are too complex, in which case the arbitrator will determine whether or not a hearing is necessary. Among the benefits of arbitration is its final binding nature.[50] One key issue in respect of appropriateness is: following the failure of the mediation process, what is the reason the parties have failed to reach a settlement? Where there are inconsistent interpretations of the facts or rules, the role of an intervening third party is interpretive, i.e. requiring an adjudicator.

The differences between arbitrators and ombudsmen

While both arbitrators and ombudsmen serve as independent and impartial umpires in a dispute, their accountability differs significantly. Arbitrators in some jurisdictions are empowered to make awards without explaining their decisions, and awards may be appealed to the courts only on very limited grounds while being binding on the parties.[51] Ombudsmen will generally have to provide reasoned decisions, and not only may they be susceptible to the oversight of the courts by way of judicial review, their awards are also not binding unless accepted by the complainant.

---

[48] S. Gilad, 'Accountability or expectations management? The role of the ombudsman in financial regulation', p. 245.

[49] Ibid., p. 246.

[50] Financial Services and the Treasury Bureau, 'Proposed Establishment of an Investor Education Council and a Financial Dispute Resolution Centre', paras. 3.15–3.16 of Part II.

[51] See FINRA rules at www.finra.org/Industry/Regulation/FINRARules/ [accessed 26 May 2012].

In two of the three common law jurisdictions studied (the United Kingdom and Australia), an ombudsman was established; in Singapore, 'adjudicators' are used. On the one hand, adjudicators bear some similarity to ombudsmen given the non-binding nature of their award on complainants. However, on the other hand, the adjudicators are functionally similar to arbitrators in that they are independent and act wholly in their own capacity and are not employees, agents or independent contractors of FIDReC.[52]

Along the dispute resolution spectrum, arbitration is next to litigation in the degree to which authority is transferred to a third party decision maker. By contrast, it is debatable whether or not ombudsmen can properly be viewed within the ambit of alternative dispute resolution, or should instead be considered a hybrid in light of the ombudsman's investigative function in the examination of grievances and the non-binding nature of his decision, as opposed to a straightforward resolution of disputes. The hybrid nature of the ombudsman between consensus building and adjudication can also be seen in its lack of formality – in contrast with the formality of arbitration.

While the arbitration process is adversarial, the ombudsman process is inquisitorial. The adversarial nature of arbitration raises the issue of whether or not the aims of deploying an alternative dispute resolution procedure, such as the preservation of the parties' relationship, might be adversely affected. It has often been noted that it is difficult for hostility not to escalate between parties in an adversarial process – which is unfortunate though perhaps not completely avoidable in a service provider–consumer relationship.

The challenge to mandatory arbitration

Unlike Hong Kong, the United States, along with Canada and Australia, allow for class actions in a number of sectors including disputes over retail financial products such as securities. However, while this litigation mechanism was originally intended to provide relief to aggrieved investors, it has become 'an inefficient and grossly incomplete means of redress for investors, a costly encumbrance to businesses, and a threat to capital formation in the United States' – in short, a hindrance on the growth of financial markets and other economic activities related to

---

[52] See www.fidrec.com.sg/website/adjudicators.html [accessed 26 May 2012].

financial markets.[53] The system of arbitration in the area of financial disputes and securities is thus intended not only as an alternative to securities litigation, but to 'facilitate capital formation, make US markets more competitive on the global stage, and ultimately spur economic growth by reducing the costs of capital'.[54] Unfortunately, with the perceptions of bias in the arbitral process, and its compulsory nature, it has been argued that the inability of aggrieved investors to enforce their rights through a more efficient mechanism has led to market inefficiency in the US, which in the context of the foregoing, has a detrimental effect on the health of the economic system.[55]

Supreme Court case law in the US appears to have gone back and forth on the issue of whether or not pre-dispute agreements to arbitrate claims under the Securities Act of 1933 are enforceable or not. In the landmark case of *Wilko v. Swan* 346 U.S. 427 (1953), the Supreme Court held that such agreements were not enforceable due to the risk of arbitrators misapplying the law, which the courts would not be able to overturn due to the Federal Arbitration Act, and as such, was against the public interest. However, in *Shearson/American Express, Inc. v. McMahon* 482 U.S. 220 (1987), the Supreme Court distinguished *Wilko v. Swan* as being decided under the Securities Act of 1933 and not the Securities Exchange Act of 1934, and 'must be read as barring waiver of a judicial forum only where arbitration is inadequate to protect the substantive rights at issue'. The Supreme Court finally expressly overruled *Wilko v. Swan* in *Rodriguez de Quijas v. Shearson/American Express, Inc.* 490 U.S. 477 (1989).[56]

However, mandatory arbitration has raised questions of fairness, resulting in the introduction of bills by the Senate and the House to enact an Arbitration Fairness Act of 2009, which reflect findings that the Federal Arbitration Act was intended to apply to disputes between commercial entities of similar sophistication and bargaining power, but that Supreme Court decisions had extended the Act to disputes between

---

[53] B. J. Bondi, 'Facilitating economic recovery and sustainable growth through reform of the securities class-action system: exploring arbitration as an alternative to litigation', pp. 607–638.

[54] Ibid.

[55] B. Stark, 'Compulsory arbitration: its impact on the efficiency of markets', p. 399.

[56] B. B. Zoltowski, 'Restoring investor confidence: providing uniformity in securities arbitration by offering guidelines for arbitrators in deciding motions to dismiss before a hearing on the merits', S. Kratsch, 'The financial crisis: arbitration as a viable option for European financial institutions'.

parties of unequal bargaining power.[57] The Act has yet to be passed due to other legislative priorities, but under s. 921 of the Dodd-Frank Wall Street Reform and Consumer Protection Act, the Securities Exchange Commission is now empowered to limit or prohibit the use of arbitration agreements.[58]

The fairness of the arbitration processes is also in doubt due to practitioner views that the discovery process is not respected by the securities industry as it is not believed that an arbitral panel is as likely as a sitting judge to sanction securities firms for discovery violations and other such behaviour.[59]

Cost and complexity

The complexity of arbitrations in the area of consumer financial disputes including securities disputes has also increased to such an extent that in many cases it now resembles judicial proceedings subject to rules of civil procedure, though the arbitral process contains none of the procedural safeguards found in civil procedure – arguably a result of the lack of judicial oversight. This has resulted in the cost of such arbitration proceedings increasing significantly: '[i]t is not atypical for a four-day arbitration evidentiary hearing, coupled with the costs of pre-hearing conferences, to produce fees and expense billings from the NASD totalling substantially in excess of $10,000.'[60]

Empirical evidence concerning arbitral fairness

Empirical evidence in respect of the arbitration process in consumer financial and securities disputes has led to the conclusions that investors have concerns about the possible bias of arbitrators, and despite the fact that arbitration is relatively well established, many investors lack knowledge of the process.[61] Empirical evidence has also shown that arbitrators who also represent brokerage firms or brokers in other arbitrations award

[57] J. I. Gross, 'The end of mandatory securities arbitration?'.
[58] B. Black, 'How to improve retail investor protection after the Dodd-Frank Wall Street Reform and Consumer Protection Act'.
[59] Ibid.
[60] Little, 'Fairness is in the eyes of the beholder'.
[61] J. I. Gross and B. Black, 'When perception changes reality: an empirical study of investors' views of the fairness of securities arbitration'.

significantly less compensation to investor-claimants than do other arbitrators.[62]

There is further empirical evidence from the United States to show that investor win rates in securities arbitration have fallen significantly, from 59 per cent in 1989–1990 to only 37 per cent in 2007. This falling win rate has been attributed to increases in settled claims rather than pro-industry bias.[63] However, it has been argued that changes to investor perception of the fairness of the FINRA arbitral process may be linked to the market itself, and the fact that in a period of market instability, more awards and damages are likely to go in favour of investors while in a period of stability, this is less likely.[64] Ironically, what this means is that it is likely that in light of the recent financial crisis, investors will receive larger and more frequent awards, and investor surveys will likely find that the users of the arbitral process believe the present form of arbitration to be fair.

Another study has also shown that there is a tendency for arbitral panels in consumer financial and securities arbitration to 'split the baby' when it comes to the amount of compensatory damages.[65]

There is also evidence to show that arbitrators may not be applying the law consistently in such arbitrations due to instructions that such application is unnecessary or because of a lack of comprehension in respect of the law or factual issues in dispute.[66]

Assessment and recommendations

The true advantage arbitration offers is that it can be customised as needed. The advantages offered by the ombudsman model do not necessarily mean that an ombudsman model need be adopted wholesale; rather, elements of the arbitration process may be customised to resemble the ombudsman model or to offer its benefits. Rather than to adopt a papers-only arbitration, which offers efficiency but may raise issues about transparency, particularly in the decision-making process, a procedure resembling the Small Claims Tribunal should be considered. Complainants should still

---

[62] S. Choi, J. E. Fisch and A. C. Pritchard (2010) 'Attorneys as arbitrators'.
[63] Ibid.
[64] S. D. Grannum, 'The faith and face of securities arbitration: after the 2008 crash' p. 111.
[65] Little, 'Fairness is in the eyes of the beholder'.
[66] Ibid.

be offered a papers-only arbitration if they prefer, with costs scaled appropriately, but complainants should not be denied the opportunity to air their grievances in person and to scrutinise the decision-making process – particularly as it appears from the experience in the United Kingdom that a more personal approach is more successful in working with consumer expectations and attitudes.

Although proponents of arbitration argue that finality may be one of the key advantages offered over the ombudsman model, serious consideration should be given to increasing the scrutiny of the courts over the arbitral process. While in the short term, this may lead to increased costs, the long-term advantage is the potential strengthening of arbitral authoritativeness through its interaction and confirmation by the courts.

Awards

In examining the jurisdictions under study, a number of distinctions can be seen with respect to the nature, scope and binding character of awards. Of significance, all ombuds models leave the complainant free to decide whether to accept the final award without prejudice. Under the ombuds model, the ombudsperson has the ability to give directions regarding the resolution of the dispute in a manner considered to be just and appropriate regardless of whether a court could have made such an order. Under both FINRA and the Hong Kong FDRC process, the final arbitral award is binding on both parties. Within the arbitration model, the only jurisdiction in which no statutory cap is imposed on the award amount is the FINRA arbitration process.

Assessment and recommendations

Given the increasing range in value of retail consumer investments, for jurisdictions with caps below £50,000, consideration should be given to raising the limit to £100,000 in order to provide greater access to financial dispute resolution services. This would also serve to ensure that the courts need not be overly burdened by smaller claims and at the same time, would enable a greater number of consumers to make use of the financial dispute resolution service rather than be forced to engage in costly litigation purely because their claims are of a sum higher than £50,000.

Table 9.6 *Comparison of award type*

Type	Service	Awards
Ombuds	FOS (UK)	The maximum money award the ombudsman may make is £100,000[a] (approx. HK$1,270,000), from which costs, interest on the principal award and interest on costs are excluded.[b] If the ombudsman considers fair compensation requires payment of a larger amount, it may recommend that the complainant be paid the balance.[c] In addition to money awards, interest awards and costs awards, the ombudsman is also empowered to give directions in respect of steps to be taken by the establishment complained against as the ombudsman considers just and appropriate, regardless of whether or not a court could have made such an order.[d] Where the ombudsman's decision is accepted by the complainant, it is binding on both parties, but if not, neither party is bound by the decision and the complainant is free to take out court proceedings.[e]
	FOS (Aus)	Since 1 January 2012, ASIC has required compensation caps from external dispute resolution schemes of at least AU$280,000 (approx. HK$2,296,000), except in the case of general insurance brokers, where the compensation cap is at least AU$150,000.[f] The remedies FOS can provide include: payment of monies; forgiveness or variation of debt, or the release of security for debt; repayment, waiver or variation of fees or other amounts paid or owed to a financial service provider; reinstatement or rectification of contract; variation of the terms of a credit contract in cases of financial hardship; and remedies dealing with privacy issues of individuals.[g] Provision is also made for financial compensation on various other bases, including costs and non-financial loss.[h] Provision is also made for the award of interest,[i] but punitive, exemplary or aggravated damages are expressly excluded.[j] If a complainant does not accept a Recommendation or Determination in respect of their dispute, they are not bound by it and may bring an action in the courts.[k]
	JFOS (Japan)	Not available.
Arbitration	FDRC (HK)	The maximum claimable amount is HK$500,000.[l]

FIDReC (Singapore)	The maximum monetary awards for compensation are S\$100,000 for claims against insurance companies, and S\$50,000 (approx. HK\$310,000) for all other disputes. Where an award is made by the adjudicator or Panel, it is binding on the financial institution but not on the complainant. The complainant's rights are thus not prejudiced in any way. He is free to choose whether or not to accept the award. Where the complainant chooses not to accept the award, he is free to pursue his other remedies such as legal action or arbitration.[m]
FINRA (US)	The FINRA Code requires the majority of the arbitrators on the panel agree on the rulings and determinations in an arbitration, but does not require written opinions be provided in respect of final awards. The limited scope for judicially reviewing such awards and not having to provide reasons allow arbitrators to reach awards based on general equitable principles. No statutory cap is imposed on the value of awards,[n] and awards are final and binding, even if new evidence surfaces later.[o]

[a] Financial Services Authority, *FSA Handbook*, DISP 3.7.4.

[b] Ibid., DISP 3.7.5.   [c] Ibid, DISP 3.7.6.   [d] Ibid., DISP 3.7.11.

[e] Financial Ombudsman Service, 'A quick guide to how we handle disputes between businesses and consumers'.

[f] Australian Securities and Investments Commission, *Regulatory Guide 139*, RG 139.156.

[g] Financial Ombudsman Service 'ASIC-approved Terms of Reference effective from 1 January 2010', amended 1 July 2010, para. 9.2.

[h] Ibid., paras. 9.3–9.4.   [i] Ibid., para. 9.5.   [j] Ibid., para. 9.6.   [k] Ibid., para. 8.9.

[l] See Financial Services and the Treasury Bureau, 'Consultation Conclusions on Proposed Establishment of an Investor Education Council and a Financial Dispute Resolution Centre', p. 23.

[m] Financial Industry Disputes Resolution Centre Ltd, *Annual Report 2005/6*.

[n] C. Alpert (2008) 'Financial Services in the United States and United Kingdom: Comparative Approaches to Securities Regulation and Dispute Resolution', p. 75.

[o] Financial Industry Regulatory Authority, 'Decision and Awards' [amended 1 July 2010], available at: www.finra.org/ArbitrationMediation/Parties/Overview/OverviewOfDisputeResolutionProcess/ [accessed 1 September 2011].

Costs

The question of costs in the context of consumer financial dispute resolution touches on the more deeply rooted principles of accessibility
and efficiency. The proposed costs of consumer financial dispute resolution services of arbitration-based services may be contrasted with the
ombudsmen in common law jurisdictions, which offer their services free
of charge, or charge a nominal case fee. The costs of such services must be
looked at in the context of the role that such fees play in filtering out vexatious or frivolous complaints as will be discussed below.

Purposes of charging

In examining the function of costs in consumer financial dispute resolution systems, fee structures may be designed in such a way that they are
affordable for complainants but at the same time be set at levels which
provide an incentive to resolve disputes at an early stage.[67]

Due to the express mandate of the regulators of the United Kingdom
and Australia in respect of consumer protection, ombudsmen services
are free of charge.

A considerably lower nominal amount is charged to consumers in
Singapore only where the dispute is escalated to the adjudication stage –
the fee is imposed to deter frivolous complaints, but is kept low in order to
ensure FIDReC is affordable for consumers.

In respect of the considerably higher costs of FINRA arbitration,
one commentator has pointed out that unlike in the case of the United
Kingdom or Australia, since FINRA complainants must pay an arbitration fee, a hearing deposit and attorneys' fees, cost deterrence serves as a
filter, and therefore strict jurisdictional prerequisites for arbitration are
unnecessary.[68]

It is thus clear that one of the purposes of charging consumers dispute
resolution service fees is to filter out certain claims, in particular, frivolous complaints, as well as to encourage settlement of disputes at an early
stage, thus preventing the draining of limited resources. However, as is

[67] Financial Services and the Treasury Bureau, 'Proposed Establishment of an Investor
Education Council and a Financial Dispute Resolution Centre', para. 3.19 of Part II.
[68] C. Alpert, 'Financial Services in the United States and United Kingdom: Comparative
Approaches to Securities Regulation and Dispute Resolution'.

noted above, jurisdictional prerequisites also serve similar purposes in respect of allocation of resources.

Aggregate costs are likewise influenced by whether or not parties are entitled to have legal representatives, particularly at the arbitration stage. In the case of the ombudsmen in common law jurisdictions, legal representation is not allowed. In the United States, the involvement of legal representatives has increased both the cost and complexity of FINRA arbitration. This is a significant issue as it has the potential to either drive up costs and formality (where legal representation is allowed) or to create an impression of inequality between the parties, particularly with respect to their experience with disputes and presenting cases (where legal representation is not allowed).

Assessment and recommendations

It is suggested that costs should be scaled for high-net-worth individuals or 'professional investors', to ensure the subsidies of the financial dispute resolution centres are allocated according to need.

Finally, in order to reduce associated costs, to maintain a level playing field between parties, and to reduce issues associated with playing for rules and over-emphasis on formalities and procedures, serious consideration should be given to the role of legal representation in the financial dispute resolution process.

Assessing consumer financial dispute resolution in a regulatory setting

In looking at the financial dispute resolution mechanisms in the context of widespread and common grievances, such as was the case in Hong Kong and Singapore with the sale and subsequent bankruptcy of Lehman Brothers, one relevant issue to examine is how well such mechanisms are suited to handling mass complaints. This question touches on broader principles of consistency and treating like cases alike.

An inherent weakness common to all models: lack of mass settlement capability

Under the majority of all financial dispute resolution systems examined, there are no provisions for mass settlements or claims brought by a class of complainants. In the United States, the existence of class action suits

Table 9.7 *Costs for consumer financial dispute resolution services*

Type	Service	Costs for Services		
Ombuds	FOS (UK)	Consumers do not pay to bring complaints to the FOS. Businesses do not pay case fees in respect of the first three complaints settled during a year, but there is a fee of £500 for the fourth and each subsequent complaint.[a] The *FSA Handbook* expressly sets out that complainants do not need to have professional advisers to bring complaints, and thus awards of costs should be uncommon.[b]		
	FOS (Aus)	Per the requirements of ASIC, external dispute resolution schemes provide their services free of charge to consumers.[c] Both FOS and COSL[d] are funded by fees from financial service providers who are members of their external dispute resolution schemes, as well as fees from the resolution of disputes.		
	JFOS (Japan)	Customers are not required to pay for dispute resolution proceedings initiated with the organisations. The operations of designated dispute resolution organisations are funded by contributions by the financial institutions in the industry.[e]		
Arbitration	FDRC (HK)	The FDRC service will be offered at a fee by both the claimants and financial institutions, under a 'pay-as-you-use' principle.[f]		
			Claimant	Financial Institution
		Making enquiries	Nil	Not Applicable
		Filing a claim form	HK$200	Not Applicable
		Mediation		
		– less than $100,000	HK$1,000	HK$2,000
		– between $100,000 and $500,000	HK$5,000	HK$10,000
		Arbitration (regardless of the amount of claims)	HK$5,000	HK$20,000

| FIDReC (Singapore) | No fees are charged to consumers where the dispute is resolved by case management or mediation. A S$50 fee is charged to consumers where the dispute is escalated to the adjudication stage – the fee is imposed to deter frivolous complaints, but is kept low in order to ensure FIDReC is affordable for consumers. The financial institution pays a flat case fee of S$500 per claim. Both parties are afforded adequate opportunity to present their case to the adjudicator or Panel. The complainant is allowed to be accompanied by his nominee, who would assist him/her in the presentation of his/her claim.[g] |
| FINRA (US) | As of 14 April 2011, the arbitration filing fee for a customer of a member firm of FINRA for an undis-closed amount and/or other relief (determined by a panel of three arbitrators per Rule 13900(b)) is US$1,250 and the estimated hearing fees for one day of hearing is US$3,000.[h] |

[a] Financial Ombudsman Service, 'The Case Fee', available at: www.financial-ombudsman.org.uk/faq/answers/research_a5.html [accessed 1 September 2011].

[b] Financial Services Authority, *FSA Handbook*, DISP 3.710.

[c] Australian Securities and Investments Commission, *Regulatory Guide 139*, RG 139.46.

[d] Credit Ombudsman Service, 'Member Fees', available at: www.cosl.com.au/Member-Fees [accessed 1 September 2011].

[e] Masako *et al.* (2010).

[f] See Financial Services and the Treasury Bureau, 'Consultation Conclusions on Proposed Establishment of an Investor Education Council and a Financial Dispute Resolution Centre', p. 16 and p.18 for the fee schedule.

[g] Financial Industry Disputes Resolution Centre Ltd, *Annual Report 2005/6*.

[h] Calculated using the 'Arbitration Filing Fee Calculator', Financial Industry Regulatory Authority, available at: apps.finra.org/ArbitrationMediation/ArbFeeCalc/1/Default.aspx [accessed 1 September 2011].

means there is a mechanism at least within the court system that can handle such issues.

In Hong Kong, as is the case with many common law jurisdictions, no such form of action exists. There is an arguable equivalent in representative actions,[69] but the test to be applied is that there must be 'a common interest, a common grievance and a remedy which is beneficial to all the plaintiffs'.[70] Representative actions cannot be brought unless the whole of the claim is appropriate to the form of action. While a general complaint of mis-selling may be common to the complainants, the variations of the Minibonds involved and the specific circumstances of sale and factors that are personal or individual, such as investment experience, level of education and so on, would enable financial institutions to raise objections to actions being brought as representative.

In the United Kingdom, the fact that the ombudsman scheme is not well designed to handle mass complaints has been commented on, though 'it may be the best of a number of alternatives'.[71] It should be noted that proposals to create class actions against financial services firms were originally included under the Financial Services Act 2010, only to be removed in order to ensure its passing.[72] According to Willmott, 'this would have facilitated a route for mass claims in court where FSA-ordered redress may not have been viable. In short, firms would have faced a redoubled threat on two fronts – from the regulator and the consumer.'[73]

This would not be the first time that such a form of action has been proposed – and rejected – in the United Kingdom. The government in July 2009 rejected a proposal by the Civil Justice Council to introduce class-action rules. In rejecting the proposal, the government stated that such changes should be made on a sectoral basis and involve reviews of the alternative dispute resolution and regulatory options in each sector.[74]

Although able to bring forward the interests of large groups of complainants at the same time, criticisms of this form of lawsuit include their cost (which make it unlikely to be the first option if others, particularly

---

[69] For further in respect of representative actions, see Order 15, Rule 12, the Rules of the High Court.
[70] *J. Bollinger S.A. v. Goldwell Ltd.* [1971] F.S.R. 405.
[71] A. Samuel, 'With arbitration facing restrictions, it's time to look at a UK solution for consumer disputes'.
[72] Willmott, 'Equipping the modern regulator: assessing the new regulatory powers under the Financial Services Act 2010'.
[73] Ibid.
[74] C. Hodges, 'Collective redress in Europe: the new model'.

alternative dispute resolution, are available), the risk of abuse, and difficulties in coping with certain types of cases, 'such as where individual
issues (reliance, causation or damage) vary widely between members of
the group, and predominate over general issues, such as in product liability or some misrepresentation claims, or over quantification, validation
or distribution of small individual sums'[75] – a description that may be
applied to complaints against financial services firms. The view of such
litigation as a hindrance to economic growth in the United States should
also be noted.[76]

The possible introduction of class actions, particularly in the financial
sector, should not be dismissed out of hand, and one can speculate as to
the effect the introduction of such litigation may have on alternative dispute resolution, including discouraging complainants from engaging in
alternative dispute resolution in favour of collectively taking the merits of
their case to court. Hodges writes about the growing interest in this form
of litigation in Europe,[77] and the weakness of an individualised approach
to complaints in the FOS (UK) because of its inability to cope with mass
complaints. In this regard, another criticism of alternative dispute resolution techniques in the financial sector (which may not specifically apply
to the FOS due to the system of adjudication and determination) is highlighted by Hodges: 'Disadvantages of ADR are said to be that settlements
can bear little relationship to underlying merits of disputes, and that
mediators can exert improper pressure in reaching settlements.'[78]

In the United Kingdom, there is a test case procedure, whereby complaints are dismissed from FOS jurisdiction without consideration of
the merits in order to allow a court to consider the complaint as a test
case if the FOS receives, from the establishment complained against, a
written statement about how and why the complaint raises an important
or novel point of law with significant consequences, and undertakes to
pay the complainant's costs and disbursements within six months of the
complaint being dismissed by the court. A test case may also be brought
where the FOS considers the complaint raises important or novel points
of law with important consequences that would be more suitably dealt
with by the courts.[79] At present, it appears that the system of test cases in
the United Kingdom may be sufficient, as the bank charges litigation in
the United Kingdom illustrates:

---

[75] Hodges, p. 19.   [76] Ibid.   [77] Ibid.   [78] Hodges, p. 24.
[79] Financial Services Authority, *FSA Handbook*, DISP 3.3.5.

Many individual complaints over allegedly unfair bank charges were initially dealt with by the FOS, and either dismissed or settled. The fact that
that Service had found in favour of a claimant in some cases was then used
to found claims in the county courts as having binding legal effect, when
it did not. The courts became clogged, and the impasse was unscrambled
when the banks and a regulator agreed to bring a test case, which had the
effect of freezing all individual cases.[80]

Hodges comments that there is a crucial difference between the
American and European regulatory systems that will need to be overcome if class-action litigation is to be deployed in the same way as it is in
the United States: 'The whole point of the US private enforcement system
is to facilitate actions in the courts as the primary means of regulatory
control: if some settlements involve over-compensation or are unfair, this
still has an intended deterrent effect on markets and actors generally.'[81]

A summary application of facts via a test case mechanism could be used
to handle large volumes of similar cases, so that where a problem appears
to be common or uniform, as was the case with the Minibonds, a financial dispute resolution mechanism could, following a test case arbitration,
apply the same award to all such cases through a summary procedure. The
burden could then be reversed back onto the financial service providers to
show why such summary awards might not apply to individual cases.

Consistency and playing for the rules

Another aspect of financial dispute resolution systems design process that
could potentially lead to complainants being at a disadvantage is the fact
that as time progresses, financial institutions will build up experience in
respect of claim amounts and settlements as 'repeat players'. By contrast,
consumers, as 'one-shotters', may be left in the dark as to the true value
of their complaint. Under the facilitative model of mediation, as mediators only facilitate discussions and are not supposed to give advice, the
experience of the mediators in this regard does not assist complainants.
Such concerns are important from the standpoint of equity, fairness and
transparency.

While in some cases financial dispute resolution systems may publish
data about disputes,[82] the confidential nature of the settlements appears

---

[80] Hodges, p. 23.   [81] Ibid.
[82] Financial Services and the Treasury Bureau, 'Proposed Establishment of an Investor
Education Council and a Financial Dispute Resolution Centre', para. 4.3 of Part II.

to mean that there will be no guidance for consumers or even arbitrators as to settlement amounts and awards for cases which involve similar facts or issues. This not only gives rise to a potential issue of uneven rates of settlement but also means that each dispute is destined to go through the same time-consuming process rather than to increase efficiency in reaching settlement of common or similar complaints.

This again highlights the limits of dispute resolution systems in dealing with mass claims – the achievement of uniform settlements. This issue is arguably better addressed under the ombudsman system due to the inquisitorial fact-finding and assessment process it involves, in contrast with the adversarial system of arbitration.

As has been noted above, one study in the United Kingdom demonstrated the effectiveness of the ombudsman model in neutralising the advantage of financial service providers due to the lack of formality and ad hoc nature of decision making. Such characteristics could well be adopted elsewhere, and in order to ensure consistency, it is suggested that financial dispute resolution centres arrange for frequent meetings of its staff, mediators and arbitrators to discuss their experiences with claims and how they handled them.

Systemic issues and parallel jurisdiction

In most cases, where an issue arises that touches on issues of systemic concern, in most cases, the financial dispute resolution centre will turn such cases over to the regulators to deal with and cease to handle them.[83]

In raising the issue of whether a given financial dispute could be characterised as systemic, a further, more pertinent question must be answered: what is a systemic concern?

In the United Kingdom, the FOS (UK) will inform the FSA of issues that appear likely to have significant regulatory implications,[84] but retains the power to resolve such cases. Such cases may also be dealt with by way of the test case procedure.

In Australia, external dispute resolution schemes approved by ASIC must report to ASIC any systemic issues and matters involving serious misconduct.[85] Systemic issues are ones that have implications beyond the

---

[83] Ibid., para. 4.8 of Part II.
[84] Ibid., para. 12.
[85] Australian Securities and Investments Commission, *Regulatory Guide 139*, RG 139.108(a).

immediate actions or rights of the parties to the complaint or dispute.[86] Serious misconduct includes fraud, gross negligence or inefficient conduct, or wilful or flagrant breaches of relevant laws.[87] It is the responsibility of the schemes to identify these matters, refer them to the financial service provider for response and action, and report the information to ASIC.[88]

In Singapore, FIDReC has the power to notify and/or to submit such information as is within its knowledge relating to systemic issues and market misconduct to the MAS.[89]

In the Consultation Conclusions, the FSTB thus altered its position from the Consultation document on cases with wider implications – the monetary part of such cases is now proposed to be dealt with under the parallel process along with cases that raise regulatory issues.[90]

In a broader financial regulatory context, the issue of identifying systemic problems has become the priority for regulators around the world following the financial crisis. It may not be immediately apparent whether or not a widespread problem is one that is 'systemic'. For example, thus far, no review of the Minibonds crisis in Hong Kong has characterised it as systemic, but whether or not its widespread nature may have led it to be considered 'systemic' at least for the purposes of early warning or until more facts about the Minibonds emerged raises questions about what actions would be appropriate in the face of a systemic concern, and what effect systemic issues will have on the private rights of complainants.

Regulator intervention and parallel jurisdiction

In both Hong Kong and Singapore, attempts to resolve Lehman-related investment disputes were all ultimately superseded by regulator-negotiated mass settlements. The mass settlement superseded all previous settlements and accordingly made adjustments to those amounts not in line with the mass settlement.[91]

---

[86] Ibid., RG 139.111.   [87] Ibid., RG 139.116.   [88] Ibid., RG 139.119.

[89] Financial Industry Disputes Resolution Centre Ltd, 'Terms of Reference', available at: www.fidrec.com.sg/resources/tor/FIDReC_TOR.pdf [accessed 1 September 2011], Rule 11 of Section 3.

[90] Financial Services and the Treasury Bureau, 'Consultation Conclusions on Proposed Establishment of an Investor Education Council and a Financial Dispute Resolution Centre', para. 55.

[91] Ali, Shahla F. and J. K. W. Kwok, 'After Lehman: international response to financial disputes – a focus on Hong Kong'.

In many jurisdictions such as Hong Kong, the financial dispute resolution centre is charged with dealing only with the monetary aspect of a complaint while the regulators deal with the regulatory aspects of a complaint in parallel. However, this begs the question as to whether or not adjustments to private settlements will need to be made in the future. Assuming that the settlement of the monetary dispute is achieved more quickly than a regulatory investigation, there is a possibility that the investigation may bring to light new facts pertinent to the settlement amount. This may arguably be less of an issue in the context of arbitration, where awards are final and binding, but in the context of mediation and certainly on the part of a consumer, a settlement may be hard to accept if fault is found by the regulator after the fact.

The setting up of a parallel process for complaints handling and removing regulatory powers from a given financial dispute resolution mechanism suggests that one way to co-ordinate the jurisdiction of the regulators and financial dispute resolution centres would be for the regulators to take a lead position, primarily in respect of fact finding, and to enable the financial dispute resolution centre to apply such facts in a summary way where appropriate.

The regulatory role

How financial dispute resolution centres are to deal with systemic issues leads to a broader question of whether or not such centres perform a regulatory function in the financial markets. The issue of the regulatory role arises from the fact that alternative dispute resolution schemes are positioned on the frontline of the interaction of consumers and financial service providers – for consumers, they are the 'first responders' on the scene of a complaint. In addition to being the first to be made aware of problems, such schemes inevitably, on some level, are engaged in a process of determination of fact and the application and upholding of certain norms or standards in order to resolve disputes. Does this necessarily lead to a regulatory role?

The FOS (UK): a quasi-regulator?

In examining the question of the role of alternative dispute resolution in financial regulation, one helpful model to look to is the one developed in the United Kingdom. In the United Kingdom, the statutory power of the FOS (UK) to determine complaints is made 'by reference to what is, in the opinion of the ombudsman, fair and reasonable in all the circumstances of the case'.[92] This unique power to 'draw on a range of extra-legal standards in a manner which operates to the benefit of consumers by mitigating the inequality of bargaining power and unfair substantive legal provisions encountered in parts of the financial services business, notably the banking and insurance sectors'[93] is one of the strengths of the FOS (UK), but gives rise to the issue of whether or not a regulatory power is being exercised.

The FOS has always maintained that it does not play a regulatory role,[94] and in his review, Lord Hunt called upon the FOS to guard against assuming a quasi-regulatory role.[95] This has been criticised as being disingenuous and misleading:

> [v]iewed in the round it is clear that the FOS in practice performs an indirect, circumscribed regulatory role: it performs an early warning function, identifying patterns in its case work which may necessitate FSA regulatory or disciplinary action; it regularly applies in its case work regulatory guidance and sectoral codes, often with a gloss added, transforming them into binding obligations; and it has started to build a corpus of persuasive precedent designed to improve standards of business practice.[96]

The recommendation against assuming a quasi-regulatory role appears to be contradicted by the recommendation in the Hunt Review for the development of a guidebook of principles and precedents as well as publishing detailed decisions. Morris identifies these recommendations as arising from criticisms from financial services firms of the lack of consistency in FOS decision making and its power to make determinations on extra-legal bases, particularly the notion of what is fair and reasonable.[97] In this regard, it is commented: 'the pleas of business should be treated with caution: the fair and reasonable standard is statutorily prescribed as the ultimate norm in FOS dispute resolution; it is inherently subjective;

---

[92] Section 228(2) of the Financial Services and Markets Act 2000.

[93] P. E. Morris, 'The Financial Ombudsman Service and the Hunt Review: continuing evolution in dispute resolution', p. 785.

[94] Financial Ombudsman Service, 'About Us', available at: www.financial-ombudsman. org.uk/about/index.html [accessed 8 September 2011].

[95] Lord Hunt (April 2008) 'Opening up, reaching out and aiming high: an agenda for accessibility and excellence in the Financial Ombudsman Service', *The Hunt Review*, available at: www.financial-ombudsman.org.uk/news/Hunt_report.pdf [accessed 8 September 2011], para. 50 of Chapter Seven.

[96] P. E. Morris, 'The Financial Ombudsman Service and the Hunt Review: continuing evolution in dispute resolution', p. 791.

[97] Ibid.

and a valuable doctrinal and practical resource in tackling unfair business practices.'[98]

This underlying tension between the need for predictability in FOS determinations and the statutory discretion of the ombudsmen raises the issue of whether or not recommendations such as the development of precedents and publishing of decisions would have the effect of eroding the otherwise unfettered discretion of the FOS, even if only by self-imposed rules of policy. It is clear, however, that this discretion has given the FOS a regulatory flavour in the United Kingdom, as the power to determine what is fair and reasonable creates an extra-legal standard to which financial service providers falling within its jurisdiction must comply with.

Distinguishing between regulatory and non-regulatory financial dispute resolution schemes in other jurisdictions

The differences in the models of financial dispute resolution utilised in other leading jurisdictions raises the issue of whether or not such schemes also play a regulatory role. In the case of the United States, for example, FINRA clearly plays a regulatory role – one of its predecessors was the regulatory arm of the NYSE, and private claims serve a regulatory function.[99] As noted above, in the United Kingdom, though the intent may not have been for the FOS (UK) to play a regulatory role, its broad discretionary power to determine cases in accordance with what is fair and reasonable, and the build-up of cases illustrating what fair and reasonable means, adds an extra-legal standard-setting dimension to its determination process. By contrast, the FOS and COSL in Australia and FIDReC in Singapore do not appear to have taken on regulatory dimensions, and their work is confined to dispute resolution – without relying on a monetary/regulatory distinction.[100]

Thus, different jurisdictions offer different answers to the question of whether or not financial dispute resolution schemes necessarily play regulatory roles. Alternative dispute resolution schemes are usually set up with efficiency in mind – in the particular context of financial markets, enhancing market efficiency by reducing the resources devoted to dispute resolution. Such schemes are supplemental to, rather than substitutive of, the court system, and lack a judicial mandate. In the absence of such a

---

[98] Ibid.   [99] Please refer to FINRA (n.d.). Rules.
[100] Please refer to The Financial Ombudsman Service (n.d.). The Jurisdiction of FIDReC and Financial Industry Disputes Resolution Centre Ltd ('FIDReC') (n.d.). About us.

mandate, is it desirable for such schemes to impose their own interpretation of the norms and standards of financial regulation in the dispute resolution process? The restrictions that are placed on the jurisdiction of the ombudsmen and FIDReC seem to imply that the answer in those jurisdictions is 'no' – cases involving large amounts, implying a certain complexity, are excluded from their purview, and to be dealt with before the courts; while complaints involving smaller amounts, and thus less likely to involve complex issues or carry serious implications, may instead be handled by a straightforward application of regulatory standards and norms by a dispute resolution scheme.[101] The non-binding nature of the ombudsmen and adjudicator's decisions (save where accepted by the complainant) is perhaps the clearest indicator that there is no intent to completely displace the judicial function. By contrast, the FINRA arbitration scheme is accepted as part of the regulatory mechanism in the United States, and its mandatory nature and unrestricted jurisdiction appear to imply a mandate to displace the court function in certain aspects of financial regulation.

It may perhaps be concluded that the exclusion of the judicial function is the touchstone of a regulatory function – an unrestricted power to make a final adjudication upon the norms and standards of financial regulation in resolving disputes between consumers and financial service providers.

In navigating the potential areas of overlap between the regulatory and non-regulatory functions of financial dispute resolution service providers, the parallel complaints procedure must be clearly established between the dispute resolution service and the regulators, and in matters of fact finding, the lead must be taken by the regulators.[102] For jurisdictions that do not have a specific consumer protection mandate such as in Hong Kong, it should be borne in mind that in the aftermath of the Minibonds crisis, there may be an expectation on the part of the public that a dispute resolution body be set up for the purposes of filling in the consumer protection gap and resolving disputes in the absence of such a regulatory mandate.

---

[101] For further discussion on matters such as eligible complainants and range of disputes of the dispute resolution schemes in the jurisdictions studied, please refer to the Table 9.1: Eligible complainants for consumer financial dispute resolution services and Table 9.2: Dispute types across ombuds and arbitration services above.

[102] Ibid., para. 4.2 of Part II.

Assessing the appropriateness of dispute resolution methods for financial regulation

Other than its place in the regulatory structure, an equally important assessment of financial dispute resolution centres is the appropriateness of alternative dispute resolution techniques for financial dispute resolution. In the course of this book, several ideas have emerged for the enhancement of financial dispute resolution centres with respect to the experience of similar schemes in other jurisdictions. This suggests that some methods of dispute resolution may be preferred over others due to the needs of disputes between consumers and financial service providers; one example of such a need is the need to bridge the power/knowledge gap between consumers and financial service providers.

Command and consensual models of dispute resolution

Methods of alternative dispute resolution can be thought of as falling within a spectrum that ranges from negotiation on one extreme end to litigation on the other – on one end, informal, consensual modes of resolving disputes, and on the other, formal, coercive 'command' models of dispute resolution. The spectrum is a useful tool to illustrate a scaled way of thinking about dispute resolution models – as one moves from the consensual end towards the command end of the scale, the formalities of the dispute resolution process increases, the processes become increasingly structured, and control over the outcome of the dispute increasingly shifts away from the disputants to a third party.

Along this spectrum, mediation is closer to the consensual end, being a form of structured negotiation in which the third party assists the disputants to reach a settlement, while arbitration is considered next to litigation on the command end due to its more formalised approach and power of the arbitrator to determine the outcome of the dispute.

One observation that may be made in respect of the dispute resolution spectrum is that as the control over the outcome of the dispute shifts to the third party, the outcome is increasingly determined based on established principles. Hence, a mediator may help disputants reach a settlement that is relatively free in form, while an arbitrator must make a determination that is based on pre-agreed principles (i.e. based on the jurisdiction of the arbitrator in accordance with the arbitration agreement). At the extreme end of the spectrum, judges are bound by law in the decisions they make.

This speaks to a need to safeguard disputants from the increasing discretion that a third party exercises over the outcome of the dispute as the mode of dispute resolution travels from the consensual end of the spectrum to the command end.

In the context of a regulatory role in financial markets indicated by a displacement of the judicial function, it may be argued that command models of dispute resolution such as arbitration more readily displace the judicial function due to the fact that the awards are generally required to be made according to legal and equitable principles.

Does the regulatory role determine appropriateness of form of dispute resolution?

In the United States, the FINRA arbitration scheme is viewed as part of the regulatory machinery, and appears to displace the function of the courts in this regard. As arbitration is considered next to litigation on the command model end of the dispute resolution spectrum, one may therefore conclude that arbitration (with its very limited grounds for recourse to intervention by the courts) aligns with the regulatory role of the scheme.

The two tiers of dispute resolution at the ombudsmen in the United Kingdom and Australia and FIDReC in Singapore arguably reflect a non-regulatory role, as mediation is less structured and formal, and the use of ombudsmen or adjudicators reflects a hybrid form of dispute resolution that despite its inquisitorial nature, is also lower in formality. The non-binding nature of the award of an ombudsman or adjudicator also speaks to a non-regulatory role, as the oversight of the courts is not excluded by the dispute resolution scheme save by election of the complainant.

Command and consensual models in mediation

When might inquisitorial mediation be preferred to interest-based mediation, being closer to the command model rather than the consensual model? In considering what forms of alternative dispute resolution are suitable for addressing disputes between consumers and financial service providers, the need for the third party intervener in any mode of dispute resolution to address the power/knowledge gap is clear. The need to address the gap may, particularly at the early stages of dispute resolution, lend itself towards the command end of the dispute resolution spectrum and the integration of relevant standards and rules, at least as touchstones, to inform an equitable negotiation process. It may suggest the need for external experts, information centres and resources to be made available to unrepresented parties. The integration of such norms, however, does not necessarily lend itself to a regulatory role.

Even in the absence of, or separate from a consumer protection mandate, the principles of equity and transparency operate to bridge the power/knowledge gap between consumers and financial service providers in order to achieve equity and fairness in the dispute resolution process. This may arguably be considered a reflection of the regulatory philosophy of disclosure that dominates financial regulation.

The premise that inquisitorial models of dispute resolution are better suited where the intent is a regulatory role, and consensual models are to be preferred in the context of non-regulatory dispute resolution schemes, must therefore be supplemented by an underlying notion of what is necessary to achieve equity and fairness between the two disputing parties in determining appropriateness. Hence, to a certain extent, command elements including the integration of relevant standards and rules, at least as touchstones, to inform an equitable negotiation process may be necessary for the resolution of financial disputes even where consensual models are being used.

Regulatory structure informing the future shape of financial dispute resolution

Another way in which financial dispute resolution schemes have come to reflect the underlying financial regulatory structure is the consolidation of sectoral schemes into super schemes with jurisdiction over much, if not all, of the financial market. Such consolidation has occurred with the Ombudsmen of the United Kingdom and Australia, FIDReC in Singapore and FINRA in the United States which are all consolidations of pre-existing, sectoral financial dispute resolution schemes.

Prior to the financial crisis, financial markets could be characterised by the increasingly blurred divisions between banking, securities and insurance products,[103] leading to a movement towards consolidated regulation and oversight – an evolution from sectoral regulation to an integrated structure. The FSA in the United Kingdom and the Monetary Authority

---

[103] D. T. Llewellyn (June 2006) 'Institutional structure of financial regulation and supervision: the basic issues', available at: http://siteresources.worldbank.org/INTTOPCONF6/Resources/2057292-1162909660809/F2FlemmingLlewellyn.pdf [accessed 8 September 2011], p. 20.

of Singapore are examples of the most fully realised embodiments of the idea of a super-regulator to oversee entire financial markets.

As financial service providers increasingly offer products and services that cross the sectoral boundaries of banking, securities and insurance, consolidation not only of regulation but also dispute resolution appears logical. Such consolidated schemes reduced confusion and enhanced convenience for consumers by creating 'one-stop shops' for all financial disputes.

Following the financial crisis, however, regulation of financial markets has now refocused on the twin peaks of financial stability and prudential regulation, and financial market conduct, with a preference for functional regulation, such as the division of labour between ASIC and the Australian Prudential Regulation Authority,[104] and the abolition of the FSA in the United Kingdom in favour of a new system of financial regulation in which the Bank of England is responsible for macro-prudential regulation, while a new Consumer Protection and Regulatory Authority takes on the regulation of the conduct of all financial services businesses.[105]

The implication for existing financial dispute resolution schemes under 'twin peaks' regulation is that systemic issues may be reported to a separate regulatory authority – financial dispute resolution being an aspect of market conduct.

While consolidated schemes have the advantage of being a 'one-stop shop' for consumers, consolidation is a complex exercise. In other jurisdictions, it has been necessary for insurance products to maintain different monetary claim limits due to their different nature.[106] The training and integration of staff to deal with different financial products and industries is another area of complexity, often requiring a restructuring of the consolidated scheme, and the establishment of uniform standards and procedures that can be applied across the board of a financial market has proven to be a time-consuming exercise in other jurisdictions.

---

[104] J. Cooper (September 2006) 'The integration of financial regulatory authorities – the Australian experience', available at: www.asic.gov.au/asic/pdflib.nsf/lookupbyfilename/ integration-financial-regulatory-authorities.pdf/$file/integration-financial-regulatory -authorities.pdf [accessed 8 September 2011].

[105] HM Treasury (July 2010) 'A new approach to financial regulation: judgment, focus and stability', available at: www.hm-treasury.gov.uk/d/consult_financial_regulation_ condoc.pdf [accessed 8 September 2011].

[106] Please refer to Table 9.6: Comparison of award type above.

Conclusion: the way forward

In examining increasingly accepted principles underlying the development of financial dispute resolution mechanisms, such underlying principles have come to include the need for an accessible grievance mechanism, accountability, efficiency, impartiality and fairness[107] as well as principles such as affordability, speediness, cost effectiveness and confidentiality, all of which are important principles in the implementation of financial dispute resolution programmes.[108]

In examining the application of such principles to financial dispute resolution systems design in a comparative context, the following specific suggestions can be made in light of experience in other jurisdictions:

1. Improving accessibility via the expansion of eligible complainants beyond individuals, while at the same time enhancing cost effectiveness by restricting the subsidised access of professional investors or scaling the charges of financial dispute resolution centres for different types of user.
2. Improving efficiency by adopting a preliminary review process that establishes the issues between the parties at an early stage; and by adopting a separate process for the exclusion of frivolous or vexatious complaints.
3. Enhancing the transparency of the decision-making process by allowing for hearings where complainants desire.
4. Where the financial dispute resolution process fails to resolve the dispute, attempts should be made to narrow down the factual disputes and issues between the parties in order to enhance the efficiency of litigation.
5. Financial dispute resolution mechanisms may consider whether the award cap is consistent with the aim of enhancing accessibility.

In examining financial dispute resolution models in the jurisdictions studied, this book finds that at the global level, due to the fact that non-binding global principles allow diverse consumer financial dispute resolution mechanisms the option of opting in to particular standards, at the substantive level, divergence in costs, regulatory role and the binding

---

[107] Note 236, see RG 139.25–139.29 of the Australian Securities and Investments Commission's Regulatory Guide.

[108] Financial Services and the Treasury Bureau, 'Consultation Conclusions on Proposed Establishment of an Investor Education Council and a Financial Dispute Resolution Centre', para. 25.

nature of awards can co-exist, to a large extent, with a relatively high degree of convergence in relation to the three-tier structure of most consumer financial dispute resolution processes.

From a review of best practices in the jurisdictions examined, efficiency of financial dispute resolution mechanisms may be enhanced through the possible adoption of a test case mechanism, the summary application of facts found under the test case mechanism, the introduction of a mechanism to consolidate complaints, frequent meetings of staff, mediators and arbitrators to share experiences and views on claims and claim handling to enhance consistency, and by financial regulators taking the lead position in respect of fact finding regarding systemic and widespread issues.

In the context of the foregoing discussion on distinguishing between regulatory and non-regulatory schemes of dispute resolution, reform considerations must take into account the intended function of the dispute resolution mechanism and whether it aims to fill a regulatory role. The appropriateness of the form of dispute resolution for a non-regulatory scheme also suggests a reduction of the command elements, or moving them down the spectrum away from the command end. The idea of non-binding awards on the complainant is one way in which such a process can be made more consensual. However, the principles that bind the majority of the suggestions together are those of fairness and equity.

Restricting professional investors' subsidised access to financial dispute resolution mechanisms, for example, not only improves cost effectiveness but also enhances the distribution of resources to where the need for them may be greater. The parallel complaints-handling mechanism operates to ensure that the knowledge gap between consumers and financial service providers will be bridged, and the facts relied upon will have a regulatory touchstone. The adoption of a separate process for dealing with frivolous or vexatious complaints should ensure that complainants are not barred from consideration on a mere prima facie basis, but at the same time, such a process should also help to protect financial service providers from frivolous and vexatious claims made by the same complainants in future.

Charging financial dispute resolution mechanisms with a further duty to narrow down factual disputes and issues between the parties even if the complaint cannot be resolved should assist in the future resolution of the dispute through formal court proceedings. Encouraging parties to agree on how disclosed information is to be dealt with prevents the abuse of positions of established information.

The importance of fairness and equity in a dispute resolution process is clear. Even absent a consumer protection mandate, the need for a financial dispute resolution scheme to be fair not only reflects broader aims of a financial regulation system, but on a practical level, furthers the aim of such schemes to increase market efficiency. Just as 'the deceived investor will not invest', complainants with no confidence in a financial dispute resolution scheme will not make use of it, which can only serve to drive the resources needed to resolve financial disputes up.

The study of financial dispute resolution schemes in different jurisdictions has, in this book, led to the conclusions that the regulatory or non-regulatory role of such schemes may be identified by whether or not they displace the judicial function. The appropriateness of the dispute resolution method is arguably informed by a regulatory or non-regulatory role – dispute resolution modes closer to the command model that displace the judicial function must incorporate safeguards for the disputants against the discretion of the third party intervener. But even for non-regulatory schemes, command elements such as the provision of regulatory and legal standards to individual complainants may still be incorporated into consensual models of dispute resolution, which speaks to a de minimis level of fairness and equity that must be achieved.

The establishment and future effectiveness of financial dispute resolution mechanisms in newly emerging jurisdictions will undoubtedly be measured against the extent to which such mechanisms effectively incorporate recognised principles of independence, impartiality, accessibility, efficiency, fairness and equity in the context of the growth of such dispute resolution mechanisms in emerging global financial markets.

BIBLIOGRAPHY

ADR FINMAC. (n.d.). Retrieved from www.finmac.or.jp (translated by Google).

Alexander, N. (ed.) (2003) *Global Trends in Mediation*. Cologne: Otto Schmidt Publishing.

Ali, S. (2010). *Resolving Disputes in the Asia Pacific Region: International Arbitration and Mediation in East Asia and the West*. Routledge (London, UK).

Ali, Shahla F. and Da Roza, A. M. (19 July 2011) 'Alternative Dispute Resolution in Financial Markets – Some More Equal than Others: Hong Kong's Proposed Financial Dispute Resolution Centre in the Context of Experience in the UK, US, Australia and Singapore', *Pacific Rim Law & Policy Journal*, Vol. 21, No. 3, 2012; University of Hong Kong Faculty of Law Research Paper No. 2012/20.

Ali, S. and Huang, H. R. (2012). Financial Dispute Resolution in China: Arbitration or Court Litigation? *Arbitration International*, Vol. 28(1), 77–100.

Ali, S. and Kwok, J. K. W. (2011). After Lehman: international response to financial disputes – a focus on Hong Kong. *Richmond Journal of Global Law and Business*, Vol. 10(2).

Alliance of Lehman Brothers Victims website. (n.d.). Retrieved from www.lbv.org. hk/content/pages/aboutus.php.

Alpert, C. (2008). Financial Services in the United States and United Kingdom: Comparative Approaches to Securities Regulation and Dispute Resolution. *BYU Int'l L. & Mgmt. Rev.*, Vol. 5, 75.

Arner, Hsu and Da Roza. (2010). Financial Regulation in Hong Kong: Time for a Change. *Asian Journal of Comparative Law*, Vol. 5, 71–114.

Attard, M. (n.d.). Resolution of Insurance Disputes. *The Law Handbook*. Retrieved from www.lawhandbook.org.au/handbook/ch23s01s10.php#.

Australian Securities and Investments Commission. (n.d.). ASIC-approved external dispute resolution schemes. Retrieved from www.asic.gov.au/asic/asic. nsf/byheadline/ASIC+approved+external+complaints+resolution+schemes ?opendocument.

(n.d.). Complaints Resolution Schemes. Retrieved from www.asic.gov.au/asic/ asic.nsf/byheadline/Complaints+resolution+schemes?openDocument.

(n.d.). Regulatory Guide. Retrieved from www.asic.gov.au/rg.

(April 2011). *Regulatory Guide 139.* Retrieved from www.asic.gov.au/asic/pdflib.nsf/LookupByFileName/rg139-published-20-4-2011.pdf/$file/rg139-published-20-4-2011.pdf.

Bank for International Settlements. (n.d.). About the Basel Committee. Retrieved from www.bis.org/bcbs/about.htm.

(n.d.). History of the Basel Committee and its Membership. Retrieved from www.bis.org/bcbs/history.htm.

(n.d.). International regulatory framework for banks (Basel III). Retrieved from www.bis.org/bcbs/basel3.htm.

Banking and Financial Services Ombudsman. (February 2008). *Review of Australia's Consumer Policy Framework, Production Commission Discussion Paper.* Retrieved from www.pc.gov.au/__data/assets/pdf_file/0010/89092/subdr170.pdf.

Banking and Financial Services Ombudsman Limited. (March 2008). BFSO Bulletin 57. Retrieved from www.bfso.org.au/ABIOWeb/ABIOWebSite.nsf/0/A2502C2CFD46FF46CA25741E001713C1/$file/Bulletin+57.pdf.

Banking Day. (11 December 2008). Ombudsman an early port of call for banking disputes. Retrieved from www.bankingday.com/nl06_news_selected.php?act=2&stream=1&selkey=7598&hlc=2&hlw=early+port+of+call&s_keyword=early+port+of+call&s_searchfrom_date=631112400&s_searchto_date=1297148660&s_pagesize=11&s_word_match=2&s_articles=1&stream=1.

(15 April 2010). Small business financial disputes on the rise. Retrieved from www.bankingday.com/nl06_news_selected.php?act=2&stream=1&selkey=9722&hlc=2&hlw=financial+ombudsman+service&s_keyword=financial+ombudsman+service&s_searchfrom_date=631112400&s_searchto_date=1297148351&s_pagesize=11&s_word_match=2&s_articles=1&stream=1.

(3 September 2010). Dispute resolution teething troubles. Retrieved from www.bankingday.com/nl06_news_selected.php?act=2&stream=1&selkey=10450&hlc=2&hlw=financial+ombudsman+service&s_keyword=financial+ombudsman+service&s_searchfrom_date=631112400&s_searchto_date=1297148351&s_pagesize=11&s_word_match=2&s_articles=1&stream=1.

Banking Ordinance (Cap. 155).

Basel Committee of Banking Supervision. (2011). Basel III: A global regulatory framework for more resilient banks and banking systems. Retrieved from www.bis.org/publ/bcbs189.pdf.

Baum, H. (2011). *Debating the Japanese Approach to Dispute Resolution. Max Planck Research.* Max Planck Institute for Comparative and International Private Law. Retrieved from www.mpg.de/4379741/W006_Culture-Society_084-091.pdf.

BBC News. (7 August 2009). Credit crunch to downturn. *BBC News.* Retrieved from http://news.bbc.co.uk/2/hi/business/7521250.stm

Beaman, L. (2010). FOS Alternative Emerges. *Money Management.* Retrieved from www.moneymanagement.com.au/news/fos-alternative-emerges.

Beeston, L. (11 October 2011). The ballerina and the bull. *The Link.* Retrieved from http://thelinknewspaper.ca/article/1951.

Bernstein, L. (2001). Private commercial law in the cotton industry: creating cooperation through rules, norms and institutions. *Michigan L. Rev.,* Vol. 99, 1724.

Bingham, Lisa Blomgren, Hallberlin, Cynthia J., Walker, Denise A. and Chung, Won-Tae. (2009). Dispute system design and justice in employment dispute resolution: mediation at the workplace. *Harvard Negotiation Law Review,* Vol. 14, 1–50.

Black, B. (2010). How to improve retail investor protection after the Dodd-Frank Wall Street Reform and Consumer Protection Act. *U. Pa. J. Bus. L.,* Vol. 13, 59–106.

Bloomberg. (21 October 2011). Ex-British Chief Brown Says Wall Street Protestors Seek Fairness. Retrieved from www.bloomberg.com/news/2011-10-21/ex-british-chief-brown-says-wall-street-protests-seek-fairness.html.

Bondi, B. J. (2010). Facilitating economic recovery and sustainable growth through reform of the securities class-action system: exploring arbitration as an alternative to litigation. *Harvard Journal of Law & Public Policy,* Vol. 33(2), 607–638.

Braithwaite, J. and Drahos, P. (2000). *Global Business Regulation.* Cambridge University Press.

Brown, R. (2011). The UN Guidelines for Consumer Protection: making them work in developing countries. *Paper for Consumers' International Congress.* Retrieved from http://a2knetwork.org/sites/default/files/un_guidelines_r_brown_paper.doc.

Caron, D. and Caplan, L. (2010). *The 2010 UNCITRAL Arbitration Rules: A Commentary.* Oxford University Press.

Carter Newell Insurance Ombudsman Service Fact Sheet 2. (n.d.). Retrieved from www.carternewell.com/media/799149/fact%20sheet%202%20-%20new.pdf.

Celnik, C. and Yakura, C. (2011–2012). Dispute Resolution Handbook 2011/12 – Japan. *Practical Law Company.* Retrieved from www.practicallaw.com/9-502-0319.

Center for Public Deliberation. (n.d.). What is deliberation? Retrieved from www.cpd.colostate.edu/what.html.

Chesterman, Simon. (2008). An International Rule of Law? *American Journal of Comparative Law,* Vol. 56, 331–361.

Cheung, F. (July/August 2003). CIETAC opens doors to financial arbitration. *China Law and Practice*.

ChinaNews. (28 December 2010). Shanghai No. 1 Intermediate People's Court warns against risks of disputes over bank investment products (上海法院: 银行理财产品纠纷多发吁加强风险防范). Retrieved from www.china-news.com/fortune/2010/12-28/2752939.shtml [Chinese].

Choi, S., Fisch, J. E. and Pritchard, A. C. (2010). Attorneys as arbitrators. *J. Legal Stud.*, Vol. 39, 109.

Clarke, D. C. (2003). Economic development and the rights hypothesis: the China problem. *Am. J. Comp. L.*, Vol. 51, 89.

Clift, R. (2009). The phenomenon of mediation: judicial perspectives and an eye on the future. *The Journal of International Maritime Law*, Vol. 15, 508–517.

Cole, T. (2007). Commercial arbitration in Japan: Contributions to the debate on Japanese non-litigiousness. *NYUJ Int'l L & Pol*, Vol. 40, 29.

Cole, C. W. (2007–2008). Financial Industry Regulatory Authority (FINRA): is the consolidation of NASD and the regulatory arm of NYSE a bull or a bear for US capital markets? *UMKC L. Rev.*, Vol. 76, 251–272.

Comparative analysis of Asian securities regulators & SROs and market characteristics (data and information provided by participating organisations in the 6th Asia Securities Forum Tokyo Round Table).

Consumers International. (n.d.). Consumer Rights. Retrieved from www.consumersinternational.org/who-we-are/consumer-rights.

Cook, J. A. and M. M. Fonow (1990). Knowledge and woman's interests: Issues in epistemology and methodology in feminist sociological research. In J.McC. Nielsen (ed.) *Feminist Research Methods: Exemplary Readings in the Social Sciences*. Boulder: Westview Press.

Cooper, J. (September 2006). The integration of financial regulatory authorities – the Australian experience. Retrieved from www.asic.gov.au/asic/pdflib.nsf/lookupbyfilename/integration-financial-regulatory-authorities.pdf/$file/integration-financial-regulatory-authorities.pdf.

COSL Member Alert. (18 June 2009). Retrieved from www.cosl.com.au/Resources/COSL/Sites/COSL/PDF/News/MemberNews-Issue22.pdf.

COSL Member News Issue 27. (1 April 2010). Retrieved from www.cosl.com.au/Resources/COSL/Sites/COSL/PDF/News/MemberNews-Issue27.pdf.

Costantino, Cathy A. and Merchant, Christina Sickles. (1996). *Designing Conflict Management Systems: A Guide to Creating Productive and Healthy Organizations*. Jossey-Bass.

Credit Ombudsman Service. (n.d.). Annual Report on Operations 2009–2010.

(n.d.). Complaint FAQs. Retrieved from www.cosl.com.au/Complaint-FAQs.

(n.d.). Complaints Process. Retrieved from www.cosl.com.au/Complaints-Process.

(n.d.). COSL Membership. Retrieved from www.cosl.com.au/ Becoming-a-member.

(n.d.). The COSL Rules. 7th edn. Retrieved from www.cosl.com.au/Resources/ COSL/Sites/COSL/PDF/About/COSL-Rules-Edition-7.pdf.

(n.d.). COSL's History. Retrieved from www.cosl.com.au/COSLs-History.

(n.d.). COSL's Role. Retrieved from www.cosl.com.au/COSLs-Role.

(n.d.). Make a Complaint. Retrieved from www.cosl.com.au/Make-a-complaint.

(n.d.). Member Fees. Retrieved from www.cosl.com.au/Member-Fees.

Credit Union Dispute Resolution Centre. (2005–2006). *2005–2006 Annual Report*. Retrieved from www.fos.org.au/public/download.jsp?id=36].

Cutler, D., Slater, S. and Comlay E. (5 November 2009). US, European Bank writedowns, credit losses. *Reuters*. Retrieved from www.reuters.com/article/ idCNL554155620091105?rpc=44.

Deason, Ellen E. (2004). Procedural rules for complementary systems of litigation and mediation – worldwide. *Notre Dame Law Review*, Vol. 80. Retrieved from http://papers.ssrn.com/sol3/papers.cfm?abstract_id=583141

Delisle, J. and Trujillo, E. (2010). Consumer protection in transnational contexts. *Am. J. Comp. L.*, Vol. 58, 135. Retrieved from http://papers.ssrn.com/sol3/ papers.cfm?abstract_id=1673945.

Dicey, A. V. (1915). *Introduction to the Study of the Law of the Constitution*. 8th edn. Macmillan.

Directive 2008/52/EC of the European Parliament and the Council of 21 May 2008 on certain aspects of mediation in civil and commercial matters OJ L136/3 24.5.2008.

Dodd-Frank Wall Street Reform and Consumer Protection Act.

Drolshammer, J. and Pfeifer, M. (2001). *The Internationalization Of The Practice Of Law*. The Hague: Kluwer Law International.

Eckstein, Harry. (1992) *Regarding Politics: Essays on Political Theory, Stability, and Change*. Berkeley: University of California Press.

Egan, L. (2009). Criticism of Expanding FOS Jurisdiction. *Money Management*. Retrieved from www.moneymanagement.com.au/news/criticism-of-expanding-fos-jurisdiction.

Ellickson, R. (1991). *Order Without Law: How Neighbors Settle Disputes*. Harvard University Press.

Federal Court of Australia. (2008–2009). *Annual Report 2008–2009*. Retrieved from www.fedcourt.gov.au/aboutct/ar2008.html.

Feeley, Malcom M. (1989). *Court Reform on Trial: Why Simple Solutions Fail*. Basic Books.

Feldman, Eric A. (2007). Legal Reform in Contemporary Japan. *University of Penn Law School, Public Law Research Paper No. 07–17*. Retrieved from http:// papers.ssrn.com/sol3/papers.cfm?abstract_id=980762.

Final Report of the Chief Justice's Working Party on Civil Justice Reform. (2004). Retrieved from www.legco.gov.hk/yr06-07/english/bc/bc57/papers/ bc570611cb2-1960-e.pdf.

Financial Industry Disputes Resolution Centre Ltd. (n.d.). Adjudicators. Retrieved from www.fidrec.com.sg/website/adjudicators.html.

(n.d.). The Jurisdiction of FIDReC. Retrieved from www.fidrec.com.sg/website/ jurisdiction.html.

(n.d.). Terms of Reference. Retrieved from www.fidrec.com.sg/resources/tor/ FIDReC_TOR.pdf.

(2005–2006). *Annual Report 2005/6.*

(2009–2010). *Annual Report 2009/10.*

Financial Industry Regulatory Authority. (n.d.). Arbitration Filing Fee Calculator. Retrieved from apps.finra.org/ArbitrationMediation/ArbFeeCalc/1/ Default.aspx.

(n.d.). Decision and Awards. Retrieved from www.finra.org/Arbitration Mediation/Parties/Overview/OverviewOfDisputeResolutionProcess/.

(n.d.). Rules. Retrieved from www.finra.org/Industry/Regulation/ FINRARules/.

(6 June 2011). Code of Arbitration Procedure for Customer Disputes Rule. Retrieved from www.finra.org/web/groups/arbitrationmediation/@ arbmed/@arbion/documents/arbmed/p117546.pdf.

(29 July 2011). Code of Arbitration Procedures for Customer Disputes. Retrieved from www.finra.org/web/groups/arbitrationmediation/@arbmed/@arbrul/ documents/arbmed/p117546.pdf.

Financial Ombudsman Service, Australia. (n.d.). Dispute Handling Process in Detail. Retrieved from www.fos.org.au/centric/home_page/resolving_ disputes/dispute_handling_process_in_detail.jsp.

(n.d.). Financial Difficulty. Retrieved from www.fos.org.au/centric/home_page/ resolving_disputes/financial_difficulty.jsp.

(n.d.). Online Form. Retrieved from https://forms.fos.org.au/OnlineDispute.

(n.d.). The Financial Ombudsman Service establishes Mutuals and Insurance Broking divisions. Retrieved from www.fos.org.au/centric/home_page/ news/the_financial_ombudsman_service_establishes_mutuals_and_ insurance_broking_divisions.jsp.

(n.d.). Submission: inquiry into collapses in the financial services industry. Retrieved from www.aph.gov.au/senate/committee/corporations_ctte/fps/ submissions/sub353.pdf.

(2008–2009). *2008-2009 Annual Review.* Retrieved from www.fos.org.au/ centric/home_page/publications/annual_reports_archive.jsp.

(2010). ASIC-approved Terms of Reference. Retrieved from www.fos.org.au/ centric/home_page/about_us/terms_of_reference_b.jsp.

(2010). Terms of Reference. Retrieved from www.fos.org.au/public/download. jsp?id=4040.

(2010–2011). *2010–2011 Annual Review.* Retrieved from www2.fos.org.au/annualreview/2010-2011/our-members.html.

'ASIC-approved Terms of Reference effective from 1 January 2010', amended 1 July 2010, available at: www.fos.org.au/centric/home_page/about_us/terms_of_reference_b.jsp [accessed 1 September 2011], para. 4 of section B.

Financial Ombudsman Service, UK. (n.d.). A quick guide to how we handle disputes between businesses and consumers. Retrieved from www.financial-ombudsman.org.uk/publications/technical_notes/QG7.pdf.

(n.d.). About Us. Retrieved from www.financial-ombudsman.org.uk/about/index.html.

(n.d.). Frequently-asked Questions. Retrieved from www.financial-ombudsman.org.uk/faq/answers/research_a5.html.

(n.d.). Online technical resource. Retrieved from www.financial-ombudsman.org.uk/publications/technical_notes/pensions.html

(n.d.). Our Organisation Chart. Retrieved from www.financial-ombudsman.org.uk/about/organisation-chart.htm.

(n.d.). The Case Fee. Retrieved from www.financial-ombudsman.org.uk/faq/answers/research_a5.html.

(1999–2000). *Annual Report 1999/2000: Laying the foundations.* Retrieved from www.financial-ombudsman.org.uk/publications/first-annual-report/ar-1999-2000.pdf.

(2009–2010). *Annual Review 2009/2010.* Retrieved from www.financial-ombudsman.org.uk/publications/ar10/ar10.pdf.

Financial Services and the Treasury Bureau. (February 2010). Proposed Establishment of an Investor Education Council and a Financial Dispute Resolution Centre: Consultation Paper. Retrieved from www.gov.hk/en/residents/government/publication/consultation/docs/2010/consult_iec_fdrc_e.pdf.

(13 December 2012). Consultation Conclusions on Proposed Establishment of an Investor Education Council and a Financial Dispute Resolution Centre. Retrieved from www.fstb.gov.hk/fsb/ppr/consult/doc/consult_iec_fdrc_conslusion_e.pdf.

Financial Services Authority. (n.d.). *FSA Handbook.* Retrieved from http://fsahandbook.info/FSA/html/handbook/DISP/2/7.

(n.d.). *Newsletter No.832010.* Retrieved from www.fsa.go.jp/en/newsletter/2010/02b.html.

(2009). The Turner Review: A Regulatory Response to the Global Banking Crisis published in March 2009. Retrieved from www.fsa.gov.uk/pubs/other/turner_review.pdf.

Fisher, R., Ury, W. and Patton, B. (1991). *Getting to YES: Negotiating Agreement Without Giving In.* Penguin Books, 2nd edn.

Flow of Consultation (translated by Google). (n.d.). Retrieved from http://translate. google.com/translate?hl=en&sl=ja&u=http://www.finmac.or.jp/&ei=fPSw TcfsMIymugPL-tSGBw&sa=X&oi=translate&ct=result&resnum=5&ved= 0CDgQ7gEwBA&prev=/search%3Fq%3Dfinmac%26hl%3Den%26rlz%3D1 R2ADFA_zh-TW%26biw%3D1003%26bih%3D628%26prmd%3Divns.

Frederick, J. (20 January 2006). The Livedoor Scandal: Tribe Versus Tribe. *Time*. Retrieved from www.time.com/time/world/article/0,8599,1151722,00.html.

Frequently Asked Questions (translated by Google). (n.d.) Retrieved from http:// translate.google.com/translate?hl=en&sl=ja&u=http://www.finmac.or.jp/ &ei=fPSwTcfsMIymugPL-tSGBw&sa=X&oi=translate&ct=result&resnum =5&ved=0CDgQ7gEwBA&prev=/search%3Fq%3Dfinmac%26hl%3Den% 26rlz%3D1R2ADFA_zh-TW%26biw%3D1003%26bih%3D628%26prmd% 3Divns.

Freshfields Bruckhaus Deringer. (June 2011). Financial Alternative Dispute Resolution System. Retrieved from www.freshfields.com/publications/ pdfs/2011/jun11/30588.pdf.

Fuller, L. (1969). *Morality of Law*, rev. edn, New Haven: Yale University Press.

Galanter, M. (1974). Why the 'haves' come out ahead: speculations on the limits of legal change. *Law & Society Review*, Vol. 9(1), 95–160.

Genn, H. (2009). *Judging Civil Justice*. The Hameline Lectures 2008, Cambridge University Press.

Gilad, S. (2008). Accountability or expectations management? The role of the ombudsman in financial regulation. *Law & Policy*, Vol. 30(2), 227–253.

    (2010). Why the 'haves' do not necessarily come out ahead in informal dispute resolution. *Law & Policy*, Vol. 32(3), 283–312.

Ginsburg, T. (2000). Does law matter for economic development? Evidence from East Asia. *Law and Society Review*, Vol. 34(3).

Grannum, S. D. (2009). The faith and face of securities arbitration: after the 2008 crash. In Robbins, D. E. (ed.) *Securities Arbitration in the Market Meltdown Era*. New York: Practising Law Institute. Chapter 4.

Gross, Jill. (2006). Securities mediation: dispute resolution for the individual investor. *Ohio State Journal on Dispute Resolution*, Vol. 21(2), 329–381.

Gross, J. I. (2010). The end of mandatory securities arbitration? *Pace L. Rev.*, Vol. 30, 1174.

Gross, J. I. and Black, B. (2008). When perception changes reality: an empirical study of investors' views of the fairness of securities arbitration. *J. Disp. Resol.*, Vol. 2, 349.

Gross, J. I. and Pekarek, E. (2010). Banks and brokers and bricks and clicks: an evaluation of FINRA's proposal to modify the 'bank broker-dealer rule'. *Alb. L. Rev.*, Vol. 73, 465.

Gullapalli, D. and Anand, S. (20 September 2008). Bailout of money funds seems to stanch outflow. *The Wall Street Journal*. Retrieved from http://online.wsj. com/article/SB122186683086958875.html?mod=article-outset-box

Gupta, D. (20 July 2009). Consent Decree in Minnesota v. NAF. *Consumer Law & Policy Blog.* Retrieved from http://pubcit.typepad.com/clpblog/2009/07/consent-decree-in-minnesota-v-naf.html.

Halliday, T. and Carruthers, B. (2007). The recursivity of law: global norm-making and national law-making in the globalization of corporate insolvency regimes. *American Journal of Sociology,* Vol. 112, 1135.

(2009) *Bankrupt: Global Lawmaking and Systemic Financial Crisis.* Stanford University Press.

Halsey v. Milton Keynes General NHS Trust [2004] 1 WLR 3002.

Haverkamp, L. (21 January 2001). Is FIDReC fair? *Singapore Business Review.* Retrieved from http://sbr.com.sg/financial-services/commentary/fidrec-fair.

Hayek, F. A. (1944). *The Road to Serfdom.* University of Chicago Press.

Heather Moor & Edgecomb [2008] EWCA Civ 642.

Hensler, D. R. (2003). Our Courts, Ourselves: How the Alternative Dispute Resolution Movement is Re-Shaping Our Legal System. 108 *Penn State Law Review,* 165–197.

Herbert Smith. (16 November 2009). ADR for financial sector retail to start soon, but it is still flawed. Retrieved from www.herbertsmith.com/NR/rdonlyres/EA8A230E-9964-48ED-B3E4-7B5E613BDB15/13439/RegulatoryNewsletterNo16ENovember2009.pdf.

Hironaka, A. and Katsube, J. (24 June 2010). Securities Litigation Picks Up. *International Financial Law Review.* Retrieved from www.iflr.com/Article/2617835/Securities-litigation-picks-up.html.

HM Treasury. (July 2009). Reforming Financial Markets. Retrieved from http://webarchive.nationalarchives.gov.uk/+/http://www.hm-treasury.gov.uk/d/reforming_financial_markets080709.pdf.

(July 2010). A new approach to financial regulation: judgment, focus and stability. Retrieved from www.hm-treasury.gov.uk/d/consult_financial_regulation_condoc.pdf.

Hodges, C. (2010). Collective redress in Europe: the new model. *Civil Justice Quarterly,* Vol. 29(3), 370–395.

Hoetker, Glenn P. and Ginsburg, Tom. (8 September 2004). The Unreluctant Litigant? An Empirical Analysis of Japan's Turn to Litigation. *U Illinois Law & Economics Research Paper No. LE04-009.* Retrieved from http://papers.ssrn.com/sol3/papers.cfm?abstract_id=608582.

Hong Kong Bar Association Circular No. 118/08. (18 November 2008). Retrieved from *Hong Kong Bar Association* database.

Hong Kong Bar Association Circular No. 097/10. (27 September 2010). *Hong Kong Bar Association* database.

Hong Kong International Arbitration Centre. (2009). HKIAC Annual Report 2009. Retrieved from www.hkiac.org/images/stories/hkiac/2009_Annual_Report.pdf.

Hong Kong Monetary Authority. (n.d.) Explanatory Note on the Scheme. Retrieved from www.hkma.gov.hk/eng/other-information/lehman/explanatory_b. shtml.

(n.d.). Notes, Lehman-Brothers-related Investment Products Dispute Mediation and Arbitration Scheme.

(n.d.) What to do if you have a complaint about banking products or services. Retrieved from www.hkma.gov.hk/eng/other-information/consumer-information/complaint_handling_leaflet_b.shtml.

(2001). Information Note for the LegCo Panel on Financial Affairs. Comparative Study on Banking Consumer Protection and Competition Arrangements in the UK, Australia and Hong Kong: An Introductory Note. Retrieved from www.legco.gov.hk/yr00-01/english/panels/fa/papers/a1112e02.pdf.

Ikeya, M. and Kishitani, S. (21 July 2009). Japan: Trends in Securities Litigation in Japan: 1998–2008 – Damages Litigation Over Misstatements on the Rise. *NERA Economic Consulting*. Retrieved from www.mondaq.com/article. asp?articleid=83300.

(2 August 2011). Japan: Trends in Securities Litigation in Japan: 2010 Update. *NERA Economic Consulting*. Retrieved from www.mondaq.com/x/140680/ Class+Actions/Trends+in+Securities+Litigation+in+Japan+2010+Update.

Interim Report of the Chief Justice's Working Party on Civil Justice Reform. (3 March 2004). Retrieved from www.info.gov.hk/gia/general/200403/03/0303195.htm/.

J. Bollinger S.A. v. Goldwell Ltd. [1971] F.S.R. 405.

Jones, H. and Hulmes, D. (15 February 2011). Basel rules to have little impact on economy – OECD. *Reuters*. Retrieved from www.reuters.com/article/2011/02/16/oecd-basel-idUSLDE71E23Q20110216.

Kagan, Robert A. (2003). *Adversarial Legalism and American Government: The American Way of Life*. Harvard University Press.

Karlberg, M. (2004). *Beyond the Culture of Contest: From Adversarialism to Mutualism in an Age of Interdependence*. Oxford: George Ronald.

Karmel, R. S. (2008). Should securities industry self-regulatory organizations be considered government agencies? *Stan. J.L. Bus. & Fin.*, Vol. 14, 151.

Klijn, W. (2008). Govt gives FOS green light. *Investor Daily*. Retrieved from www.investordaily.com.au/cps/rde/xchg/id/style/4653. htm?rdeCOQ=SID-0A3D9633-A6FEA22A.

Koebel, J. T. (2010). Trust and the investment adviser industry: Congress' failure to realize FINRA's potential to restore investor confidence. *Seton Hall Legis. J.*, Vol. 35, 61.

Konish, L. (1 March 2011). All-public Panels Approved For Arbitrations; A step in the right direction-or just a cost increase? *onwallstreet*. Retrieved from www.onwallstreet.com/ows_issues/2011_3/all-public-panels-approved-for -arbitrations-2671609-1.html.

Kratsch, S. (2010). The financial crisis: arbitration as a viable option for European financial institutions. *Arbitration*, Vol. 76(4), 680–685.

Lande, John. (2002). Using dispute system design methods to promote good-faith participation in court-connected mediation programs. *UCLA Law Review*, Vol. 50, 69–141.

Law on Civil Proceeding Costs (MinjiSoshouHiyouTou Ni KansuraHouritsu) (Law No. 40 of 1971, amended through 1996). Retrieved from www.houko. com/00/01/S46/040.HTM#s4.

Little, W. B. L. (2008). Fairness is in the eyes of the beholder. *Baylor L. Rev.*, Vol. 60, 73.

Llewellyn, D. T. (June 2006). Institutional structure of financial regulation and supervision: the basic issues. Retrieved from http://siteresources. worldbank.org/INTTOPCONF6/Resources/2057292-1162909660809/ F2FlemmingLlewellyn.pdf.

Lord Hunt. (April 2008). Opening up, reaching out and aiming high: an agenda for accessibility and excellence in the Financial Ombudsman Service (The Hunt Review). Retrieved from www.financial-ombudsman.org.uk/news/ Hunt_report.pdf.

Lord Justice Jackson. (December 2009). Review of Civil Litigation Costs: Final Report. Retrieved from www.judiciary.gov.uk/NR/rdonlyres/8EB9F3F3-9C 4A-4139-8A93-56F09672EB6A/0/jacksonfinalreport140110.pdf.

Love, L. P. (2000). Images of justice. *Pepperdine Dispute Resolution Law Journal.* Retrieved from http://papers.ssrn.com/sol3/papers. cfm?abstract_id=229990.

Lynch, Katherine. (2003). *The Forces of Economic Globalization: Challenges to the Regime of International Commercial Arbitration.* The Hague, Netherlands: Kluwer Law International.

Martinez, Janet and Smith, Stephanie. (2009). An analytic framework for dispute system design. *Harvard Negotiation Law Review*, Vol. 14, 123.

Miyatake, M. and Andriotis, T. (2010). Japan's New Financial ADR System. *Bloomberg Law Reports.* Retrieved from www.hugheshub-bard.com/files/Publication/e66266f4-0130-4416-ae75-accafffcde78/Presentation/PublicationAttachment/4792b24e-4239-4 5b5-a62a-b7b03488f6df/Japan's%20New%20Financial%20ADR%20 System%20-%20Andriotis%20Bloomberg%20Article.pdf.

Menkel-Meadow, Carrie J. (2009). Are there systemic ethics issues in dispute system design? And what we should [not] do about it: Lessons from international and domestic fronts. *Harvard Negotiation Law Review*, Vol. 14, 195–231.

Millennium Project. (n.d.). What they are. Retrieved from www.unmillenni-umproject.org/goals/index.htm.

(2006). Goals, Targets and Indicators. Retrieved from www.unmillenni-umproject.org/goals/gti.htm.

Ministry of Internal Affairs and Communications, Statistics Bureau. (2011). 25–11 Cases Newly Receive and Cases Disposed of Litigation Cases and Conciliation Cases by Type (2005–08). In Chapter 25 Justice and Police. *Japan Statistical Yearbook 2011*. Retrieved from www.stat.go.jp/english/data/nenkan/back60/1431-25.htm.

Ministry of Justice. (March 2010). *Annual Pledge Report 2008–9: Monitoring the effectiveness of the government's commitment to using alternative dispute resolution 2/3/10*. Retrieved from www.justice.gov.uk/publications/docs/alternative-dispute-resolution-08-09.pdf.

Moffit, M. and Schneider, A. K. (2008). *Dispute Resolution: Examples and Explanations*. Aspen.

Monetary Authority of Singapore. (October 2004). Policy Consultation on the Financial Industry Disputes Resolution Centre.

Moody's Analytics. (2011). Implementing Basel III: Challenges, Options & Opportunities. *White Paper September 2011*. Retrieved from www.moodysanalytics.com/Contact-Us/ERM/Contact-Form-Basel-III-Implementation/~/media/Insight/Regulatory/Basel-III/Thought-Leadership/2011/11-01-09-Implementing-Basel-III-Whitepaper.ashx.

Morris, E. (2008). The Financial Ombudsman Service and the Hunt Review: continuing evolution in dispute resolution. *J.B.L.*, Vol. 8, 785–808.

Murphy, C. (2005). Lon Fuller and the moral value of the rule of law. *Law and Philosophy*, Vol. 24, 240.

Muskal, M. (15 November 2011). Occupy Wall Street camps are today's Hoovervilles. *The Los Angeles Times*.

Nagashima Ohno and Tsunematsu. (2010). Japan: Financial Alternative Dispute Resolution. *International Financial Law Review*. Retrieved from www.iflr.com/Article/2713008/Financial-alternative-dispute-resolution.html.

National Alternative Dispute Resolution Advisory Council. (2003). ADR Statistics – Published Statistics on Alternative Dispute Resolution in Australia. Retrieved from www.nadrac.gov.au/www/nadrac/rwpattach.nsf/VAP/(960DF944D2AF105D4B7573C11018CFB4)~ADRstats+2003.pdf/$file/ADRstats+2003.pdf.

New South Wales Government Lawlink. (n.d.). Other complaint handling agencies. Retrieved from www.lawlink.nsw.gov.au/lawlink/olsc/ll_olsc.nsf/vwPrint1/OLSC_othercomplaint.

North, D. (1990). *Institutions, Institutional Change And Economic Growth*. New York: Cambridge University Press.

Norio Nakazawa and Yasuo Nakajima. (2009). The summary of alternative dispute resolution system in the financial field (financial ADR system). *Shoji Homu No. 1876*, 48.

Nottage, Luke R. (2005). Civil Procedure Reforms in Japan: The Latest Round. *Ritsumeikan University Law Review*, Vol. 22, 81–86.

Occupy Wall Street. (n.d.). About. Retrieved from www.occupywallst.org/about/.

(29 September 2011). Declaration of the Occupation of New York City. Retrieved from www.nycga.net/resources/declaration/.

Ombudsman News Issue 62. (June/July 2007). Retrieved from www.financial-ombudsman.org.uk/publications/ombudsman-news/62/62.htm.

Operating rules for mediation and complaint resolution assistance (translated by Google). (n.d.). Retrieved from http://translate.googleusercontent.com/translate_c?hl=en&prev=/search%3Fq%3Dfinmac%26hl%3Den%26rlz%3D1R2ADFA_zh-TW%26biw%3D1003%26bih%3D628%26prmd%3Divns&rurl=translate.google.com&sl=ja&u=http://www.finmac.or.jp/html/kujyo/pdf/kisoku02.pdf&usg=ALkJrhghIeGYq4zrAocrK9sgFn_sg2pupQ.

Overseas Development Institute. (April 2010). The MDGs fundamentals: improving equity for development. *Briefing Paper.* Retrieved from www.odi.org.uk/resources/docs/5833.pdf.

Pardieck, A. M. (2001). The formation and transformation of securities law in Japan: from the bubble to the big bang. *UCLA PAC. BASIN L.J.*, Vol. 19, 1.

Petrick, J. A. (2011). Sustainable stakeholder capitalism: a moral vision of responsible global financial risk management. *J. Bus. Ethics*, Vol. 99(1), 93–109.

Platto, C. (1999). *Economic Consequences of Litigation Worldwide.* Kluwer Law International.

Pokrajac, M. (20 August 2010). FOS upgrades dispute resolution approach. Retrieved from www.moneymanagement.com.au/news/fos-upgrades-dispute-resolution-approach.

Powell, K. (2008). Business law: what Montana lawyers need to know about FINRA. *Montana Lawyer*, Vol. 33, 31.

Press, Sharon. (1992–1993). Building and maintaining a statewide mediation program: a view from the field. *Kentucky Law Journal*, Vol. 81, 1029–1065.

Provisional Measures on the Administration of the Members of the China Futures Association. (Promulgated 29 December 2000). Retrieved from www.csrc.gov.cn/n575458/n4239016/n6634558/n9768113/10011976.

Raz, J. (1979). *Authority of Law.* Oxford: Clarendon Press.

Review of the Financial Industry Complaints Service 2002 – Final Report.

Reuben, Richard C. (2005). Democracy and dispute resolution: systems design and the new workplace. *Harvard Negotiation Law Review*, Vol. 10, 11.

(15 October 2010). How ADR can foster the rule of law: beyond the fundamental tension. Symposium on ADR and the Rule of Law: Making the Connection. Missouri School of Law.

Riles, A. (2011). *Collateral Knowledge.* University of Chicago Press.

Riskin, L. L. (1997). Understanding mediators' orientations, strategies, and techniques: a grid for the perplexed. *Harvard Negotiation Law Review*, Vol. 1(7). Retrieved from http://ssrn.com/abstract=1506684.

Rodriguez de Quijas v. Shearson/American Express, Inc. 490 U.S. 477 (1989).

Rosette, A. and Cheng, L. (1991). Contract with a Chinese face: socially embedded factors in the transformation from hierarchy to market, 1978–1989. *J. Chin. L.*, Vol. 5, 219–233.

Samuel, A. (2010). With arbitration facing restrictions, it's time to look at a UK solution for consumer disputes. *Alternatives to the High Cost of Litigation: the Newsletter of the International Institute for Conflict Prevention & Resolution*, Vol. 28, 111–113.

Sander, F. E. A., Goldberg, S. B., Rogers, N. H. and Cole, S. R. (2007). *Dispute Resolution Casebook*. Aspen 5th edn.

Schneider, Andrea Kupfer. (2008). The Intersection of Dispute Systems Design and Transitional Justice. *Harvard Negotiation Law Review*. Retrieved from http://papers.ssrn.com/sol3/papers.cfm?abstract_id=1296183.

Securities and Futures Commission. (n.d.). Code of Conduct for Licensed Persons by or Registered with the Securities and Futures Commission.

(December 2008). Issues Raised by the Lehman Minibonds Crisis: Report to the Financial Secretary.

Securities and Futures Ordinance (Cap. 571).

Sharp, A. (2008). One-stop Shop to Help Consumers. *The Age*. Retrieved from www.theage.com.au/business/onestop-shop-to-help-consumers-20080710-3d96.html.

Shearson/American Express, Inc. v. McMahon 482 U.S. 220 (1987).

Singapore Department of Statistics. (n.d.). Key Annual Indicators. Retrieved from www.singstat.gov.sg/stats/keyind.html.

Slaughter, A. M. (2004). *A New World Order*. Princeton University Press.

Smith, Stephanie and Martinez, Janet. (2009). An analytic framework for dispute system design. *Harvard Negotiation Law Review*, Vol. 14, 123.

Soo, G., Zhao, Y. and Cai, D. (2010). Better ways of resolving disputes in Hong Kong – some insights from the Lehman-Brothers related investment product dispute mediation and arbitration scheme. *J. Int'l Bus. & L.*, Vol. 9, 137.

South China Morning Post. (10 December 2008). 60 investors get HK$30m from banks on minibonds.

Stark, B. (2009). Compulsory arbitration: its impact on the efficiency of markets. In Robbins, D. E. (ed.) *Securities Arbitration in the Market Meltdown Era*. New York: Practising Law Institute. Chapter 9.

Sturn, S. and Gadlin, H. (2007). Conflict resolution and systemic change. *J. Disp. Resol.*, Vol. 1, 1.

Supreme Court of Japan website. (n.d.). Retrieved from www.courts.go.jp/english/.

Supreme Court of New South Wales. (2008). *Annual Review 2008*. Retrieved from www.lawlink.nsw.gov.au/lawlink/Supreme_Court/ll_sc.nsf/vwFiles/SCNSW_AnnualReview08.pdf/$file/SCNSW_AnnualReview08.pdf.

Susskind, Lawrence, McKearnan, Sarah and Thomas-Larmer, Jennifer. (1999). *The Consensus Building Handbook: A Comprehensive Guide To Reaching Agreement*. SAGE.

Takeyoshi Kawashima. (1963). Dispute resolution in contemporary Japan. In von Mehren, A. T. (ed.) *Law In Japan: The Legal Order In A Changing Society*. Cambridge: Harvard University Press, 41–72.

Tamanaha, B. (2004). *On Rule of Law: History, Politics, Theory*. Cambridge University Press.

(2007). A concise guide to the rule of law. *Legal Studies Research Paper Series Paper # 07-0082*. Retrieved from http://ssrn.com/abstract=1012051.

The Equator Principles Association. (June 2006). The Equator Principles. Retrieved from www.equator-principles.com/resources/equator_principles.pdf.

(2011). About the Equator Principles. Retrieved from www.equator-principles.com/index.php/about-the-equator-principles.

(September 2011). Members & Reporting. Retrieved from www.equator-principles.com/index.php/members-reporting.

(January 2012). History of the Equator Principles. Retrieved from www.equator-principles.com/index.php/history.

The Hon McClellan J. (15–16 April 2010). Civil Justice in Australia – Changes in the Trial Process. 'Civil Justice Reform – What Has It Achieved?', jointly hosted by the University of Hong Kong and the University College of London in Hong Kong.

The Japan Times Online. (31 March 2005). Pension fund group to sue Seibu Railway. Retrieved from www.japantimes.co.jp/text/nn20050331a2.html.

The Navigator Company Pty Ltd. (November 2004). Independent Review of the Banking and Financial Services Ombudsman. Retrieved from www.fos.org.au/public/download.jsp?id=2812.

(November 2005). Independent Review of the Credit Union Disputes Resolution Centre. Retrieved from www.fos.org.au/public/download.jsp?id=3665.

(May 2006). Independent Review of the Credit Ombudsman Service Ltd. Retrieved from www.cosl.com.au/Resources/COSL/Sites/COSL/PDF/Publications/IndependentReview-2006.pdf.

The Online Citizen. (2 January 2009). FIDReC – more symbolism than substance? Retrieved from http://theonlinecitizen.com/2009/01/fidrec-more-symbolism-than-substance/.

The Reagan Administration and Multinationals. (August 1984). *Multinational Monitor*, Vol. 5, No. 8. Retrieved from www.multinationalmonitor.org/hyper/issues/1984/08/reagan.html.

Thornton, P. (June 2007). A Review of Pensions Institutions: An Independent Report to the Department for Work and Pensions. Retrieved from www. dwp.gov.uk/docs/institutionalreviewfinalreport180507.pdf.

Tolley's Company Law and Insolvency Newsletter. (July 2010). Vol. 10, Bulletin 1.

Trubek, D. M. (1972). Toward a social theory of law: an essay on the study of law & development. *Yale L. J.*, Vol. 82, 1.

——— (1973). Max Weber on law and the rise of capitalism. *Wisconsin Law Review*, Vol. 3, 720.

Turner, G. (2008). *The Credit Crunch: Housing Bubbles, Globalization and the Worldwide Economic Crisis.* London: Pluto Press.

UN Department of Economic and Social Affairs. (1999). Part II. *UN Guidelines for Consumer Protection.* Retrieved from www.un.org/esa/sustdev/publications/ consumption_en.pdf.

UN Division for Sustainable Development Department of Economic and Social Affairs. (1998). Consumer protection and sustainable consumption: new guidelines for the global consumer. *Background paper for the United Nations inter-regional expert group meeting.* Retrieved from www.un.org/esa/ sustdev/sdissues/consumption/cppgoph4.htm.

United Nations. (n.d.). Background. Retrieved from www.un.org/millennium-goals/bkgd.shtml.

United Nations Rule of Law. (2004). What is the rule of law?. Retrieved from www. unrol.org/article.aspx?article_id=3.

Upham, F. (2002). Mythmaking in the rule of law orthodoxy, Carnegie Endowment for international peace. Rule of Law Series, Democracy and Rule of Law Project, Number 30.

Ury, William L., Brett, Jeanne M. and Goldberg, Stephen B. (1988). *Getting Disputes Resolved: Designing Systems to Cut the Cost of Conflict.* Jossey-Bass.

Vella, J. (26 March 2012). *The EU's Commission for a Proposed Financial Transaction Tax.* The University of Hong Kong.

Vella, J., Fuest, C. and Schmidt-Eisenlohr, T. (2011). The EU Commission's Proposal for a Financial Transaction Tax. *British Tax Review*, Issue 6.

Victorian Law Reform Commission. (2008). *Civil Justice Review: Final Report.* Retrieved from www.lawreform.vic.gov.au/html-reports/Civil%20Justice/ index.htm.

Weber, M. (1968). *On Charisma And Institution Building.* S.N. Eisenstadt (ed.), University of Chicago Press.

Wiegand, S. A. (1996). A just and lasting peace: supplanting mediation with the ombuds model. *Ohio St. J. on Disp. Resol.*, Vol. 12, 95.

Wilko v. Swan 346 U.S. 427 (1953).

Willmott, N. (2010). Equipping the modern regulator: assessing the new regulatory powers under the Financial Services Act 2010. *Compliance Officer Bulletin*, Vol. 78, 1–28.

Wong, E. (2008). Singapore: financial regulation – dispute resolution schemes. *J.I.B.L.R.*, Vol. 23(1), N10–11.

World Justice Project. (2011). Rule of Law Index. Retrieved from http://worldjusticeproject.org/rule-of-law-index-data.

Yokoi-Arai, M. (2004). A comparative analysis of the Financial Ombudsman Systems in the UK and Japan. *Journal of Banking Regulation*, Vol. 5, 333–357.

Zhu, S. (2009). Legal aspects of the commodity and financial futures market in China. *The Brooklyn Journal Of Corporate, Financial & Commercial Law*, Vol. 3, 377–430.

Zoltowski, B. B. (2008). Restoring investor confidence: providing uniformity in securities arbitration by offering guidelines for arbitrators in deciding motions to dismiss before a hearing on the merits. *Syracuse L. Rev.*, Vol. 58(3), 375–396.

INDEX